Upholding Mystery

Upholding Mystery

An Anthology
of Contemporary
Christian Poetry

Edited by

David Impastato

NEW YORK   OXFORD

Oxford University Press

1997

OXFORD UNIVERSITY PRESS

Oxford   New York   Athens   Auckland   Bangkok   Calcutta
Cape Town   Dar es Salaam   Delhi   Florence   Hong Kong   Istanbul
Karachi   Kuala Lumpur   Madras   Madrid   Melbourne   Mexico City
Nairobi   Paris   Singapore   Taipei   Tokyo   Toronto
and associated companies in
Berlin   Ibadan

Copyright © 1997 by Oxford University Press, Inc.

Published by Oxford University Press, Inc.
198 Madison Avenue, New York, New York 10016

Oxford is a registered trademark of Oxford University Press, Inc.

Design by Omega Clay

Pages ix–xiv constitute an extension of the copyright page.

Library of Congress Cataloging-in-Publication Data

Upholding mystery : an anthology of contemporary Christian poetry / edited by
    David Impastato.
        p.   cm.   ISBN 0-19-510400-5
        1. American poetry—20th century.   2. Christian poetry, American.   3. Eng-
lish poetry—20th century.   4. Christian poetry, English.   I. Impastato, David.
PS595.C47U6   1996
811'.54080382—dc20   96-19968

1 3 5 7 9 8 6 4 2
Printed in the United States of America
on acid-free paper

For Nancy,
with love and appreciation,

and for David John and Michael,
the best of minds and hearts,

and for our beautiful growing families

Acknowledgments

I wish to thank all of my friends and family who have touched me
with their enthusiasm for this project. Special thanks go to my astute ed-
itor at Oxford, Cynthia Read, and to Jonathan Holden for his personal
encouragement. His excellent book, *The Fate of American Poetry*, point-
ed me to several of the poets ahead and in many ways inspired the idea
of an anthology of this kind. My warmest gratitude as well to Bill Barr,
Chris Herbert, Tom Powers, and Steve Smith, for their fraternal support
and invaluable practical advice, and to Peggy McDonald, whose listen-
ing illuminated. Lastly, I thank the poets themselves for their generosity
and constant good will, to say nothing of the pleasure their verse has
given me.

Credits

reprinted by permission of The University of Arkansas Press. "Sister Mary Appassionata Lectures the Bible Study Class: *Homage To Onan*," "Sister Mary Appassionata Lectures the Eighth Grade Boys and Girls on the Nature of The Candle," "Sister Mary Appassionata Lectures the Folklore Class: *Doctrines of the Strawberry*," "Sister Mary Appassionata Lectures the Home Ec Class: *The Feast*," and "Sister Mary Appassionata Proves to the Entomology Class that Women and Men Descended from the Cricket" from *The Appassionata Doctrines*, Cleveland State University Poetry Center, 1983, 1986, copyright ©1983 by David Citino; reprinted by permission. "Whole Wheat, Decaf Black, A Morbid Curiosity" printed by kind permission of the author.

    David Craig. "Francis Helps A Brother Who Is In Sin," and "John Says Mass on All Souls Day," from *The Sandaled Foot* by David Craig, Cleveland State University Poetry Center, copyright ©1980 by David Craig; reprinted by permission. "Apple Fools," "Gospel Poem #1," "Gospel Poem #2," "Gospel Poem #3," "The Presence of God," "Pentecost," and excerpts from "Peter Maurin (1877–1949)" and "Prothalamion," from *Peter Maurin and Other Poems* by David Craig, Cleveland State University Poetry Center, copyright ©1985 by David Craig; reprinted by permission. "'Christ Bearing the Cross' by El Greco," "Gethsemane," "Hyperbole," "Litany," "Nursing Home, 3rd Shift," "Our Father," "The Apprentice Eats Glass," "The Apprentice Is Amazed," "The Apprentice Prophecies," "The Apprentice Sees Himself in The Sunset," "Young Monk (Denver)," and excerpt from "Marian Sector," from *Like Taxes: Marching Through Gaul*, by David Craig, Scripta Humanistica, copyright ©1990 by David Craig; reprinted by permission. "Hewn Hands" from *The Widening Light*, and versions of "Peter Maurin" and "Pentecost" prepared for this volume, printed by kind permission of the author.

    Maura Eichner. "A Woman Is Waiting for a Bus," "Back Porch Fundamentalist," "Dream Songs Concluded," "Eclogue and Elegy," "From a Woman's Life," "Imagist at Coney Island," "Litany for The Living," "Message from Inland," "The Father," and excerpts from "Out of Cana" and "What My Teachers Taught Me I Try To Teach My Students" from *Hope Is A Blind Bard* by Sister Maura Eichner, copyright ©1989 by Sister Maura Eichner; reprinted by permission. "Letter from Santa Cruz" from *What We Women Know* by Sister Maura Eichner, copyright ©1980 by Sister Maura Eichner; reprinted by permission.

    Louise Erdrich. "Portrait of the Town Leonard," "Leonard Commits Redeeming Adulteries with All the Women in Town," and "Leonard Refuses to Atone" from *Jacklight* by Louise Erdrich, copyright ©1984 by Louise Erdrich; reprinted by permission of Henry Holt and Co., Inc. "Angels," "Christ's Twin," "Fooling God," "Mary Kröger," "Saint Clare," "The Sacraments," and "The Savior" from *Baptism of Desire* by Louise Erdrich, copyright ©1990 by Louise Erdrich; reprinted by permission of HarperCollins Publishers, Inc.

xi

Contents

Introduction

Why would anyone want to read more contemporary Christian poetry when so much of it is clearly bad? Our answer has little to do, as some may think, with whether we agree or disagree with a belief system. Poetry can never escape a poet's conviction about how life is. But "good" poets create a language and imagery whose suggestiveness ripples outward in all directions. Regardless of its ideological support, its flesh and voice still argue to our hearts. "Bad" Christian poetry is bad, like any bad poetry, because it has failed to do this—failed for whatever reason to reach beyond its premise to our common life. This volume testifies that there are Christian poets today writing poetry that is "good," whose work can provide a source of pleasure and discovery for Christian and non-Christian readers alike.

Even so, some may still question *any* poetry of religious transcendence in a postmodern age. Spiritual seekers, Christians, and others in the received traditions will have no such qualms, of course. But the irony is that postmodernism as an intellectual climate proves far more congenial to the Christian poet than, for example, the romantic empiricism that nourished poets Wallace Stevens and William Carlos Williams in the 1920s and '30s. For them and for many in the decades following, ultimacy was the "the" of physical objects, as Stevens himself put it, and transcendence, especially in the form of a Judeo-Christian "God," was pretty much ruled off-limits as a subject for respectable poetry.

But postmodernism has ruled *everything* off-limits. It declares that we have only language, and a language of bias at that. All fabrications of language like poetry, therefore, are equally suspect, but at the same time equally worthy of our investigation. In other words, *nothing* is off-limits, and the Christian poet today advances an appeal to scrutiny from the same equitable zero-point as any other member of the writing community.

In many ways, the Christian embrace of "the word" of its scripture anticipates postmodern concerns about text and authorship. As critic Northrop Frye has pointed out, Judeo-Christian scripture is a presentation of "language events" fussed over by so many authors, redactors, and editors that all individuality of authorship in the modern sense has been smashed out if it, and for that it is all the more powerful. So at this level at least the Christian poet is comfortable with the "polyphony of self" that language is said to mirror. Equally untroubling is the postmodern notion of history as a web of narratives floating rather free of historical fact, if there is such a thing as fact, since for most Christians the "inspiration" of scripture is what gives it authority, not the precise historical status of its narrative referents.

Further and largely unacknowledged kinship between Christianity and postmodernism exists in other ways. Granting the difference of their guiding faith-statements—Christianity's witness of metaphysical presence against postmodernism's presumption of absence—both proceed by radically interrogating the world's wisdoms and its power arrangements. Both seek to understand human personhood less in the conventional realms of "self" than in relation to the "other," to community, and to the shaping powers of tradition. Finally, both are highly suspicious of the Enlightenment deification of reason, and ultimately accept the universe, and our sense of it, as a mystery beyond the reach of rational or scientific constructs.

Christianity's special relationship to the word, for all its postmodern elusiveness and presumption, is what makes poetry a natural touchstone for the Christian experience. Christianity's most inclusive term for Jesus, its visible dimension of Godhead, is Logos, the Greek for "word," a conceptualizing of Christ as God's utterance. The Bible is referred to, in a more usual linguistic sense, as "God's word," a word that its multiple witnesses cast in lyric and verse. A Christian worship tradition utters words back to the Word in the poetry of its rituals, in which metaphorical, mantric, and ecstatic language is employed, as in all poetry, to break the confines of ordinary meaning. For the Christian, this theological and rhetorical link between Word and word privileges language, and especially the language of poetry, with an engendering power.

The present volume focuses in depth on the work of fifteen poets, currently writing and publishing, who are recognized equally for the stature of their verse and for their illumination of the way of being and perceiving known as Christian. Instead of a "broad survey" of the occasional lightning strike, which many anthologies of Christian verse already present, the collection offers the maturity and depth of sustained bodies of work. Moreover, instead of highlighting one poet at a time, again the conventional practice, *Upholding Mystery* gathers the combined verse into major areas of Christian attention. Each chapter is accompanied by a brief introduction and commentary, and the sequence of chapters is an evolving one, with subjects foundational to Christianity coming first. The resulting volume, then, is both an anthology and an overview of contemporary Christianity revealed through poetry, the native tongue of Christian revelation.

What the overview finally discloses is the paradox of a vision that can be grasped only in diversity, in the very contrast between the poets from whose work the vision comes into being. Humor, for example, is a prominent feature of the poetry of both David Citino and Scott Cairns, but their imagery explores vastly different terrain. Citino is drawn to the organic and physiological, to human body-ness in its vitality and decay. He is just as fascinated by the body's processes, like sex, which trace "the lineaments of God," as he is by its diseases, like cancer, which break the body down only to anatomize a mysterious wholeness. The speaker of a number of Citino's poems is Sister Mary Appassionata, whose teachings of an ethnic Christianity become the perfect vehicle for the poet's mix of satire, wit, and serious moral reflection. Scott Cairns's poetic counterpart to Sister Mary is Raimundo Luz. Chef, jazz enthusiast, and writer of postmodern Portuguese verse, Luz admits to be suffering from "an acute lack of despair," especially for a contemporary poet. More than anyone in the collection, Cairns's humor and playful openness to mystery sound the "bass note of joy" often identified as a primary Christian stance.

The work of Louise Erdrich testifies to the mingling of Christian and Native American spiritual traditions to which she was born. Erdrich spins her magic-realist images and fables in a poetry of intense "negative capability" attuned to the uncanny, to the shadow side, and to human suffering. A spirituality like Erdrich's that clings to the earth also finds a natural home in the poetry of Wendell Berry, who has spent the past two decades living and working in Kentucky as a farmer. Berry's poetry connects the natural supernaturalism of the romantic tradition and Henry David Thoreau with a specifically Christian response to nature. His lyrics evoke a particularity of place—a place in the physical terrain where the spiritual and historical somehow find ground as well. David Craig, by contrast, is essentially an urban poet, a mystical voice of the street. Craig's heady tone is fueled by an ordinary diction that mirrors his enthusiasm for the ordinary object, scene, or moment, which are all, for him, carriers of the sacred. He often explodes his language syntactically, as ecstasy explodes sequence and time, or as ego dissolves in the glare of spiritual illumination.

Andrew Hudgins is linked with a Southern Gothic tradition that has roots in his Alabama childhood. The narrative content of his poetry is by turns violent, funny, erotic, and compassionate. His characters and the "speakers" of his poems battle against their frailties, often without success, as they do against the pull of circumstance, broken relationships, and the past. One of the hallmarks of Hudgins's work, unusual in an almost mandatory climate of free verse, is the use of an iambic line, frequently a classic five-beat pentameter, to sustain his intimate, colloquial voice.

In a poetry of candor and irony, Kathleen Norris draws on her pilgrimage from New York City to the prairie of South Dakota, sharing a woman's experience of love, family, death and historic memory. A spirituality of surprises, even incongruities, is in keeping with Norris's participation as a lay member, though married and Protestant, in the monastic order of Saint Benedict. Pilgrimage has left its traces in the life and work of Denise Levertov as well. As a child she witnessed the conversion of her Jewish father and his ordination to Anglican ministry. Levertov rejected his faith and emigrated to the United States from England, but over the years the agnostic naturalism informing her verse slowly evolved into the Christian poetics by which she is known today. Levertov carries over from her earlier work a keen alertness to the immediacy of the moment. In fact, like her literary mentor and co-pilgrim in the spirit, Austrian poet Rainer Maria Rilke, staying present to the moment, "being here now" as recent spiritualities phrase it, may well describe the undercurrent of all Levertov's verse in the coming pages, despite subjects as varied as Lady Julian of Norwich, animal rights, Renaissance painting, Rilke, and the new physics.

Like the prophecy of scripture, the work of Daniel Berrigan and Geoffrey Hill, poets close in age and temperament, prophetically challenges both world and God. Advocate for the poor, antiwar protester, hospice worker, writer, and poet, Berrigan foregrounds issues of justice and personal integrity. His tone, ever impatient, often rises to indignation. Like Berrigan in the fierceness of his faith, Geoffrey Hill rejects all compromise with an imperfect world, including the imperfection in himself. Frequently compared to the visionary William Blake, Englishman Hill composes in British and continental traditions, his impassioned verse intensified by the rigor of its forms.

The sprawling landscapes of Australia, the drollery of its people, and its distinctive take on English-language rhythms all resound in the poetry of Les Murray. Murray's interests range from the mores and folk of rural Australia to nature and the behavior of species, to themes of the Bible and classical mythology. These he fashions into an intricate, bardic verse that echoes both the English ballad and Anglo-Saxon poetry. Though calling on many of the same literary and historical resources as Murray's, the work of American poet Richard Wilbur more explicitly seeks out traditional methods of rhyme and meter. Wilbur's literary strategy parallels a philosophical one. He strives to marshal not just the sensibility of the present but also the instincts of the past in a verse of broad inquiry, an instrument he uses more than once to weigh the implications of relying too much or too little on the data of the senses.

Wilbur's "things that are," or seem to be, also occupy the concerns of Maura Eichner and Annie Dillard. Eichner's haiku-like meditations on suffering and grace recall the "plain speech" prosody with which American poet William Carlos Williams assailed the literary formalism of contemporaries T. S. Eliot, Ezra Pound, and others in the first half of the twentieth century. But Williams, much like his colleague Wallace Stevens, confessed to "unquenchable exaltation" when regarding the absoluteness of physical objects and phenomena. Eichner might rule this the empirical fallacy of modernism. Her objects, events, and literary personages are absolutely present too, but present both to us and to the mystery in which Eichner senses that they move and have their being. The same holds true for Annie Dillard, a modern mystic who again and again is surprised by the invisible in the trappings of the material world. Though her poetry contains episodes of rapture similar to the "divine espousals" of Saint Teresa of Avila, Dillard's encounter with mystery is always acknowledged as itself a mystery, and always shares in rapture for what she can see and touch.

The verse of David Brendan Hopes unveils allegories of human and divine struggle in the forces of nature. Hopes stands in the English lyric tradition, his musicality often resembling that of Gerard Manly Hopkins or Dylan Thomas. But Hopes's music celebrates a nature that exists in continual tension with its darker enactments, just as it sings of a human nature haunted by its failed idealisms and its loss of innocence. Through it all, the poet attains a sometimes ecstatic intensity of spiritual affirmation.

As stated earlier, these fifteen poets have been chosen for *Upholding Mystery* because their work is not only "Christian" but "good." They have been writing poetry long enough to have brought to it the struggle, contradiction, change, and depth that characterizes spiritual journey. Christian poets of promise, then, of which there are a good number, whose work is modest in volume did not qualify, though their absence should not be taken as a judgment against their excellence. Also not represented are poets who can perhaps be named "Christian" but whose work does not give voice to specific Christian concerns. Passed over too is poetry that conscientiously wrestles with Christian identity but on the whole, for reasons of style or intent, fails the needs of the mainstream literary reader. Finally, arguments could be made for including poets of "Judeo-Christian sensibility" along the lines, say, of a Donald Hall or Seamus Heany, but again such unarguably "good" work fails to articulate Judeo-Christian spirituality, thought, and culture in any focused way.

It is that spiritual landscape, unfolding by its own logic, or mysterious illogic, which the poems of the opening chapter, "The Cross," begin to reveal. Only in the scandal of crucifixion can Christian poets find an authentic, if paradoxical, place of beginning for a spirituality of rebirth and wholeness. Hence the title of the second chapter, "Transformation," the heading for poetry about the resurrection and its legacy for Christians in the patterns of nature and human life. The ultimate challenge to the power of transformation, of course, is death, and as the subject of the third grouping of poems, death appears to meet that challenge for Christians, transforming the unimaginable with meaning. But the poetry in the chapter that follows, "Injustice," is left to grapple with the meaning, or lack of it, of undeserved suffering and the persistence of evil.

The enigmas of cosmic and human injustice beg the question of what spiritual seekers can really know or, rather, *how* they can know. The chapter entitled "Presence" contains poems about the felt experience of the transcendent in the everyday world; the chapter "God's Body," of presence in nature. "Fools" comes next in the sequence, for experiential contact with a transcendent, christic presence can plant the idea of actually living out the christic example given in scripture. Poems reflecting on the Christian obsessions of "doing good and being good," of being "fools for Christ," are followed, in the chapter "Wayfarers," with an account of the Christian fool's dilemma. By circumstance a pilgrim, it seems the Christian not only is rejected as an irksome countersign but is torn by love for a transient world that is both home and not home.

Whatever their heartache, estrangement, or hope, Christians seek to hold fast to love, that divine height of foolishness. The chapter "Love" contains poems about the four dimensions of human loving proposed by English author C. S. Lewis, and the ensuing verse is grouped into chapters that take their measure from love: "The Dark," love eclipsed by sentient evil, variously personified; "Grace," the Christian experience of God's gratuitous love for humankind; and "Praise," the Christian response—God's love returned to God in love.

Because praise is a central communal act of Christianity, what follows is "The Mystical Body," a scriptural term for the interdependent community of Christian believers alive and dead. Poems in this chapter consider the so-called communion of saints, its accumulated identity or "tradition," and its cultural manifestation as "church." Bound up with both praise and worship is "Sacrament," the next chapter, presenting poetry that relates the mystical body's rituals of grace to the sacraments observed by Christians in creation and humanity.

The final two chapters are reserved for poetry about the first and last moves of the Christian journey. "The Leap" offers verse about faith, the necessary point of entry in the spiritual quest. Poets confront faith with issues of despair, the mystic's dark night, epistemology, volition, and the phenomenon of grace. This chapter appears here after the path has been marked, rather than up front, because the leap of faith is made not blindly but by enlightened assent. "The Holy" is the leap's omega-point, the consummation of the Christian way in the wholeness of the holy life. Poetry about the saints and holy ones, who by and large are a fairly eccentric lot, chronicles the effort to live out the universal Christian calling of perfected love.

As separated by tone, attitude, and style as the poems of this anthology are, taken together they create what critic Jonathan Holden calls a "revolutionary core" of work. By offering a vision not just to a single interpretive community but to the cultural mainstream, they may begin, Holden feels, "a partial desecularization of the modernist hegemony." We need neither fear nor welcome such a prospect to recognize how all of us are enriched by the language of these poets, and by an encounter with Christian mystery that evokes the mysteries of human experience.

Author's Note

Because I intend this anthology for the widest audience, certain readers may find some of my explanatory notes and comments unnecessary. To them I apologize in advance for any appearance of condescension or for simply plying the obvious. I also apologize to certain others who may have wished for even more orientation at various points in the book. Not all the poems, for example, are introduced or annotated. In a number of cases I felt that a poem's mere place in the sequence was enough to cast light. If shadows linger, I regret my presumption. In all cases, my goal has been to foreground the poems with no more talk, or less, than I thought was necessary for the reader to personally enter them and be at ease in their spiritual and literary settings. Breaks in poetic text for which I am responsible will be indicated by unspaced ellipsis, thus: .... Ellipses appearing by poet's intention will be indicated by normally spaced points, or: .... The distinction between these markings may be subtle, but I feel that more elaborate indicators ignore the needs of flow and appearance. Though my breaks are few, the occasional exerpt or abridgment is a practical necessity in a collection of this scope.

Upholding Mystery

This is my pigeon
and I its prophet.
No one but I
found it. It died
for me to find,
to lift like the Host
and place aloft, a soft
weight on my naked scalp,
where one more time
flailing wings can
contest with the wind.
I am a column, a pillar of
righteousness, upholding
mystery....
            —Denise Levertov, "Man Wearing Bird"

The comfort lies in fingering the incoherent for the true.
The comfort lies in suspecting more than evidence allows.
My only rule: If I understand something, it's no mystery.
      —Scott Cairns, "My Good Luck"

If you didn't hear the wind speak you were not listening.
If the stars did not warn you, you were
safe at home with the doors locked tight.
If you sought your soul and didn't find
a small bird beating straight home forever
where there is no road, you were seeking something else.
         —David Brendan Hopes, "Birdbones"

To possess nothing,
all of it.
This is your end.
         —David Craig, "Marian Sector"

The Cross

*I*t would be evasive, though more pleasant, to begin this volume on a subject other than Christ's suffering. But the paradox of the cross is the dark center of Christian light, the spring of its central meaning. All reflection on the Christian experience starts here because without Christ's passion there is no Christianity beyond useful precept, a reality that baffled and disgusted even Christ's closest associates. Like so much else in Christianity, the cross is designated by Christians as a mystery. But certainly it ranks among their most mysterious, which may help to explain why the Christian gaze is fixed on it so constantly, struggling among other things to comprehend its horror, absurdity, and inescapable necessity.

The speaker of Andrew Hudgins's "Dead Christ" studies the corpse after its removal from the cross. The finality of dead human flesh overcomes all notions of messianic return. Hudgins proposes what many eyewitnesses must have felt. His images argue Christ's full share in human experience, a crucial aspect of Christian understanding. An eyewitness speaks in "Ecce Homo" too, but on behalf of the crowd that calls for Christ's execution. Humanity's complicity in the death of Christ is further developed in "Crucifixion." Concluding that each of us, at different times, is crucifier and crucified, the poet sees the crucifixion as an inclusive event revealing the human condition.

Dead Christ Andrew Hudgins

There seems no reason he should've died. His hands
are pierced by holes too tidy to have held,
untorn, hard muscles as they writhed on spikes.
And on the pink, scrubbed bottom of each foot
a bee-stung lip pouts daintily.
No reason he should die—and yet, and yet
Christ's eyes are swollen with it, his mouth
hangs slack with it, his belly taut with it,
his long hair lank with it, and damp;
and underneath the clinging funeral cloth
his manhood's huge and useless with it: Death.

One blood-drop trickles toward his wrist. Somehow
the grieving women missed it when they bathed,
today, the empty corpse. Most Christs return.
But this one's flesh. He isn't coming back.

Ecce Homo Andrew Hudgins

Christ bends, protects his groin. Thorns gouge
his forehead, and his legs

are stippled with dried blood. The part of us
that's Pilate says, *Behold the man.*
We glare at that bound, lashed,
and bloody part of us that's Christ. We laugh, we howl,
we shout. *Give us Barabbas,*
not knowing who Barabbas is, not caring.
A thief? We'll take him anyway. A drunk?
A murderer? Who cares? It's better him
than this pale, ravaged thing, this god. Bosch knows.
His humans waver, laugh, then change to demons
as if they're seized by epilepsy. It spreads
from eye to eye, from laugh to laugh until,
incited by the ease of going mad,
they go. How easy evil is! Dark voices sing,
You can be evil or you can be good,
but good is dull, my darling, good is dull.
And we're convinced: How lovely evil is!
How lovely hell must be! *Give us Barabbas!*

Lord Pilate clears his throat and tries again:
I find no fault in this just man.
It's more than we can bear. In gothic script
our answer floats above our upturned eyes.
O crucify, we sing. *O crucify him!*

Crucifixion (Montgomery, Alabama) Andrew Hudgins

In the hot dark they dug a hole—
quickly and with some panic dug
a small hole, tipped in the cross, braced it.
Flames surged through burlap soaked in kerosene.
A short lopsided, crude, half-burning cross.

Ah, Lord—each day, each breath, you're back
on some cross or another, nailed,
jabbed, taunted. And one eternal cross

burns through a hot night on this scorched
patch of suburban lawn. Judge Johnson's lawn.

I went to college with his son,
who, one fall day six months removed from Easter,
went in his room, shotgunned himself.

I would have said he died for us, our sins,
but I no longer know who Jesus is.
He's someone walking through his life—or hers—
until God whispers, *It's you.* And God's ignored.

Two boys—one fourteen and one fifteen—
heave their homemade cross onto a truck.
God's voice grows louder as the truck
turns down Christ's street. God's shouting now.
God roars. The boys ignite the cross, run off,
run hide, and wait to see whom God has chosen.

Or does God simply choose us all?

In Revelations of Divine Love, *fourteenth-century English mystic and
theologian Lady Julian of Norwich details an experience of eight super-
natural visions. In "On a Theme from Julian's Chapter XX," her words
help Denise Levertov grasp the meaning of the cross in the light of all
human suffering.*

On a Theme from Julian's Chapter XX Denise Levertov

Six hours outstretched in the sun, yes,
hot wood, the nails, blood trickling
into the eyes, yes—
but the thieves on their neighbor crosses
survived till after the soldiers
had come to fracture their legs, or longer.

Why single out the agony? What's
a mere six hours?
Torture then, torture now,
the same, the pain's the same,
immemorial branding iron,
electric prod.
Hasn't a child
dazed in the hospital ward they reserve
for the most abused, known worse?
The air we're breathing,
these very clouds, ephemeral billows
languid upon the sky's
moody ocean, we share
with women and men who've held out
days and weeks on the rack—
and in the ancient dust of the world
what particles
of the long tormented,
what ashes.

But Julian's lucid spirit leapt
to the difference:
perceived why no awe could measure
that brief day's endless length,
why among all the tortured
One only is "King of Grief."
The oneing, she saw, *the oneing
with the Godhead* opened Him utterly
to the pain of all minds, all bodies
—sands of the sea, of the desert—
from first beginning
to last day. The great wonder is
that the human cells of His flesh and bone
didn't explode
when utmost Imagination rose
in that flood of knowledge. Unique
in agony, Infinite strength, Incarnate,

empowered Him to endure
inside of history,
through those hours when he took to Himself
the sum total of anguish and drank
even the lees of that cup:

within the mesh of the web, Himself
woven within it, yet seeing it,
seeing it whole. *Every sorrow and desolation*
He saw, and sorrowed in kinship.

Christ suffered for six hours on the cross before dying. But his "passion"
spans a forty-eight-hour period that begins in Gethsemane, a garden on
the Mount of Olives about a half mile from Jerusalem. Christ was ar-
rested there after a night of "agony" in which he sought to be reconciled
to the coming torment that scripture prophesied. Scott Cairns's poem on
the subject is inspired by a phrase from Luke's gospel, "And being in
agony he prayed more earnestly..." Denise Levertov has quoted Lady
Julian saying that Christ took on "every sorrow and desolation" in his
suffering. David Craig bears this out in "Gethsemane," finding no sorrow
too great or desolation too small for the "Kinship" of Christ's passion.

The More Earnest Prayer of Christ Scott Cairns

> *And being in an agony he prayed more earnestly...*
> *—Luke 22.44*

His last prayer in the garden began, as most
of his prayers began—*in earnest,* certainly,
but not without distinction, an habitual... what?

Distance? Well, yes, a sort of distance, or a mute
remove from the genuine distress he witnessed
in the endlessly grasping hands of multitudes

and, often enough, in his own embarrassing
circle of intimates. Even now, he could see
these where they slept, sprawled upon their robes or wrapped

among the arching olive trees. Still, something new,
unlikely, uncanny was commencing as he spoke.
As the divine in him contracted to an ache,

a throbbing in the throat, his vision blurred, his voice
grew thick and unfamiliar, his prayer—just before
it fell to silence—became uniquely earnest.

And in that moment—perhaps because it was so
new—he saw something, had his first taste of what
he would become, first pure taste of the body, and the blood.

Gethsemane David Craig

Damp wind, the innocent
movement of grubs at the roots of trees.

The moon, a moth
caught fluttering in wet branches:
    white wings, slowing.

Then the angel, gathering
the pieces of Jesus, large hand caressing His head,
the rumpled folds of hair
to his chest, blood on the snow-white gown.
    The slow, unearthly movement
    of giant wings.

He cried out, for the ones to follow:
    … in a haze He saw
bodies, twistings in a thin
dark oil. Voices, the sucking

of flesh away from flesh, the relapse.
     Waves of voices, in time:
Abraham's lament, Napoleon
cursing in the snow, the rumble of horses.
A cut-off arm in high weeds, box lunch
of Kentucky Fried, the spiked sound
of the Avon lady, her heels up the walk...

In "Christ Bearing the Cross," Craig encounters the Man of Sorrows on the road to Calvary, as El Greco painted the scene in the early seventeenth century. The poet's speech falters in "Gospel Poem #2" when noting the futility of the cross ("Your fibula   now cow's head along the Nebraskan roads"), a futility spawned by want of "listening." Daniel Berrigan shares Craig's dismay in "Facing It." Setting aside history's response (or its lack of response) to the "case of Christ," Berrigan's "The Crucifix" visualizes the intent of the cross against the horizon of human experience.

"Christ Bearing the Cross" by El Greco David Craig

The honey-red hue of the picture.
along with the eyes (left one, wetter),
suggest the greater temptation:
the prospect of creation, evidence of God's love,
breaking apart.

There is no logic here. Only
loss. That face, bruised, is calm.
The calm. The red in the clock, the sky
is also blood, suggested.
The body that was of earth, the earth
changed.

     Bright red berries
     in the fall. How here, in western Ohio,

the whole sodden scene becomes
tinted. A tree brimming, and yet,
bare. Red leaves among the fallen brown,
yellow. Grey sky, trees, the whole
terrible fecundity,
as if the earth were too loaded, too late.

His neck is thick, masculine.
His shoulders, too broad, long muscle somehow
speaking an unhurried pace.
The hands in contrast, are delicate. The left one,
down the cross He not so much bears
as becomes, toward the bottom of the painting.
Only the smallest finger, almost an afterthought,
crooked, notes Hell's harrowing.

Fixed, submissive. He wears an angular halo.
A geometry of wood, and the clouds
opening above the cross' raised arm, which might,
from this frontal view (the long beam, across His Back,
hidden), easily, wittily, be the top,
instead, of a
smaller cross.

Gospel Poem #2 David Craig

Jesus
Good Friday blood on the teeth night a
steel trap Blades of amber grass
the stoney reach of cliffs along Herod's lacquered pate
The blue ranches within your mortgaged veins
angry house licensed ache
Your fibula now cow's head along Nebraskan roads
Call on us dead one we will not answer
Call on us and watch our bruised mouths negotiate
ivory steps The gears of our gospel survive us

14

Talk to us of holiness we were not listening
our hands are angry and run like mice
along our beetled bones

Facing It Daniel Berrigan

Who could declare your death, standing
obedient as Stylites, empty as death's head
moving gently as the world's
majestic sun into light?

It was a hollow death; men
dread it like a plague. Thieves die this way,
charlatans, rejects. A good man's thought recoils;
his best years, aspiration, children

beckon a different road. To grow old yes,
gently one day to stop breathing, home and faces
drifting out of mind. Abrupt violence even
he can countenance, a quick mercy on disease

but not this, not this. The mother's face
knotted, mottled with horror.
A vision,
a few men destroyed.

It is always like this; time's cruel harrowing,
furies at the reins of fortune
wild horses dragging
the heroic dishonored body on time's ground.

O for an act of God! we cry, before death utterly
reduce to dust
        that countenance, that grace and beauty.

But
come wild hope, to dead end. War, murder,
anguish, fratricide.

No recourse. The case of Jesus Christ
is closed. Make what you will
desire, regret, he lies
stigmatized, a broken God
the world had sport of.

Risen? we have not turned that page.

---

*Berrigan compares Christ to Saint Simeon Stylites, the fourth-century
ascetic who lived the last twenty years of his life atop a pillar* (stylos) *in
extreme penitence, preaching to the crowds who sought him out.*

The Crucifix Daniel Berrigan

I

I remember today a Quebec roadside, the crucifix
raised crude as life among farming people,
its shadow creeping, dawn and twilight, over their lives.
Among wains, haycocks and men it moved like a savior.

So old, so scored by their winters, it had been staked out
perhaps by a band of ruffians on first Good Friday.
The way it endured, time would have bruised his fist in striking it.

What time had done, breaking the bones at knee and wrist,
washing the features blank as quarry stone,
turning the legs to spindles, stealing the eyes

was only to plant forever its one great gesture
deeper in furrow, heave it high above rooftops.

Where time had done his clumsy worst, cracking its heart,
hollowing its breast inexorably,—he opened this Burning-glass
to hold the huge landscape: crops, houses and men, in Its fire.

II

He was irremovably there, nailing down the landscape,
more permanent than any mountain time could bring down
or frost alter face of. He could not be turned aside
from his profound millennial prayer: not by birds
moved wonderfully to song on that cruel bough,
not by sun, standing compassionately at right hand or left.

Let weather tighten or loosen his nails: he was vowed to stand.
Northstar took rise from his eyes, learned constancy of him.

Let cloudburst break like judgement, sending workmen homeward
whipping their teams from field, down the rutted road to barn

still his body took punishment like a mainsail
bearing the heaving world onward to the Father.

And men knew nightlong: in the clear lovely morning he will be
    there,
not to be pulled down from landscape, never from his people's
    hearts.

---

*In Geoffrey Hill's "Canticle for Good Friday," the apostle Thomas, the
"doubter" who will have to search the wounds of a risen Christ in order
to believe, here reacts to Christ's execution. He is close enough to smell
both the blood of the wounds and the vinegar offered in mockery to
quench Christ's thirst. Good Friday is the Friday before Easter Sunday
and commemorates the day of the crucifixion.*

Canticle for Good Friday Geoffrey Hill

The cross staggered him. At the cliff-top
Thomas, beneath its burden, stood
While the dulled wood
Spat on the stones each drop
Of deliberate blood.

A clamping, cold-figured day
Thomas (not transfigured) stamped, crouched,
Watched
Smelt vinegar and blood. He,
As yet unsearched, unscratched,

And suffered to remain
At such near distance
(A slight miracle might cleanse
His brain
of all attachments, claw-roots of sense)

In unaccountable darkness moved away,
The strange flesh untouched, carrion-sustenance
Of staunchest love, choicest defiance,
Creation's issue congealing (and one woman's).

---

*As a follower of Christ, the Christian will be called to follow wherever
Christ has led, including the "way of the cross." This proves even more
of an enigma perhaps, especially to non-Christians, than the cross itself.
David Citino recognizes the challenge, and asks just how far along the
way of the cross Christ's followers would be willing to go. Andrew Hud-
gins tells how far a preacher went one night at an Alabama revival.*

Situation No. 33: The Feast David Citino

You're told the ingredients
have been assembled: for the sake of love,
wine and bread, fennel, honey and leeks;
laurel and bay to represent
your political importance and way with words;
a sampling of fabulous beasts and birds.
Fruits and meats to symbolize labor;
salt, the apple and lamb.

You're told the entertainment
will consist of your slow dismemberment
to the pulse of bass drums,
the plodding cadence of Gregorian chant,
screams of your parents and children.

You're told it will hurt
like nothing else, but after it's over
your very best friends will take you
home with them and place you
on altars in the midst of music and yearning,
place you near fire, teach their children
to sing your name.

Do you accept?

At the Piano Andrew Hudgins

One night two hunters, drunk, came in the tent.
They fired their guns and stood there stupidly
as Daddy left the pulpit, stalked toward them,
and slapped them each across the mouth. He split
one's upper lip.

19

                              They beat him like a dog.
They propped their guns against the center pole,
rolled up their sleeves as Daddy stood and preached
about the desecration of God's house.
They punched him down, took turns kicking his ribs,
while thirty old women and sixteen men
sat slack-jawed in their folding chairs and watched.
Just twelve, not knowing what to do, I launched
into "Amazing Grace"—the only hymn
I knew by heart—and everybody sang.
We sang until the hunters grew ashamed
—or maybe tired—and left, taking their guns,
their faces red and gleaming from the work.

They got three years suspended sentence each
and Daddy got another tale of how
Christians are saints and strangers in the world.
I guess he knows. He said that I'd done right
to play the song. God's music saved his life.
But I don't know. I couldn't make a guess.
Can you imagine what it means to be
just barely twelve, a Christian and a girl,
and see your father beaten to a pulp?
Neither can I, God knows, and I was there
in the hot tent, beneath the mildewed cloth,
breathing the August, Alabama air,
and I don't know what happened there, to me.
I told this to my second husband, Jim.
We were just dating then. I cried a lot.
He said, *Hush, dear, at least your father got*
a chance to turn all four of his cheeks.
I laughed. I knew, right then, I was in love.
But still I see that image of my father,
his weight humped on his shoulders as he tried
to stand, and I kept plunging through the song
so I could watch my hands and not his face,
which was rouged crimson with red clay and blood.

Transformation

The cross marks the end of Jesus' life and the beginning of the christic affirmation, witnessed by Christ's immediate followers as his transformed bodily presence among them. Transformation thus becomes for Christians the primary sign of the power of the cross, as much for themselves as it was for Christ. The first four poems of this chapter observe the initial "Easter event," a crucified Jesus transformed to a risen Christ. The remaining poems examine the Christian awareness of transformation in the life of humans and in nature.

Les Murray's "Easter 1984," like Andrew Hudgins's "Ecce Homo," ex-
poses the human impulse to destroy Jesus but sees in it, almost by way of
ironic praise, the force that "raised up evolution." Beneath the rough
grain of his language, Murray's precise strategies guide the poem's move-
ment toward a structural transformation that supports its transforma-
tive theme. A sequence of three sonnets, each containing various combi-
nations of three rhymes, most of them slant or half rhymes, provides an
appropriately trinitarian symmetry. The first two sonnets are built
mostly of four-beat lines, but the third sonnet raises the beat to five, even
six beats per line, as the poet signals the implications of the risen Christ.

Easter 1984 Les Murray

When we saw human dignity
healing humans in the middle of the day

we moved in on him slowly
under the incalculable gravity

of old freedom, of our own freedom,
under atmospheres of consequence, of justice

under which no one needs to thank anyone.
If this was God, we would get even.

And in the end we nailed him,
lashed, spittled, stretched him limb from limb.

We would settle with dignity
for the anguish it had caused us,

we'd send it to be abstract again,
we would set it free.

.   .   .

23

But we had raised up evolution.
It would not stop being human.

Ever afterwards, the accumulation
of freedom would end in this man

whipped, bloodied, getting the treatment.
It would look like man himself getting it.

He was freeing us, painfully, from freedom,
justice, dignity—he was discharging them

of their deadly ambiguous deposit,
remaking out of them the primal day

in which he was free not to have borne it
and we were free not to have done it,

free never to torture man again,
free to believe him risen.

. . .

Remember the day when life increased,
explainably or outright, was haloed in poignancy,

straight life, given not attained, unlurching ecstasy,
arrest of the guards for once, and ourself released,

splendour taking detail, beyond the laughter-and-tears
as if these were gateway to it, still or moving utterness

in and all around us? Some have seen this human
night and day, steadily. Flashes of it have drawn others on.

A laser of this would stand the litter-bound or Lazarus
upright, stammering, or unshroud absent Jesus

whose anguish was to be for a whole day lost to this,
making of himself the companionway of our species

up from where such love is an unreal, half-forgotten
peak, and not yet the baseline of the human.

---

*"The Say-but-the-Word Centurion Attempts a Summary" is a medita-
tion by the Roman soldier whom Jesus had credited with a faith greater
than the Israelites'. His servant near death, the centurion had declared
himself unworthy to receive Christ under his roof, certain if Jesus would
"say but the word" the servant would be healed. In Murray's monologue,
the centurion speaks after Christ's death in a boundary moment of West-
ern religious thought, when the Olympian pantheon bumps against the
"Saturnalia and paradox" of a transforming Christian consciousness.*

The Say-but-the-Word Centurion Attempts a Summary Les Murray

That numinous healer who preached Saturnalia and paradox
has died a slave's death. We were maneuvered into it by priests
and by the man himself. To complete his poem.

He was certainly dead. The pilum guaranteed it. His message,
unwritten except on his body, like anyone's, was wrapped
like a scroll and dispatched to our liberated selves, the gods.

If he has now risen, as our infiltrators gibber,
he has outdone Orpheus, who went alive to the Shades.
Solitude may be stronger than embraces. Inventor of the mustard
      tree,

he mourned one death, perhaps all, before he reversed it.
He forgave the sick to health, disregarded the sex of the Furies
when expelling them from minds. And he never speculated.

If he is risen, all are children of a most high real God
or something even stranger called by that name
who knew to come and be punished for the world.

To have knowledge of right, after that, is to be in the wrong.
Death came through the sight of law. His people's oldest wisdom.
If death is now the birth-gate into things unsayable

in language of death's era, there will be wars about religion
as there never were about the death-ignoring Olympians.
Love too, his new universal, so far ahead of you it has died

for you before you meet it, may seem colder than the favors of
    gods
who are our poems, good and bad. But there never was a bad
    baby.
Half of his worship will be grinding his face in the dirt

then lifting it up to beg, in private. The low will rule, and curse by
    him.
Divine bastard, soul-usurer, eros-frightener, he is out to monopo-
    lize hatred.
Whole philosophies will be devised for their brief snubbings of
    him.

But regained excels kept, he taught. Thus he has done the impos-
    sible
to show us it is there. To ask it of us. It seems we are to be the
    poem
and live the impossible. As each time we have, with mixed cries.

The centurion's characterization of believers as Christ's "poem" puts a naively literal but very Christian spin on the creative dynamic of the resurrection. It plays off a favorite Christian pun instigated by the Gospel of John's "In the beginning was the Word [logos]." Just as God in the beginning speaks the embodied Logos-Word of Christ, so Christ in turn speaks a transforming word that believers embody, becoming his "poem" in the centurion's sense. That Murray's multiple reflection on God's Word and Christ's poems and the healing power of Word and word is itself in the form of a poem creates a final level of pun on the kinship between Christianity and poetic language.

For the woman in "The Emperor Has No Clothes!" by Kathleen Norris, power manipulation of the Jesus poem by "men" begins even as witnesses strain for a look at the empty tomb. The story gains poignancy in light of the gospel accounts, where Christ after his death appears first to women, entrusting himself to their spiritual authority. His early appearance to Mary Magdalene is recalled by Andrew Hudgins in "Christ as a Gardener."

The Emperor Has No Clothes! Kathleen Norris

After she said it,
the crowd grabbed her roughly.
The emperor
was spirited off
by Secret Service men
disguised as angels.

"Wait a minute," she said,
"I just want to
think this through."
But they bound her wrists
with rope
and prodded her with irons.
"By whose authority?"
they demanded.

She couldn't answer,
being bound and gagged,
so they invented for her
a man with horns
and supernatural cock,
much bigger
and more talented than theirs.

She was still saying it
as priests approached
with notepads and pills.
"You're overwrought,"
one said gently
as he took her by the arm.
She tried to turn her head
back toward the empty tomb
but men were putting neon signs
around it.

Christ as a Gardener Andrew Hudgins

The boxwoods planted in the park spelled LIVE.
I never noticed it until they died.
Before, the entwined green had smudged the word
unreadable. And when they take their own advice
again—come spring, come Easter—no one will know
a word is buried in the leaves. I love the way
that Mary thought her resurrected Lord
a gardener. It wasn't just the broad-brimmed hat
and muddy robe that fooled her: he was *that* changed.
He looks across the unturned field, the riot
of unscythed grass, the smattering of wildflowers.
Before he can stop himself, he's on his knees.
He roots up stubborn weeds, pinches the suckers,
deciding order here—what lives, what dies,
and how. But it goes deeper even than that.

His hands burn and his bare feet smolder. He longs
to lie down inside the long, dew-moist furrows
and press his pierced side and his broken forehead
into the dirt. But he's already done it—
passed through one death and out the other side.
He laughs. He kicks his bright spade in the earth
and turns it over. Spring flashes by, then harvest.
Beneath his feet, seeds dance into the air.
They rise, and he, not noticing, ascends
on midair steppingstones of dandelion,
of milkweed, thistle, cattail, and goldenrod.

---

*Hudgins's imagery associates a transforming nature with the risen
Christ. In "Sabbaths: 1979 II," Wendell Berry goes further and actually
names the image of "resurrection" in nature's cycles of death and re-
birth. In "The Handing Down" and "An Anniversary," the transforma-
tive natural process, "life that only lives by dying," merges with the hu-
man experiences of hope and married love.*

---

from **Sabbaths: 1979 II** Wendell Berry

Another Sunday morning comes
And I resume the standing Sabbath
Of the woods, where the finest blooms
Of time return, and where no path

Is worn but wears its makers out
At last, and disappears in leaves
Of fallen seasons. The tracked rut
Fills and levels; here nothing grieves

In the risen season. Past life
Lives in the living. Resurrection
Is in the way each maple leaf
Commemorates its kind, by connection

Outreaching understanding. What rises
Rises into comprehension
And beyond. Even falling rises
In praise of light....

from **The Handing Down** Wendell Berry

7. *The heaviness of his wisdom*
The incredible happens, he knows.
The worst possibilities are real.
The terrible justifies

his dread of it. He knows winter
despondences, the mind inundated
by its excrement, hope gone

and not remembered.
And he knows vernal transfigurations,
the sentence in the stems of trees

noisy with old memory made new,
troubled with the seed
of the being of what has not been.

He trusts the changes of the sun and air:
dung and carrion made earth,
richness that forgets what it was.

He knows, if he can hold out
long enough, the good
is given its chance.

He has dreamed of a town
fit for the abiding of souls
and bodies that might live forever.

He has seen it in a far-off
white and gold evening
of summer, the black flight

of swifts turning above it
in the air. There's a clarity
in which he has not become clear,

his body dragging a shadow,
half hidden in it.

An Anniversary Wendell Berry

What we have been becomes
The country where we are.
Spring goes, summer comes,
And in the heat, as one year
Or a thousand years before,
The fields and woods prepare
The burden of their seed
Out of time's wound, the old
Richness of the fall. Their deed
Is renewal. In the household
Of the woods the past
Is always healing in the light,
The high shiftings of the air.
It stands upon its yield
And thrives. Nothing is lost.
What yields, though in despair,
Opens and rises in the night.
Love binds us to this term
With its yes that is crying
In our marrow to confirm
Life that only lives by dying.
Lovers live by the moon
Whose dark and light are one,

Changing without rest.
The root struts from the seed
In the earth's dark—harvest
And feast at the edge of sleep.
Darkened, we are carried
Out of need, deep
In the country we have married.

The patterns of nature are also the subject of Kathleen Norris's "The Monastery Orchard in Early Spring" The poem's speaker seeks to imitate them, seeing there the "idea of change" that moves in all things, including the unseen "forces, principalities, powers" of the spiritual realm. Norris alludes to the time Saint Augustine stole fruit from an orchard as a boy, described in a famous passage from his Confessions.

The Monastery Orchard in Early Spring Kathleen Norris

God's cows are in the fields,
safely grazing. I can see them
through bare branches,
through the steady rain.
Suddenly, fir trees seem ashamed
and tired, bending under winter coats.

I, too, want to be light enough
for this day: throw off impediments,
push like a tulip
through a muddy smear of snow.

I want to take the rain to heart
and feel it move
like possibility, the idea
of change,
through things

seen and unseen:
forces, principalities, powers.

Newton named the force that pulls the apple
and the moon with it,
toward the center of the earth.
Augustine found a desire as strong; to steal,
to possess, and then throw away.
Encounter with fruit is dangerous:
the pear's womanly shape forever mocked him.

A man and a woman are talking.
Rain moves down
and bare branches lift up
to learn all over again
to hold their fill of green
and blossom, and bear each fruit to glory,
letting it fall.

---

*In "Alatus," a word meaning wingèd in Latin, Richard Wilbur watches
the leaves of autumn making their "rash consent to change." Their
transformation is elicited by "the hid pulse of things," much as the
seascape in "The Beacon" is transformed by a lighthouse beam whose
sweeping pulse brings clarity and order to the darkness. Like Alexander
the Great who severed the intricate knot at Gordium with his sword,
thus becoming ruler of Asia, the beacon "solves" the benighted waters,
revealing, among other things, the playful spray of sea-nymph Nereids.*

Alatus Richard Wilbur

Their supply lines cut,
The leaves go down to defeat,
Turning, flying, but

Bravely so, the ash
Shaking from blade and pennon
May light's citron flash;

And rock maple, though
Its globed array be shivered,
Strews its fallen so

As to mock the cold,
Blanketing earth with earnest
Of a summer's gold.

Still, what sumac-gore
Began, and rattling oak shall
End, is not a war;

Nor are leaves the same
(Though May come back in triumph),
Crumpled once by flame.

This time's true valor
Is a rash consent to change,
To crumbling pallor,

Dust, and dark re-merge.
See how the fire-bush, circled
By a crimson verge

Of its own sifting,
Bristles aloft its every
Naked stem, lifting

Beyond the faint sun,
Toward the hid pulse of things, its
Wingèd skeleton.

The Beacon Richard Wilbur

Founded on rock and facing the night-fouled sea
A beacon blinks at its own brilliance,
Over and over with cutlass gaze
Solving the Gordian waters,

Making the sea-roads out, and the lounge of the weedy
Meadows, finding the blown hair
As it always has, and the buxom, lavish
Romp of the ocean-daughters.

Then in the flashes of darkness it is all gone,
The flung arms and the hips, meads
And meridians, all; and the dark of the eye
Dives for the black pearl

Of the sea in-itself. Watching the blinded waves
Compounding their eclipse, we hear their
Booms, rumors and guttural sucks
Warn of the pitchy whirl

At the mind's end. All of the sense of the sea
Is veiled as voices nearly heard
In morning sleep; nor shall we wake
At the sea's heart. Rail

At the deaf unbeatable sea, my soul, and weep
Your Alexandrine tears, but look:
The beacon-blaze unsheathing turns
The face of darkness pale

And now with one grand chop gives clearance to
Our human visions, which assume
The waves again, fresh and the same.
Let us suppose that we

See most of darkness by our plainest light.
It is the Nereid's kick endears
The tossing spray; a sighted ship
Assembles all the sea.

---

*In "My Farewell," the poet is undergoing a transformation he cannot
entirely understand. Scott Cairns translates from the Portuguese of
Raimundo Luz, whom he introduces as "the greatest postmodern poet"
writing in that language. Luz is also, according to Cairns, "a radical
theologian, identifying himself paradoxically as a Christian-Marxist.
He is a devoted family man, a fan of American rhythm and blues, an
accomplished cook, and a fiction." His verse will appear throughout
this anthology in Cairns's exclusive translation. Accompanying the
complete Luz sequence is an inscription from St. Paul's letter to the
Corinthians: "I show you a mystery. We shall not all sleep, but we shall
all be changed."*

The Translation of Raimundo Luz: My Farewell Scott Cairns

Things are happening. Daily.
I come across new disturbances
in my routine. I am curiously
unsettled. I dress myself
and the clothes fall to the floor.
I scratch my head. Dust
in my hand. All morning
arranging flowers, and for what?
Petals fallen, litter
on the pretty cloth. I march
straightway to the mirror
and shake my fist. My hand
is a blue maraca scattering petals.
I shout my rage
and hear my words praising

the vast goodness of the world.
This is beyond control.

Even so, I am slowly learning one thing;
of one thing I am slowly becoming
aware: whether or not I would
have it so, whether I sleep
or no, I will be changed.
I am changing as I speak. Bless you all.
Suffer the children. Finished. Keep.

Another frequent voice in the present volume is Sister Mary Appassion-
ata, David Citino's composite folk pedagogue, who offers with varying
degrees of satire the kind of religious lore that was often an accompani-
ment of Catholic elementary education before the Second Vatican
Council (1962–1965). Like Cairns's Raimundo Luz, Sister Mary serves
us a whimsical front for serious theological ideas. In "Doctrines of the
Strawberry," Mary the mother of Jesus is the instigator of an organic
process by which Sister Mary illustrates the transformative powers asso-
ciated with Christ. In "The Nature of the Candle," Sister Mary relates
transformation to the action of a flame.

Sister Mary Appassionata Lectures the Folklore Class:
Doctrines of the Strawberry David Citino

Mary, full of the mercy only
mothers know, hides the souls
of unchristened infants, guilty
as sure as they're born, in seeds
of strawberries, Jesus' favorite fruit,
and when He's picked and had His fill,
walking out into heaven's
misty meadows and groves weeping over
the gross appetites of the wicked,
thinness of the good, and after

nature's run its course, their beauty
passing through Him like too much
of any good thing, the seeds are left
to be covered with the dirt of paradise,
time's never ceasing tide, but soon
to rise again in blossoms of white flower
and plump red fruit, bitter and sweet
as blood, as life,
waiting for Him to come again.

Sister Mary Appassionata Lectures the Eighth Grade Boys and Girls on the Nature of the Candle David Citino

> There are many instances during the Middle Ages
> of persons having a candle made, as a special
> devotion, of the same height or the same weight
> as themselves.
> —Curiosities of Popular Customs

It stands to reason. Wax crafted by bees,
tallow of vegetable or beast rendered just hard enough
to stand, to support the flame that dances
dangerously before the slightest breath, wick
running the body's length, spinal cord
that makes all parts a whole, intelligence
warming whatever comes near, touch of love,
to dispel the sentence of night after night,
only need to be, but eating a hole
in the center, faith consuming flesh from the inside,
running toward the heart, a fuse,
utter dark biding its time under the tongue,
inside each tooth and bone, life drowning
in the rising tide of life, deadly depth
of every day, price we're made to pay
for our season of light, last breath
a hiss or sigh as sun floods windows
to bear the soul away, what's left of us lying

gutted, guttered, cold, scents
of our brief wisdom lingering in the room.

---

*For Sister Mary the burning away of the candle is as much about hu-
man life giving way to death, the physical body giving way to "the soul,"
as it is about the self that "stands to reason" giving way to a new self in
the flame of faith. With Citino, the phenomenon of rebirth, though an
obvious good, can never be separated from the loss and suffering in-
volved. He betrays a kind of Gethsemane foreboding, even a squea-
mishness, at the prospect of "life drowning / in the rising tide of life." In
all cases a breaking down or brokenness, like the body crucified, precedes
an experience of wholeness. Citino takes this idea to the extreme in
"The Analysis," in his account of what is happening to his speaker's
body and mind, and in his metaphors like cancer, an agent of radical
alteration.*

The Analysis David Citino

> *I existed frequently without a stomach; I expressly told
> the attendant…I could not eat because I had no stomach.*
> —*Daniel Paul Schreber*

Yes there was a visitor again last night
but whether it was an incubus or succubus
I can't tell until you tell me who I am.
    It began, Doktor, last Mother's Day
    with the customary denial of paternity.
  Russians and Poles in one-man subs
    make daring night raids into my testicles.
Thin people the world over
are engaged in a conspiracy to eat
at my marrow until I too
am thin and conspiratorial.
    Can I enjoy any meal knowing as I do
    that three times each day all mothers
    become larger?

My nerves before meals exalt themselves so loudly
they mingle with the nerve of God: cell and ganglion,
synapse, axon, dendrite, dynamo.
Yes! And radio interference
from the planet Venus, Israel and the Vatican.
    Each night I stumble from
    my aged wife's bed, my feet swollen big
    as tombstones, the riddle of the sphinx
    in my pajamas.
  My parents employ earwigs and termites
  to sabotage the wires inside my head.
    She's wonderfully aggressive in a way
    I wasn't born to be, her teeth are relics.
When self splits as I so often do into man and not-man
the partners embrace—this is holy love
    and I love myself to watch me love one
    another in others' eyes and mirrors
    under God's approving rays
  his energy a cancer in my soul
    his love my downfall and rising
tearing apart to make me whole.

The ivory-tower priest of Daniel Berrigan's "In Memoriam II" failed in his short life to embody Christ, to know him in the "singulars, odd-ments, smells" of the world. Berrigan insists that the brokenness of poverty and suffering, the choice of Jesus, transforms, drawing compassionate life from the "crotch of being"—the "needle's eye" of simplicity through which the bloated rich have no more chance of passing than a camel. But in a sonnet from his "Genesis" sequence, Geoffrey Hill wonders if any Christian follower is capable of embodying Christ, of responding to the light of transformation for which the cross was endured.

In Memoriam (II) Daniel Berrigan

A young priest, dead suddenly
at forty years
taught a metaphysic of the world.
His mind was lucid, ingrained. He would say,
it is deductibly verified
that God is immutable; and,
universal order converges on one being.

So be it. This priest, alas for poetry, love and priests
was neither great nor evil.
The truths he spoke
being inert, fired no mind to a flare;
a remote world order
of essence, cause, finality,
invited submission to his God.

He never conveyed a man, Christ, or himself—
His cleric's eye
forbade singulars, oddments, smells,
sickness, pushcarts, the poor.
He dwelt in the fierce Bronx, among a university's
stone faced acres
hemmed in by trucks and tumbrels. No avail.

Yet it could not be borne
by those who love him, that having passed
from unawareness to light
he should be denied
the suffering that marks man
like a circumcision, like unstaunched tears; *saved.*

Heaven is everything earth has withheld.
I wish you, priest, for herald angel,
a phthisic old man

beating a tin can with a mutton bone—
behold he comes!

For savior,
unsavory men
a wino's dime
a Coxey's army, a Bowery 2 A.M.
For beatific vision
an end to books, book ends, unbending minds,
tasteless fodder, restrictive order.

For eternal joy
veins casting off, in a moment's
burning transfiguration
the waste and sludge of unrealized time.

Christ make most of you!
stitch you through
the needle's eye, the grudging gate.
Crawl through
that crotch of being;
new eyes, new heart, the runner's burning start.

from **Genesis** Geoffrey Hill

On the sixth day, as I rode
In haste about the works of God,
With spurs I plucked the horse's blood.

By blood we live, the hot, the cold,
To ravage and redeem the world:
There is no bloodless myth will hold.

And by Christ's blood are men made free
Though in close shrouds their bodies lie
Under the rough pelt of the sea;

Though Earth has rolled beneath her weight
The bones that cannot bear the light.

---

*In "The Way of Pain," Wendell Berry considers how the experience of
the cross in the brokenness of personal anguish leads to "the extremity of
love." "The Slip" relates how human "pain / perceives new possibility"
in the same way a river surges over farmland and "an awful clarifica-
tion occurs / where a place was."*

The Way of Pain Wendell Berry

For parents, the only way
is hard. We who give life
give pain. There is no help.
Yet we who give pain
give love; by pain we learn
the extremity of love.

I read of Abraham's sacrifice
the Voice required of him,
so that he lead to the altar
and the knife his only son.
The beloved life was spared
that time, but not the pain.
It was the pain that was required.

I read of Christ crucified,
the only begotten Son
sacrificed to flesh and time
and all our woe. He died
and rose, but who does not tremble
for his pain, his loneliness,
and the darkness of the sixth hour?
Unless we grieve like Mary

at His grave, giving Him up
as lost, no Easter morning comes.

And then I slept, and dreamed
the life of my only son
was required of me, and I
must bring him to the edge
of pain, not knowing why.
I woke, and yet that pain
was true. It brought his life
to the full in me. I bore him
suffering, with love like the sun,
too bright, unsparing, whole.

Berry cites the examples of Jesus, Jesus' mother, Mary, and their ances-
tor Abraham. According to the scripture story, when Abraham raised
the knife that would sacrifice his son Isaac in obedience to divine com-
mand, an angel, for Abraham's faithfulness, intervened.

The Slip Wendell Berry

The river takes the land, and leaves nothing.
Where the great slip gave way in the bank
and an acre disappeared, all human plans
dissolve. An awful clarification occurs
where a place was. Its memory breaks
from what is known now, begins to drift.
Where cattle grazed and trees stood, emptiness
widens the air for birdflight, wind, and rain.
As before the beginning, nothing is there.
Human wrong is in the cause, human
ruin in the effect—but no matter;
all will be lost, no matter the reason.
Nothing, having arrived, will stay.
The earth, even, is like a flower, so soon

passeth it away. And yet this nothing
is the seed of all—the clear eye
of Heaven, where all the worlds appear.
Where the imperfect has departed, the perfect
begins its struggle to return. The good gift
begins again its descent. The maker moves
in the unmade, stirring the water until
it clouds, dark beneath the surface,
stirring and darkening the soul until pain
perceives new possibility. There is nothing
to do but learn and wait, return to work
on what remains. Seed will sprout in the scar.
Though death is in the healing, it will heal.

---

*David Craig celebrates transformation in giddy, transformed language
that mimics the cadences of the pentecostal sermon. In "Gospel Poem
#1" the poet calls for change that brings enlightenment ("take the owl
from the pumpkin" . . . "flower the walls with tutors of lost languages")
and fullness ("in a munch of apples in / every trumpet's blaze"). In
"Gospel Poem #3" he modulates his tone somewhat as, at the foot of the
cross ("Furnished Ash") we wait, paralyzed by spiritual inertia.*

Gospel Poem #1 David Craig

Jesus
Loaded Jowl Cakes Mother of seismic dreams
if only I could touch Your pebbled face
Coax the clamshell
lunch time read-out
Come   take the owl from the pumpkin march
the skins of the old days out the necessary door
You are the Mother walker candle tongue
bee thread Take the lies
exchange them for jazz on Barnaby street
flower the walls with tutors of lost languages

Let me shout your blare-root
over the beams of every mule house
Come   Come   Come
in a munch of apples in
every trumpet's blaze through keys of ivy
under sun-dusted sleeves

Gospel Poem #3 David Craig

Jesus
Risen
past the amphibial claws
the promontories of self all
governing bodies Pious instruments will
chase hatted seeds Holy files
of presbyters will rejoice alphabetically
and even the coldest thumb-tied road unwinds
O Dark Embrace Your
wings blood-tipped sun-dipped curl
around the rumpled cloth the rock hard
earth Jesus
we hear persimmon voices out over the water
We bud under snowcake in trees
out over heretical streets
We are thoughtful seals and our chorus
runs in timber down steel beams
fuels the electron span beneath bankers   billboards
Furnished Ash we wait

from **Metamorphoses** Geoffrey Hill

Through scant pride to be so put out!
But feed, feed, unlyrical scapegoat;
Plague shrines where each fissure blows
Odor of laurel clouding yours.

46

Exercise, loftily, your visions
Where the mountainous distance
Echoes its unfaltering speech
To mere outcry and harrowing search.

Possessed of agility and passion,
Energy (out-of-town fashion)
Attack every obstacle
And height; make the sun your pedestal.

Settle all that bad blood;
Be visited, touched, understood;
Be graced, groomed, returned to favor
With admirable restraint and fervor.

Death

Christians view Christ's experience of death as a paradigm of their own. For them death is a passage, not a terminus rendering earthly life ironic or futile. The Christian poet variously welcomes, mocks, even praises death in ways the non-Christian may think unseemly. Images of light abound. Death also furnishes the Christian with imagery that finds a philosophical counterpart in Plato's world of ideas, death as a metaphor of an eternal perfection imperfectly present in the everyday, like glimmerings on the wall of a cave.

Coming Forth Scott Cairns

I'm sorry. I have a hard time not laughing
even now. This ridiculous grin

won't get off my face. Dying did it,
though I don't remember much about

being dead. Sometimes, horrible things happen:
children die, famine sets in, whole towns

are slapped down and turned to dust by earthquake.
I can't help it, but these things start me

laughing so I can't stop. My friends all hate me.
The morning my sister cracked her hip,

I was worthless; I had to run clear out
to the clay field to keep anyone from seeing

how it broke me up. I know. You think
I'm trash, worse than a murderer

or a petty god. I suppose I am.
I just get this quiver started

in me every time someone I know dies and stays dead.
I tremble all over and have to hold

myself, as if some crazy thing in me
were anxious to get out. I told you

I can't remember being dead. I can't.
But this weakness in my knees, or in my throat

keeps me thinking—whatever comes next
should be a thousand worlds better than this.

Last Rites David Citino

When death dances in,
tap-shoes rattling like dice
on the floor of your room,
assure him there's been no mistake;
ask if you may borrow
his faded straw hat, his grin.
Ask if you may lead;
waltz him out the door.

Stake your claim early
to a plot of bright earth.
Bleak ground at dawn, sowing
the seeds your father left unplanted;
reap a future in crisp green bunches.
At the close of the harvest day
lie down in the soil, head to the east,
the ancient scent rising all around.
As the sun falls from the edge of earth
let the darkness race across your body.

A corposant, from the Latin corpus sanctus, *is a "holy body," the human person transfigured in death. In "Situation No. 9," Citino visualizes how the corposant identity of the reader folds into nature's rhythm. Likewise, the corposant of Wendell Berry's friend in "Three Elegaic Poems" lives on in the landscape, "hidden among all that is." Scott Cairns's "Surprise" recounts a similar metamorphosis, while the victim transfigured at the stake in "The Martyr" is received into rapture, "a new / consideration of light / on its objects." These images tap the Christian expectation of the greater completeness, the "radiances" awaiting in an order of being beyond death.*

Situation No. 9: The Corposant David Citino

You wake at the end of night
young again, all things new:
the celebration of moonlight and wind
in the pine-tops, the kindness
between a sleeping lover's legs.

You walk out alone
over the fallow fields that ring your home
rubbing a stone big as a child's skull
and marred by a fossil or the harrow's tooth,
carrying in your pockets
the few relics you've decided
you can't leave to others.

You see your body
grown lovely as candlelight
or moonlit mist move out to walk
beside you, then change direction
to go off alone, a diminishing place
glowing with sculpted tissue—
the bones of the face and the hands
a geometry precise enough
to make you cry.

Tell me, what's the difference now
between what's left of you
and dawn?

from **Three Elegiac Poems** Wendell Berry

Harry Erdman Perry, 1881–1965

II.

I stand at the cistern in front of the old barn
in the darkness, in the dead of winter,

53

the night strangely warm, the wind blowing,
rattling an unlatched door.
I draw cold water up out of the ground, and drink.

At the house the light is still waiting.
An old man I've loved all my life is dying
in his bed there. He is going
slowly down from himself.
In final obedience to his life, he follows
his body out of our knowing.
Only his hands, quiet on the sheet, keep
a painful resemblance to what they no longer are.

III.

He goes free of the earth.
The sun of his last day sets
clear in the sweetness of his liberty.

The earth recovers from his dying,
the hallow of his life remaining
in all his death leaves.

Radiances know him. Grown lighter
than breath, he is set free
in our remembering. Grown brighter

than vision, he goes dark
into the life of the hill
that holds his peace.

He's hidden among all that is,
and cannot be lost.

Surprise Scott Cairns

A voice calling from the trees
or a gun-blast. You must answer
and you do, catching your breath.
You catch your breath and you answer.
It is easy as breathing.
You discover your father or a child.
You discover your god wandering.
You uncover the body of a friend. You uncover
your own body, freshly scrubbed and eager
to move on. There is a lost crowd
of townspeople browsing on the land.
Behind a cedar stump, your mother
sings and washes clothing.
The day continues, drawing light
from all angles, tossing light harshly
into eyes. There is a rain
of light. There is a woman dressed in sheepskin.
There are a dozen soldiers knocking trees.
There is a tribe of blind men whose eyes
are blood-oranges.
There is no one in the wood at all.
No one is among the trees and no one
will be coming. You are caught in a forest
like a sound; you are expanding like a sound
in a forest. You are a stretch of light.
Something has called you to an exit
and you have come; so now
you must continue on the way.

The Martyr Scott Cairns

set to flame, his eyes
discovering new color, a new

consideration of light
on its objects:

A guard dropping his eyes
to avoid his vision. A blind man
fingering his sightless eyes. The eye
of the needle, its requisite motion.
The cat's eye. A dead man's eyes
in a jungle. The blue space
beyond the trees, which is an eye.

This ecstatic death that sends his eyes
rolling back into his head,
and further back.

---

*More circumspectly, the speaker of Cairns's "Prospect of the Interior"
acknowledges that we are given pause, as Hamlet was, by "the undis-
covered country from whose bourn no traveller returns."*

Prospect of the Interior Scott Cairns

A little daunting, these periodic
incursions into what is, after all,
merely suspected territory.

One can determine nothing from the low
and, I'm afraid, compromised perspective
of the ship, save that the greenery is thick,

and that the shoreline is, in the insufficient
light of morning and evening, frequently
obscured by an unsettling layer of mist.

If there are inhabitants, they've chosen
not to show themselves. Either they fear us,
or they prefer ambush to open threat.

We'd not approach the interior at all
except for recurrent, nagging doubts
about the seaworthiness of our craft.

So, as a matter of course, necessity
mothers us into taking stock of our
provisions, setting out in trembling parties

of one, trusting the current, the leaky
coracle, the allocated oar.

---

*American poet John Berryman sets out before his necessary time in
Maura Eichner's "Dream Songs Concluded." What finally claims him is
"mercy and truth." Berryman, whose life ended in suicide in 1972, is
perhaps best known for his two volumes of* Dream Songs *which won
him the Pulitzer Prize for poetry. The speaker and protagonist of the
songs is Henry, the poet's alter ego.*

Dream Songs Concluded Maura Eichner

   in memory of John Berryman 1914–1972

Henry was sick of winter, John dying of
living. Together they walked across the bridge

to the library. Following truth, no doubt,
John said. Truth detoured,

going home the short way—under water.
John followed like a bulging sack.

Henry turned,
fled back to the printed page.

Under black water truth cored the river.
John sucked the dark totality into his lungs.

Truth absorbed the pull of tide, plunged
into the root of water. John followed,

gained momentum in desire, felt the coldness
of the fire, brilliant burning of the root.

While sirens stopped to let the grappling
nets into the river, someone gave the story

to the press, the pictures to T.V.
"He chose the wrong way."

Not so John said not so. Mercy and truth
are one in the root of the river.

At last I am free.
I am free.

---

*Eichner's use of water imagery invites comparison between death by
drowning and "death" by baptismal immersion. For the Christian,
both mark the passing from one life, bound by time and self, to a life of
spiritual freedom. But for flesh itself there is only decay, as Eichner tells
in "Eclogue and Elegy," a lyric in the* vanitas *tradition.*

Eclogue and Elegy Maura Eichner

Before the ants,
before the crows,

before the old hunting dog,
I found the bird.

The black mask
stared upward from the
olive gray head.

The yellow breast
shone in the sun.
The sound of *witchery, witchery*
in marshy land, in tall grass,
stilled.

From the clear memory
of what I saw,
I speak a universal word.

Though Geoffrey Hill often peoples his verse from history or biography, the namesake of "In Memory of Jane Fraser" exists solely as the dogged victim of her poem's wintry fate.

In Memory of Jane Fraser Geoffrey Hill

When snow like sheep lay in the fold
And winds went begging at each door,
And the far hills were blue with cold,
And a cold shroud lay on the moor,

She kept the siege. And every day
We watched her brooding over death
Like a strong bird above its prey.
The room filled with the kettle's breath.

Damp curtains glued against the pane
Sealed time away. Her body froze

As if to freeze us all, and chain
Creation to a stunned repose.

She died before the world could stir.
In March the ice unloosed the brook
And water ruffled the sun's hair.
Dead cones upon the alder shook.

---

*Richard Wilbur's "In a Churchyard" protests romantic idealization,
"bright thoughts uncut by men," the cutting loose of our awareness from
"time and sound" to which meditations on death so often lead. The
eyesockets of the dead are filled with their "unseenness," their obscurity
to the living. The living cannot know what the dead may know beyond
the "sill of sense." Wilbur specifically indicts Thomas Gray's famous "El-
egy in a Country Churchyard," written in 1751. He pilfers from its oft-
quoted stanza comparing the unknown graces of the anonymous poor
with the unseen beauties of nature:*

> *Full many a gem of purest ray serene*
> *The dark unfathomed caves of ocean bear;*
> *Full many a flower is born to blush unseen,*
> *And waste its sweetness on the desert air.*

*Wilbur argues that such reveries "charm" us away from the beauty of
the known and present moment, the "ken" of our mortality. The con-
clusion of his poem rings out in contrast to Gray's curfew bell that wist-
fully "tolls the knell of parting day." The "mauled boom" of Wilbur's
bell returns the mind from the "pulseless clangor" of what may be or
might have been to the "things that are."*

In a Churchyard Richard Wilbur

That flower unseen, that gem of purest ray,
Bright thoughts uncut by men:
Strange that you need but speak them, Thomas Gray,
And the mind skips and dives beyond its ken,

Finding at once the wild supposèd bloom,
Or in the imagined cave
Some pulse of crystal staving off the gloom
As covertly as phosphorous in a grave.

Void notions proper to a buried head!
Beneath these tombstones here
Unseenness fills the sockets of the dead,
Whatever to their souls may now appear;

And who but those unfathomably deaf
Who quiet all this ground
Could catch, within the ear's diminished clef,
A music innocent of time and sound?

What do the living hear, then, when the bell
Hangs plumb within the tower
Of the still church, and still their thoughts compel
Pure tollings that intend no mortal hour?

As when a ferry for the shore of death
Glides looming toward the dock,
Her engines cut, her spirits bating breath
As the ranked pilings narrow toward the shock,

So memory and expectation set
Some pulseless clangor free
Of circumstance, and charm us to forget
This twilight crumbling in the churchyard tree,

Those swifts or swallows which do not pertain,
Scuffed voices in the drive,
That light flicked on behind the vestry pane,
Till, unperplexed from all that is alive,

It shadows all our thought, balked imminence
Of uncommitted sound,

And still would tower at the sill of sense
Were not, as now, its honed abeyance crowned

With a mauled boom of summons far more strange
Than any stroke unheard,
Which breaks again with unimagined range
Through all reverberations of the word,

Pooling the mystery of things that are,
The buzz of prayer said,
The scent of grass, the earliest-blooming star,
These unseen gravestones, and the darker dead.

In the note accompanying "To His Skeleton," Wilbur defines a phlebo-lith as a vein-stone.

To His Skeleton Richard Wilbur

Why will you vex me with
These bone-spurs in the ear,
With X-rayed phlebolith
And calculus? See here,

Noblest of armatures,
The grin which bares my teeth
Is mine as yet, not yours.
Did you not stand beneath

This flesh, I could not stand,
But would revert to slime
Informous and unmanned;
And I may come in time

To wish your peace my fate,
Your sculpture my renown.

Still, I have held you straight
And mean to lay you down

Without too much disgrace
When what can perish dies.
For now then, keep your place
And do not colonize.

One of Annie Dillard's "found" poems, "Deathbeds" is arranged from quotations in Dictionary of Last Words, *edited by Edward S. Le Comte, 1955.*

from **Deathbeds** Annie Dillard

> *The poet essentially* can't *be concerned with the act of dying.*
> —Henry James, *preface to* The Wings of the Dove

This is too tight; loosen it a little. I pray
You give me some sack! Bring me last year's apple,
If you can, or any new melon. A dozen cold oysters.
My children! My papers! My book, my unfinished book!

From my present sensations, I should say I was dying
—And I am glad of it. The world is bobbing around.

Do you know the Lord's Prayer? Cover me.
Shut the door. Can't see you any more.
I must go home. I am very forlorn at the present
Moment, and wish I was at Malvern.

Am I still alive? Do I drag my anchors?

So here it is at last, the distinguished thing!
Is this dying? Is this all? Is this
All that I feared, when I prayed against a hard death?
O! I can bear this! I can bear it!
Now I have finished with all earthly business

—High time, too. Yes, yes,
My dear child, now comes death.
Is it come already? Here, here is my end.
Wait a moment. Do you not hear the voices?
And the children's are the loudest! The chariots
And horses! I do not know how this happened.
I can account for it in no way....

I am coming, Katie! John, it will not
Be long. Supremely happy! Excellent!
My dearest, dearest Liz. We are all going;
We are all going; we are all going.

This is it, chaps. Take me home.
I believe, my son, I am going. That's it.
Good-bye—drive on. Cut her loose, Doc.

I'm going, I'm going. At a gallop!
Clear the way. Good-bye, God bless you!
Good-bye, everybody. A general good-night.

Wendell Berry wishes to say good-bye from a simple grave on his farm in Port Royal, Kentucky.

---

from **Testament** Wendell Berry

> *And now To the Abbyss I pass*
> *Of that Unfathomable Grass...*

1.

Dear relatives and friends, when my last breath
Grows large and free in air, don't call it death—
A word to enrich the undertaker and inspire
His surly art of imitating life; conspire
Against him. Say that my body cannot now
Be improved upon; it has no fault to show

To the sly cosmetician. Say that my flesh
Has a perfection in compliance with the grass
Truer than any it could have striven for.
You will recognize the earth in me, as before
I wished to know it in myself: my earth
That has been my care and faithful charge from birth,
And toward which all my sorrows were surely bound,
And all my hopes. Say that I have found
A good solution, and am on my way
To the roots. And say I have left my native clay
At last, to be a traveler; that too will be so.
Traveler to where? Say you don't know.

2.

But do not let your ignorance
Of my spirit's whereabouts dismay
You, or overwhelm your thoughts.
Be careful not to say

Anything too final. Whatever
Is unsure is possible, and life is bigger
Than flesh. Beyond reach of thought
Let imagination figure

Your hope. That will be generous
To me and to yourselves. Why settle
For some know-it-all's despair
When the dead may dance to the fiddle

Hereafter, for all anybody knows?
And remember that the Heavenly soil
Need not be too rich to please
One who was happy in Port Royal....

4.

Beneath this stone a Berry is planted
In his home land, as he wanted.

He has come to the gathering of his kin,
Among whom some were worthy men,

Farmers mostly, who lived by hand,
But one was a cobbler from Ireland,

Another played the eternal fool
By riding a circus mule

To be remembered in grateful laughter
Longer than the rest. After

Doing what they had to do
They are at ease here. Let all of you

Who yet for pain find force and voice
Look on their peace, and rejoice.

---

*Kathleen Norris experiences the power of life over death as an infant in
"The Blue Light." As an adult, she calmly faces down the "angel of
death" in "Desert Run Scenario." The poem combines a surreal parody
of the American Western with an ecstatic vision of deliverance. Cows
serve as trumpets of the apocalypse in a cameo appearance by the Book
of Revelation. For David Craig's spiritual apprentice, who speaks in
several of Craig's reflections in the pages ahead, the end is friend and
guest. The apprentice will have more to say about his cryptic taste for
glass in the chapter "Presence."*

The Blue Light Kathleen Norris

1.
The angels stood
with their backs to me.
I was six months old
and dying.

I had no name for them,
or anything.
They were cold,
not like my mother.

Just beyond the angels
was a blue light
and like any child
I reached for it
because it was pretty.
I wanted to curl my fingers
around it and hold on.

The angels didn't move,
but the blue light receded.
Children are easily disappointed,
and I wanted it so much.

I lay in the hospital, angry,
rolling my head
and crying.
It may have been one of the angels
who picked me up
and returned me to my mother:
I don't know. But I knew my parents
were helpless as I.

I learned it too soon.

2.

I learned to keep moving,
back through pain.
I had no word for it.

And the nurse who fed me a bottle
all through the operation,
the doctor working helplessly

with all his skill:
it was their world
I learned to want.

The love that moved me then
still moves me.
I saw the perfect backs of angels
singed with light:

I turned from them,
I let them go.

Desert Run Scenario Kathleen Norris

You are caught pulling the brake,
Throwing pride and jealousy out at the back of the train;
People look as if they are startled,
They hadn't expected so much pain, and
The angel of death stops by, expecting to blow in
All the windows. You look up over your shoulder,
And ask it to please move on.
People look annoyed; they know by now
It's just another delay.

Your eyes move carefully around the engine,
Your shadow serves drinks in the dining car;
The light outside is dazzling,
And washes things red when you look at them

In the last town, you asked for some supplies
And were not understood.
The devil there was a dilettante,
With nothing much to offer
Except a passion for analysis
And self-deceit;
You aimed a crystal bullet,

You expected to shoot it clean through his clothing,
Clean through his heart,
But for miles all around cows turned to trumpets,
You saw the lost wagons of Death Valley, glazed blue with age,
Waiting patiently in another dimension
To be set free.

You ran for days,
You managed to catch the last train out

The Apprentice Eats Glass David Craig

Your friend, the end, comes every day:
doorbells and flowers.
He eats your grass, spackles your chimney.
Let him. He is your guest.

Invite him to sit on the porch
to share your melon, spit the seeds.
Barefoot, the two of you can collect
the dirt from between your toes,
use it against yourselves,
become halls of angry voices.

Tell him the red razor
scratches you where you itch.

He'll get serious for a moment,
tell you the radical laws of departure
are everywhere in evidence, everywhere
a bus stops on the corner of Hollywood and time.
Join in the fun.
Tell him that half the passengers there
are dead, but to ignore them,
there is little they can say.

The longing for death in David Brendan Hopes's "Planxty Irwin" is informed as much by political fatalism as by a thirst for spiritual apotheosis. Hopes re-creates the jaunty cadences of this traditional Irish dance-tune or planxty—his lyric could almost be set to the music. Meanwhile he embellishes themes of oppression and dread. The poet sounds a gentler note in "Something of the Flowers," which rhapsodizes death as a sensuous love recurring from before the "broken garden" of Eden. The kind of welcome that Hopes extends to death is interpreted by Andrew Hudgins as a sign of identity with Christ in "As a Child in the Temple."

"Planxty Irwin" David Brendan Hopes

Sometimes the music's in the room
and you're alone and there's nothing
but to let it down and dance.
And I tell you it's fierce to dance
when your father's on your back
and your mother's on your back
and seven hundred years when
your people were alive with nothing to tell
but beaten princes and the bare hills.

They say the best tune's scratched
from the fiddles of blind men,
for the blind can see the worst coming
hump and bump over the dark fields.
Who plays must dance,
and the blind can jig off—cliff and sea—
too far ever to come back, just music in their ears.
I want to go that way, I said.
So did they all.

from **Something of the Flowers** David Brendan Hopes

If the flowers could ask me,
I would want to dream their dreams with them one night.
How simple it must be to flower!
What is there to it but to let light in,
light, first, simple love, palpable, everywhere,
descending, from before the broken garden.
I would dream of someone bending
as I bend over us, watching, tasting,
his breath in my throat, wondering how the bee feels,
how I fill the field.
My love comes and I can tell him nothing.
Arms of the night press me.
Rain licks me open.
When I awake the sky is clear above me.

Lord, who so simple made the flowers,
so laborious made me,
You were wrong to suppose that out of
the tasks and missteps I should want,
at the end, anything but death.
I have earned something of the flowers,
some mortal gratitude....

As a Child in the Temple Andrew Hudgins

"I'm looking forward to my death," she said.
I sat upright. I watched her blond hair sway,
this college girl who taught our Sunday School.
"In death, we'll see God face to face," she said.
"Now through a glass darkly. Then, face to face."
She cried a tear or two, composed herself,
and said. "Let's turn our Bibles to First John..."

I didn't. "Hell," I whispered to a friend,

"if she's so hot to die, who's stopping her?"

But now I'm older than that girl, by far,
and she's become her wish to die, some tears,
and now, most vividly, that swaying length
of ash-blond hair—that hair, and my relief.
Not understanding meant I wasn't Christ.
I didn't have to love death. I was reprieved,
saved, not for the last time, by my ignorance.

The first-person narrator of Hudgins's book-length poem, After the Lost
War, *is American poet Sidney Lanier (1842–1881), who served in the
Confederate army during the Civil War. In the passage "What Light
Destroys," Lanier contends that death reveals the deathless, the perfect
light bound in all things that finally "destroys" earthly appearances.
This distinction between the "world of forms" and the "world of ideas,"
between the temporal and eternal, is given an even more explicit neo-
Platonic formulation in David Brendan Hopes's "The Cave."*

What Light Destroys   Andrew Hudgins

Today I'm thinking of St. Paul—St. Paul
who orders us, *Be perfect.* He could have said,
Touch your elbow to your ears, except
that if you broke your arm, then snapped your neck,
you might could manage it. The death inside
the flawed hard currency of what we touch
bamboozles us, existing only for that flaw,
that deathward plunge that's locked inside all form,
till what seems solid floats away, dissolves,
and these poor bastard things, no longer things,
drift back to pure idea. And when, at last,
we let them go we start to pity them,
attend their needs: I almost have to think
to keep my own heart beating through the night.

I have a wife and four pink boys. I spin
on all this stupid metaphysic now
because last afternoon we visited
some friends in town. After the pecan pie,
I drank until my forehead smacked the table,
and woke to find my shirt crusted with blood.
When Mary didn't yell at me, I knew
she finally understood that I was gone,
dissolving back. As we rode home, I tried
to say, *I'm sorry, Hon.* The carriage bucked
across the mud-dried ruts and I shut up.
And she, in August heat, just sat, head cocked
as if for chills hidden in the hot, damp breeze,
as if they were a sound, time merely distance.
O Death, I know exactly where it is—
your sting. And Grave, I know your victory.

That night, around the tents, the boys caught fireflies,
pinched them in half, and smeared them on their nails,
then ran through pine-dark woods, waving their hands.
All I could hear was laughter, shouts. And all
that I could see for each one of my sons
were ten blurs of faint, artificial light,
never too far apart, and trembling.
Like fairies, magic, sprites, they ran and shouted.
"I'm not real! I'm not real!" The whole world fell
away from me—perhaps I was still drunk—
as on the night Titania told dazed Bottom,
"Put off your human grossness so, and like
an airy spirit go." But even then
the night could not hold long against the light,
and light destroys roots, fog, lies, orchids, night,
dawn stars, the moon, delusions, and most magic.
And light sends into hiding owls, fireflies,
and bats, whom for their unerring blunder, I
adore the most of all night fliers. But owls,
hid in a hickory, will hoot all day,

and even the moon persists, like my hangover,
some days till almost noon, drifting above
the harsh, bright, murderous morning light—so blue,
so valuable, so much like currency
that if the moon were my blue coin, I'd never spend it.

from **Five Neo-Platonic Commentaries** David Brendan Hopes

2 The Cave
We entered from the north.
There were two sounds: water, bees.
There was one engorging dark.
The water came both from outside
and from farther down,
splashing, flowing. The bees
moled in from the field above,
laid down their honey in live rock
where cold and enemies never come.
We had not seen them in the field,
not seen them dropping, laden,
where there grew no flower.
We heard them droning on the roof,
the sound, if we did not keep our
thoughts on edge, like the cave
speaking one syllable, invariable, continuous.
It was purple beyond the reach of our lamps.
We aimed the flashlights out, pretending
to look for blocks or ways,
but looking at the purple,
purple like the robe of someone leading us
just out of sight.
At what seemed the bottom was a clear pool
shallow over pebbles. I dipped my hand in.
Under the water I was the color of the stones,
pale, clean. At that moment
I was frightened, and at home.

Injustice

*U*njust suffering and the forces of destruction within nature and humanity stun human conscience. Injustice appears to be at worst an intention or at best a passive allowance of the creative principle Christians call God. "The facts are pain and horror," writes David Brendan Hopes in a poem recalling the argument of the Book of Job, a pivotal text in the Judeo-Christian dialogue on moral injustice, inequities of fate, and the afflictions of nature.

While the Christian poet refuses to deny injustice, at the same time an existential choice is made against despair, however closely despair might seem to hound the indignation of a Daniel Berrigan. For other poets here, the occasion of injustice reveals the endurance of the human spirit, while it challenges still others to transcend the limits of purely human judgment. None of the poets claim a status of exemption or privilege in relation to injustice, or a special understanding of it, by virtue of being Christian. Even Christ protested, "My God, my God, why have you abandoned me?"

In "Mary Kröger," Louise Erdrich documents the frustration and suffering of a small-town housewife at the turn of the century. Tormented by rage at her husband, Otto the butcher, Mary asks God, "Why don't you just / fix the damn thing and be done with it?" Another small-town housewife, Marta, also suffers the injustice of her circumstance, though in a very different time and place, in Maura Eichner's "Letter from Santa Cruz."

Mary Kröger Louise Erdrich

1

Sometimes I had such fury I would choose
the knife and hone it keen, I thought his heart
was small and dark, a whetstone for my tooth.
I thought his eyes had character at first,
but that was just exhaustion, schnapps, the truth
is that I left him in my sleep,
traveling through the whiteness where he could not follow,
descending through the lovely danger,
to where the waves boomed and hissed.
Those dreams were nothing. I had barrels
to unload each morning. I had salt
to plunge my hands in till they shrank.
I talked to him, let hot words bloom and smoke
like ashen flowers fragile in the sheets.
Beneath his hand I faltered and my rage
was managed for me, blown to particles
that came together again and hardened
in the slow, unfiltered afternoons.

2

I had my nerve, my shackles, and those dreams
that killed me with their vehemence, and him,
who lit red votive candles for my womb,

but I was barren that way, it's just one
way to be empty, Otto, one,
and I've a thriving scheming mind
that's good with numbers.
He did not relent,
so hounded past all sense,
I threw the twenty-dollar roasts to dogs.
A wasted animal, my anger healed
all wrong. It walked on elbows,
ate and screamed,
until there was no living with it.

God, who in your pity made a child
to slaughter on a tree, why don't you just
fix the damn thing and be done with it?
I prayed. That year the mayflies came
or angels, take your pick, in haste to crush
themselves together in a cloudy paste
and clog our engine parts.

There's luck, there's luck, I've seen luck pass and fall
on less deserving strangers. There's poor Clare
who bore her child then threw it down a well.
The sorry fool. She had a creed, a name,
a hand to look for in a cloud,
a purpose in a fast distilling life
that comes to this—a stone, a knife,
ten years, and the slow patience of steel.

Letter from Santa Cruz Maura Eichner

I do not know the date.
Calendars have no meaning here.
One hundred miles north (or
maybe more) from Santa Cruz

our families live or try to live
(and fail) farming rice.

Five years ago only monkeys
talked and swung in jungle trees.
There is a road, but not
when there is rain. It had been
raining long when Marta died.

Months ago, a doctor passing
through, told Marta that she ought
to get to Santa Cruz. Some time, some
time, Marta said, she would.

She was busy at the well when
the growth was big enough
to stop the last thin breath
from edging up her throat.

Sunsets in the tropics go like
that—gold, amber, scarlet—
then the dark.

That night Felipe came, sat
in silence, said the child
must be removed from Marta's body
otherwise Marta would be too
heavy to rise up to heaven.

No one argued. What must be done
is always done. Twenty four
hours after her death, Marta
was buried with her child
born as no one living has been
born.

Think of us sometimes. We have
Some medicines, and a syringe.
We have a mirror—will it
cloud with breath? We choose
a feather from the breast of some
small bird. Will it stir?

Fires burn holes in darkness
when the living wait upon
the dead.
        We push at memories
as at a wilful strand of hair.
Somewhere, you are at a desk
trying to splice language to
reality.
        And I am here,
my feet wrapped in wet grass,
my hands open to receive
whoever comes.

In his impatient, prophetic voice, Daniel Berrigan in "Astonishment"
wonders why "Transcendent God does nothing" while the "membrane
of life," and the entire christic promise with it, is defiled. The startling
finish, or failed finish, of the poem is a recognition, stopping just short of
outright condemnation, of the ultimate incomprehensibility of Berri-
gan's God. But whatever his moral outrage and bewilderment, the
spectacle of unjust suffering in "Prague: Old Woman in the Street" leads
Berrigan, the social activist, not to paralysis but into profound solidar-
ity with the victim. In turn, it is in such impulses of the human heart
that Christians like Berrigan sense the presence of a God of justice.

---

from **Astonishment** Daniel Berrigan

Wonder
    why illness
an odious plague dispersed,
settles again after deep knives made
of the loved face a tragic mask.

Wonder
    why after one
tentative promise
raised like a green denial of death,
life resumes
its old mortician method after all.

Wonder
    why men break
in the kiln, on the wheel; men made of the sun,
men sprung from the world's cry; the only men,
literal bread and wine, the crucial ones
poured out, water among dogs....

Wonder
    at incapacity of love;
a stern pagan ethic, set against Christ at the door
(the discomfiting beggar, the undemanding poor).

Wonder
    woman and man, son and father
priest and sacrifice—to all right reason
one web of the world, one delicate
membrane of life. Ruptured.

Wonder.
Transcendent God does nothing.
The Child plays
among stocks and stones

A country almanac
records
moon phase, sun phase
hours and elements, grey dawn and red;
He sleeps and stands again,
moony, at loss, a beginner in the world....

Wonder, wonder,
          across his eyes
the cancerous pass unhealed, evil
takes heart monstrously. What use
the tarrying savior, the gentle breath of time
that in beggars is contentious and unruly,
that in dumb minds comes and chimes and goes
that in veins and caves of earth
sleeps like a tranced corpse, the abandoned body
of violated hope?

Wonder
given such God, how resolve the poem?

Prague: Old Woman in the Street Daniel Berrigan

In the country saying, she was only
doing what must be done, as a stone falls
or a wheel turns; punished
by a man's labors, to man's shape.

Childbearing done, not for twilight peace
but for this; pulling a cart, sweeping cobbles
stolid in the killing cold. Suffering?
hands were made for it, blood warmed to it.

I tell you, I stood stupefied
as though a flare went up in the foul street,
some ikon Christ casting rags off for glory.

Woman I never knew, I kneel,
I am born of you. For you, my heart keeps
like an unhealed leper's, stint of hope—

Christ is not hard as stone, cold as my doubt.
You neared. Unbearably, the quick dead cried out.

from **Of Commerce and Society** Geoffrey Hill

Statesmen have known visions. And, not alone,
Artistic men prod dead men from their stone:
Some of us have heard the dead speak:
The dead are my obsession this week

But may be lifted away. In summer
Thunder may strike, or, as a tremor
Of remote adjustment, pass on the far side
From us: however deified and defied

By those it does strike. Many have died. Auschwitz,
Its furnace chambers and lime pits
Half-erased, is half-dead, a fable
Unbelievable in fatted marble.

There is, at times, some need to demonstrate
Jehovah's touchy methods that create
The connoisseur of blood, the smitten man.
At times it seems not common to explain.

The log church at Shiloh, Tennessee, marks the site of the first major conflict of the American Civil War. The battle's 23,000 casualties exceeded the combined total of those killed in the nation's three previous wars: the Revolution, the War of 1812 and the Mexican War. In "Shiloh Church, 1862," Geoffrey Hill levels his rage against himself as much as at "Geneva's tribe," the religious reformers in whose inheritance he stands. The poet makes no excuses in defense of historical Christianity, as others might be tempted to do, for racist and exploitative ideologies that were inescapably linked to the wider culture in which they were forged. The prophetic conscience reckons only the injustices a "shod Word" visited on the New World. Shiloh is a biblical name meaning "place of peace."

Shiloh Church, 1862: Twenty-three Thousand Geoffrey Hill

O stamping-ground of the shod Word! So hard
On the heels of the damned red-man we came,
Geneva's tribe, outlandish and abhorred—
Bland vistas milky with Jehovah's calm—

Who fell to feasting Nature, the glare
Of buzzards circling; cried to the grim sun
'Jehovah punish us!'; who went too far;
In deserts dropped the odd white turds of bone;

Whose passion was to find out God in this
His natural filth, voyeur of sacrifice, a slow
Bloody unearthing of the God-in-us.
But with what blood, and to what end, Shiloh?

In "Watching Dark Circle," Denise Levertov condemns a savage incident of animal experimentation. The injustice of it cries out the louder because the violence is gratuitous, its victims wholly powerless and wholly innocent. Annie Dillard's found poem on the subject is composed from the text of Observations and Experiments in Natural History, *a book written in 1962 by Alan Dale.*

Watching Dark Circle Denise Levertov

> *"Why, this is hell, nor am I out of it."*
> —*Marlowe,* Dr. Faustus

Men are willing to observe
the writhing, the bubbling flesh and
swift but protracted charring of bone
while the subject pigs, placed in cages designed for this,
don't pass out but continue to scream as they turn to cinder.
The Pentagon wants to know
something a child could tell it:
it hurts to burn, and even a match
can make you scream, pigs or people,
even the smallest common flame can kill you.
This plutonic calefaction is redundant.

Men are willing
to call the roasting of live pigs
a simulation of certain conditions. It is
not a simulation. The pigs (with their high-rated intelligence,
their uncanny precognition of disaster) are real,
their agony real agony, the smell
is not archetypal breakfast nor ancient feasting
but a foul miasma irremovable from the nostrils,
and the simulation of hell these men
have carefully set up
is hell itself,
                    and they in it, dead in their lives,
and what can redeem them? What can redeem them?

Observations and Experiments Annie Dillard

Observations

1. Trout seem to learn that danger
   Is associated with artificial flies;
   Perhaps it is the hook in them.

2. I once saw a frog attacked
   And turned over by my dog
   And it lay quite still on its back.

   I am positive it made quite
   A separate movement to put
   Its front feet over its ears.
   Why did it?

Experiments

1. Catch butterflies and clip
   Their wings with scissors.
   Do your observations
   Outside, where butterflies are numerous.

2. Pinch through ten worms.
   Obtain a fresh herring and place it
   On an open plate. Leave it.

3. Liberate a grasshopper and cause
   It to jump by touching it. Make
   It jump again—and again.

   Do its leaps get more feeble?
   Does the insect become more reluctant
   To jump after each leap?

Last Personal Note

Once I was walking across fields in Shropshire
To a river which, because of a rise
In the ground, I could not see.

I have preferred to know
Less and less about more and more.

---

*Wendell Berry denounces capital punishment as a violation of funda-
mental moral justice in "The Morning's News." He is "sickened by the
complicity" of human beings in this killing "by design." His outrage
drives him away from human institutions to a "deathlier knowledge" of
nature that reveals his own end. Berry's ambivalence even toward the
institution of church is of a piece with his independent, earthy Chris-
tianity. David Citino's reading of the morning news in "Whole Wheat,
Decaf Black, A Morbid Curiosity" leads him to the place where talk
about injustice properly begins.*

The Morning's News   Wendell Berry

To moralize the state, they drag out a man,
and bind his hands, and darken his eyes
with a black rag to be free of the light in them,
and tie him to a post, and kill him.
And I am sickened by the complicity in my race.
To kill in hot savagery like a beast
is understandable. It is forgivable and curable.
But to kill by design, deliberately, without wrath,
that is the sullen labor that perfects Hell.
The serpent is gentle, compared to man.
It is man, the inventor of cold violence,
death as waste, who has made himself lonely
among the creatures, and set himself aside,
so that he cannot work in the sun with hope,

or sit at peace in the shade of any tree.
The morning's news drives sleep out of the head
at night. Uselessness and horror hold the eyes
open to the dark. Weary, we lie awake
in the agony of the old giving birth to the new
without assurance that the new will be better.
I look at my son, whose eyes are like a young god's,
they are so open to the world.
I look at my sloping fields now turning
green with the young grass of April. What must I do
to go free? I think I must put on
a deathlier knowledge, and prepare to die
rather than enter into the design of man's hate.
I will purge my mind of the airy claims
of church and state. I will serve the earth
and not pretend my life could better serve.
Another morning comes with its strange cure.
The earth is news. Though the river floods
and the spring is cold, my heart goes on,
faithful to a mystery in a cloud,
and the summer's garden continues its descent
through me, toward the ground.

Whole Wheat, Decaf Black, a Morbid Curiosity David Citino

We study the paper, fingers
darkening with the stinking ink
of the daily news,
as Dad bangs Mommy's head
against the bedroom wall,
the thud like coming thunder,
as baby's shaken until
the crying stops,
as the sniper's scope X's-out
another enemy of the tribe,
all for ethnic cleansing,

as, at the mall, boys dressed
in street colors change
forever the face of other boys
with semi-automatic rage,
as women of the village
bind the girl, legs spread
wide, the oyster cut
from its delicate shell,
so she can know holiness.

It's not that we relish
the blood, as the Romans did—
is it? Somewhere, someone
knows a suffering too terrible
for words, nearly.
Thank God it's not us.
There but for fortune.
Give us the details,
What was she wearing?
Did she struggle, weep, plead?
And then what happened?

David Craig's meditation on human need and suffering partially echoes
an ancient prayer, The Litany of the Blessed Virgin Mary. But Craig's
"Mother of" sequences leave off the mantric supplication, "pray for us,"
that concludes each phrase of the traditional Marian text. His blues-
like "Litany" therefore becomes more lamentation than intercessory
prayer, his "Mother" more a silent companion of sorrow than a refuge
or source of mercy.

Litany David Craig

Mother of Sorrow,
Mother of stars and night fires, arroyos,
tossed tequila bottles,

the dead drunk.
Mother of the streets, of the violent,
weekend golfers, cut off,
and a windshield smashed with bare fists;
the knife, the absurdity, the day in court.
Mother of amphetamines, the aging
speed freak, who looks to kick
around an oval track in a beat up
stock car. Mother of the subways,
the swaying lost.
Mother of day laborers, children,
early mornings, in the fields.
Mother of Guatemala,
of empty Ohio River steel towns
where no more black soot seeps
into the cracks of houses.
Mother of Cleveland, of every neon bar,
honky tonk. Mother of Hank Williams,
late night pick-ups that end in
anguish or bruises.
Mother of every redneck,
alone and crossed at closing,
every liberal who circles a silo
in protest, crying out
to be loved.

Les Murray couches a eulogy for his cousin Frederick Samuel, dead at 56, in the stumbling rhythms and rhymes of an improvised pub ballad. Discovered as graffiti, its title, "The Misery Cord," is a boozy pun on misericord, *a corruption of the Latin word for mercy,* misericordia, *literally "merciful heart." The Latin itself plays on* miserabilis *(wretched) and* miseratio *(pity and compassion), poignantly mating the requisites of the miserable/merciable/merciful heart. But in Murray's mock ditty the pun is robbed of mercy. The cord is all misery, pulling the poet's heart out through his eyes. "Grief," he rules, "is nothing you can do, but do."*

The Misery Cord (In Memory of F. S. Murray) Les Murray

Misericord. The Misery Cord.
It was lettered on a wall.
I know that cord, how it's tough to break
however hard you haul.

My cousin sharefarmed, and so got half:
half dignity, half hope, half income,
for his full work. To get a place
of his own took his whole lifetime.

Some pluck the misery chord from habit
or for luck, however they feel,
some to deceive, and some for the tune—
but sometimes it's real.

Milking bails, flannel shirts, fried breakfasts,
these were our element,
and doubling on horses, and shouting Score!
at a dog yelping on a hot scent—

but an ambulance racing on our back road
is bad news for us all:
the house of community is about
to lose a plank from its wall.

Grief is nothing you can do, but do,
worst work for least reward,
pulling your heart out through your eyes
with tugs of the misery cord.

I looked at my cousin's farm, where he'd just
built his family a house of their own,
and I looked down into Fred's next house,
its clay walls of bluish maroon.

Just one man has broken the misery cord
and lived. He said once was enough.
A poem is an afterlife on earth:
Christ grant us the other half.

The chaos in nature and human history belies a rationale of cosmic or-
der based strictly on the norms of human justice. In Denise Levertov's
"The Task," God sustains a cosmic order based instead on the norms of
beauty. An analogy can be made to music, where a music of beauty
rather than monotony honors the contrasts of assonance and disso-
nance, disturbance and clarity, tension and release. Locally troubling
and unaesthetic elements become aesthetic in the larger synthesis. Just
so is human lamentation a necessary dissonance in a tapestry of cosmic
beauty woven and imagined by Levertov's God.

The Task Denise Levertov

As if God were an old man
always upstairs, sitting about
in sleeveless undershirt, asleep,
arms folded, stomach rumbling,
his breath from open mouth
strident, presaging death ...

No, God's in the wilderness next door
—that huge tundra room, no walls and a sky roof—
busy at the loom. Among the berry bushes,
rain or shine, that loud clacking and whirring,
irregular but continuous;
God is absorbed in work, and hears
the spacious hum of bees, not the din,
and hears far-off
our screams. Perhaps
he listens for prayers in that wild solitude.
And hurries on with the weaving:

till it's done, the great garment woven,
our voices, clear under the familiar
   blocked-out clamor of the task,
can't stop their
                    terrible beseeching. God
imagines it sifting through, at last, to music
in the astounded quietness, the loom idle,
the weaver at rest.

For David Brendan Hopes, nature spins the ultimate allegory of God's
justice and our human responses to it. The nuthatch endures the cold
weather that drives the other birds away in "October." The geese com-
plain, "bleating / on God's doorstep how He has wronged us." In the
cold, an old woman with outstretched "talon" peddles religious pamph-
lets on Syracuse's Salina Street. As far as we can tell, her cry of "Jesus,
Jesus, come and be saved" goes unheeded. Only the spring, five months
away, promises any sure respite for her or the returning birds. Mean
time the nuthatch stays the winter, and will either perish or survive.

   "Birdbones" praises the delicate but powerful structure that gives
birds, "with that furious heart behind them," their genius to endure.
Hopes equates the human soul with "a small bird beating straight home
forever." Against birds "there is no force," he marvels. "Hammered,
they leap; / tumbled, they gather and bunch back; / galed, they seize the
whirlwind and rise." It is only because the "sky stops," and not because
they lack spirit or stamina, that they fly no higher.

October David Brendan Hopes

It's nuthatch on the box elder outside the window.
He's making his clown's voice, *nnink, nning, nnink,*
pecking for grubs, seeds, scraps.
The first snow powdered down
last night while he slept, and as
birds have dreams there's snow in his song now.

Nighthawk heard it. He is gone.
Warbler heard it. She is gone.
Thrasher went. Finch went.
You could hear them at night, little bells
so far off you thought they were the stars ringing.
I sat on an empty hill and said goodbye.

The geese, like tragic actresses, keep nothing to themselves.
They beat down the center of the air
crying, and crying, how the white north
snaps behind them, how their nests are shoveled under,
how their circle is broken
by fox, bullet, and cold.

The geese, like the practiced keeners my great-grandmothers
used to pay when they had
no more salt to cry with,
bark for us all, uninhibited, bleating
on God's doorstep how He has wronged us,
how we suffer in His circles, round and round.

On Salina Street the hag with a hollow for a left eye
cries Jesus, Jesus, come and be saved.
She puts on her black coat.
Her old hand is nail and January to the bone.
Put a coin in her talon, a cold coin.
Take her pamphlet and let it ride the wind

as the geese ride, flapping, rattling.
Put a coin in the black mouth
and hear it cry Jesus Jesus,
hear it cry Jesus Jesus.
I swear the geese and the nighthawks and the hags
must cry something different when they come home

with the sun pulled up behind them
and the long hills waking from the five month bad dream.

94

I have not heard it in so long.
I have heard the nuthatch in the box elder outside the window,
laughing, scrounging. He stays and dies,
or stays, and stays.

Birdbones David Brendan Hopes

The girdle is a grass leaf dried and curled.
Spine's whittled to a splinter, a thorn.
Clavicle is a taut hair holding without weight.
Wing blades are a folded feather, in a stiff wind
almost flying by themselves:
girder, crossbeam, strut, the bones of birds,
swallow bones, catbird bones, willing to bear nothing,
made to lift; with that furious heart behind them,
lighter than air, nimbler than light, made to
hover, veer, power, descend, home in, stoop, evade.
Against them there is no force: hammered, they leap;
tumbled, they gather and bunch back;
galed, they seize the whirlwind and rise.

Wind sledged the ash tree.
Its leaves went up and its wood went down,
a great wind, and the limbs were sailing.
In the space from which the ash had fallen
I saw swifts climb like black sparks
from a steel-gray stack.
They were safe where they had been,
under eaves, in chimneys, but the wind taunted
and they laid their bones against it for delight,
those strands, those parings. They spiraled up
the funnel of the wind, black, gray, blue,
climbed to the shine above it,
took their pastime in the storm.

What is small enough to get around,
light enough to rocket over,
quick enough to enter by the worst door?
Cardinal, whipped by fire that first day,
steeped into the fire;
wren, seeing her smallness among the beasts,
put on fury like a coat of knives;
bunting lost heaven, brought it down;
kingfisher saw how the world prepares and
comes to nothing, poised above the water,
hovered, blue on blue, neither diving nor departing;
chickadee snatched seeds beneath the beating axe,
ripped thistle from the bear's pelt,
it is my world, my world;
thrush stole the songs, that night might think
the world sings against it all together;
killdeer learned deceit, drew the hunters
from her generations;
swift felt the hammer, stepped aside.

Remember this: there are no fables.
If you didn't hear the wind speak you were not listening.
If the stars did not warn you, you were
safe at home with the doors locked tight.
If you sought your soul and didn't find
a small bird beating straight home forever
where there is no road, you were seeking something else.
And each day impossible they lie down in air.
They take their bit of earth up
high enough to serve, insubstantial, indestructible,
come down because the sky stops, not their bones.

Hopes's themes of implacable destiny and endurance can be found in the Book of Job, "patient" Job who was instructed to "gird up his loins" before the mystery of unknowable justice. But after his final exchange with God, Job moves toward a sabbath vision, a mystical grasp of creation beyond ego and the narrowly human. He comes to understand the cosmic sense in which God calls creation good. The wholeness and intimacy of his sight resembles Adam and Eve's before they tasted the fruit of the knowledge of good and evil, before they sought to know the principles of cosmic justice knowable only to God. "Now my eyes have seen you," says Job in Stephen Mitchell's translation, "therefore I will be quiet, comforted that I am dust."

David Brendan Hopes longs for such a vision in "The Swimmers." The "storybook" scenes inhabited by the poem's ducks disguise realities of "pain and horror." God is surely present, shivering the waters of the lake. But when a swimmer paddles out to the center he fails, like the ducks, to learn the secrets of the "secret heart / that he will have or die." For now, bound by his anger, he may find no more than a "white clown face hidden in the depths and in the heavens." What ego and human justice seek but cannot find, says the poet, "is what we wanted always," the visionary experience of "earth, wind, water," outside the forbidden knowledge of good and evil, that once enabled us, and may again, "to walk proud upon our home."

The Swimmers David Brendan Hopes

Even at night the ducks are at work,
   quiet and duck-shaped on the lake,
like complications in enormous black silk.
   Night is heavier than day.
   The waves are round-shouldered
   where they shove the shore.
In storybook weather, the purple-brown light,
   the water and the ducks discuss
      their storybook histories:

how there is right,
how there is natural,
  how a bird might rest sometimes upon the water
  and the water delight in its diadem of bird.
  The ducks and the water laugh.
Fire is in a bolt of black silk.
  One voice bubbles from the bottom of the lake
  and hawks down from the iron stars
  and it cries *lie! lie! lie!*

The facts are pain and horror.
  Ask duck bones secret in the lake.
   ice-crushed and starved to paper
  when the north stomped them down.
Ask ghost elm riddled with her worms.
  Ask these cliffs down-blow of the everlasting hammer.
  When did sweet Christ put thorns
  between the roses and the north wind?
Lake's eaten with stars.

  Brown ducks ride in a field of coals.
   There are moments when the story book seems true.
  Carp descends among the water lilies,
gold hidden in shadow,
  stir of blossom not of any wind.
  A child fishes from a willow-knee
  and is fire between dark water and dark leaves.
The moment is a steel jaw. What lets down its fear
  is swallowed. What lets its hate rest

  is plowed under new snow
  with the mice, trilling its blood to glass.
Christ, when did you make
  your enemies a liar and come down
   against all theories on the clockwork earth,
  flail asphalt to dark flowers,
transform blizzard to a curtain of descending light?

Horror and pain have grown to us
like arms to push the world away.

Dawn. A boy flies a kite,
a silvery kite, like a hook.
It floats over the lake and therefore in the lake.
Kite and shadow, hook and hook.
I see God coming like a carp
among the shapeless lilies. He moves them without touching.
I see God rising in the lake, shivering
the waters that shoot through the earth.
He sniffs hook with his great snouts and moves on.

I see a swimmer on the lake.
It is cold there, but he seeks for God.
Ducks on the surface, paddling, pretending
to believe they are droll and happy.
Perch, carp, shiner beneath, sucker, dace,
bluegill, sunfish, cat, large-mouth, small-mouth,
loon when there's trouble in the north.
God's jokes but not God. Perhaps in the tension
between water and air, the dime-thin borderland.

He looks. Nobody lives there.
It is a fence to keep the lake from leaping to the sky.
In his fury the swimmer swims out, out,
beating the underwater with his arms,
cutting the glaze away until he must be
dead center, the secret heart
that he will have or die. He descends.
He stands up with his shoulders showing.
Duck shit. Shore mud. He has missed the middle.

The ducks close him in a little circle.
They want to share with him the stories
they have made against the hour of their horror.
They see the swimmer eye-to-eye now. They understand.

99

If he swims out again they follow him.
If he trudges home they sit on the shore and watch.
They want to say there is no right ever, so be at peace.
They wish to celebrate that he too failed
   conspicuously. That is the armor, the cloak.

It is too ridiculous for anything but our
smirk beaks and loony voices, they say,
   how lake boiled out of glacier
      when glacier seemed a tall flame in the sun,
   how bird beats from a shell into a shell,
the white clown face hidden in the depths and in the heavens,
   how the swimmers cut cold water thinking to find
      what we wanted always, earth, wind, water,
   once to walk proud upon our home.

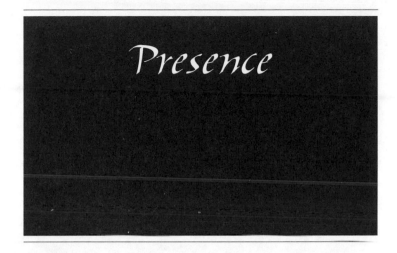

Presence

Nearly all great spiritual traditions testify to Presence, the intimation of transcendence in the everyday world. What gives the experience a christic dimension for Christians is the sense of personal contact with the spirit of the risen Logos or Christ of scripture, whose personhood embodies the "pure positivity" of God. Any encounter with Presence points Christians theologically to what they consider its primal disclosure, the mystery of the Incarnation. The word's Latin roots spell out the unreasonable demands of the proposition: transcendence "made into meat" (*carnis*), specifically in Jesus born of Mary at Bethlehem. For many in the West, this action ascribed to God signifies the penetration of all matter by spirit, a sacralizing of the physical universe. Thus is the Christian in search of spiritual meaning turned again and again to the world.

The selections begin with the nativity, the Incarnation event itself. The remaining poems chronicle the legacy of Presence in day-to-day life, in the flesh of the world. The Presence or immanence of God in nature, a dominant theme of both Western and Eastern civilization, inspires the poetry of the next chapter, "God's Body."

Hewn Hands David Craig

Little Mary
she's a buried cargo
wrapped in so many blankets I
   have to smile
she reminds me of the circus fat
   lady
who sweats chin over chin
while the donkey bears in silence
his retribution

at the hotel
a drunk swings out a second story
   window
it was two in the morning as he sang
to the cheering crowd below
Is it so much to ask for?
some clean floor to have our son
is it so much to ask for?
a room for a beggar and his family

Mary muffles her time
Lord God it is her time!
shall we have Your son on the side
   of the road
invite the beasts of the field
every straggler every all-night
   pilgrim?

The Savior Louise Erdrich

When the rain began to fall, he rolled back
into the clouds and slept again.
Still it persisted, beating at every surface,
until it entered his body

103

as the sound of prolonged
human weeping.

So he was broken.
His first tears dissolved
their mask of white stone.
As they traveled through the bones of his arms,
his strength became a mortal strength
subject to love.

On earth, when he heard the first rain
tap through the olive trees,
he opened his eyes and stared at his mother.
As his father, who had made the sacrifice,
stood motionless in heaven,
his son cried out to him:

I want no shelter, I deny
the whole configuration.
I hate the weight of earth.
I hate the sound of water.
Ash to ash, you say, but I know different.
I will not stop burning.

Les Murray speaks to several Christian ideas in "Animal Nativity." The animals' recognition of the infant's Presence suggests a new dispensation extending to all of nature and its creatures, "even humans." The "Iliad of peace" brings to mind the "sword" of Christ's call for justice, and the fourth stanza's images of Eden tell of the restored hope and freedom from death wrought by the "new Adam." Likewise, the "child-king" brings peace to the sea-creatures in Geoffrey Hill's "Picture of a Nativity." But Hill assails the domestication of the event by pretty nativity scenes crowded with angels, the iconography of the Christmas card. The poem's final "picture" reduces to deadening "familiar tokens" of art and sentiment the "marvel" that is the Incarnation of the wholly Other, theology's mysterium tremendum.

Animal Nativity Les Murray

> The Iliad of peace began
> when this girl agreed.
> Now goats in trees, fish in the valley
> suddenly feel vivid.
>
> Swallows flit in the stable as if
> a hatching of their kind,
> turned human, cried in the manger
> showing the hunger-diamond.
>
> Cattle are content that this calf
> must come in human form.
> Spiders discern a water-walker.
> Even humans will sense the lamb,
>
> He who frees from the old poem
> turtle-dove and snake
> who gets death forgiven
> who puts the apple back.
>
> Dogs, less enslaved but as starving
> as the poorest human there,
> crouch, agog at a crux of presence
> remembered as a star.

Picture of a Nativity Geoffrey Hill

> Sea-preserved, heaped with sea-spoils,
> Ribs, keels, coral sores,
> Detached faces, ephemeral oils,
> Discharged on the world's outer shores,
>
> A dumb child-king
> Arrives at his right place; rests,

105

Undisturbed, among slack serpents; beasts
With claws flesh-buttered. In the gathering

Of bestial and common hardship
Artistic men appear to worship
And fall down; to recognize
Familiar tokens; believe their own eyes.

Above the marvel, each rigid head,
Angels, their unnatural wings displayed,
Freeze into an attitude
Recalling the dead.

---

*While for Hill the créche motif deadens the power of its subject, for poet
Andrew Hudgins a masterwork by Sandro Botticelli (1444–1510)
brings life and resonance to an earlier moment in the story, the moment
in the gospel account of Luke when "this girl agreed," as Les Murray
puts it. With Mary's assent to the news that she is to bear God's son,
Murray points out, the Incarnational mystery has its beginning. In
"The Cestello Annunciation," Botticelli captures for Hudgins the hu-
man struggle, the reckoning of the cost of faithfulness, that precedes
Mary's words of affirmation, "Behold, I am the handmaid of the Lord,"
spoken in response to the angel Gabriel's message. The locale of "She
Said Yeah," a meditation on Mary's words by Kathleen Norris, is a
Benedictine monastery on the Great Plains that the poet attends as an
oblate, or lay member. Part of the monks' day is the praying of the An-
gelus, a devotion recalling the angelic annunciation to Mary.*

The Cestello Annunciation Andrew Hudgins

The angel has already said, *Be not afraid.*
He's said, *The power of the Most High*
will darken you. Her eyes are downcast and half closed.
And there's a long pause—a pause here of forever—

as the angel crowds her. She backs away,
her left side pressed against the picture frame.

He kneels. He's come in all unearthly innocence
to tell her of glory—not knowing, not remembering
how terrible it is. And Botticelli
gives her eternity to turn, look out the doorway, where
on a far hill floats a castle, and halfway across
the river toward it juts a bridge, not completed—

and neither is the touch, angel to virgin,
both her hands held up, both elegant, one raised
as if to say *stop,* while the other hand, the right one,
reaches toward his; and, as it does, it parts her blue robe
and reveals the concealed red of her inner garment
to the red tiles of the floor and the red folds

of the angel's robe. But her whole body pulls away.
Only her head, already haloed, bows,
acquiescing. And though she will, she's not yet said,
Behold, I am the handmaid of the lord,
as Botticelli, in his great pity,

lets her refuse, accept, refuse, and think again.

Mysteries of The Incarnation: "She Said Yeah" Kathleen Norris

The land lies open: summer fallow, hayfield, pasture. Folds of
cloud mirror buttes knife-edged in shadow. One monk smears
honey on his toast, another peels an orange.

A bell rings three times, as the Angelus begins, bringing to
mind Gabriel and Mary. "She said yeah," the Rolling Stones
sing from a car on the interstate, "She said yeah." And the bells
pick it up, many bells now, saying it to Metchtild, the barn cat,
pregnant again; to Ephrem's bluebirds down the draw; to the

107

grazing cattle and the monks (virgins, some of them) eating silently before the sexy tongue of a hibiscus blossom at their refectory window. "She said yeah." And then the angel left her.

In "A World Without Objects Is a Sensible Emptiness," Richard Wilbur rejects what is known in the contemplative world as desert spirituality, a striving for heightened consciousness by the shedding of attachment to all things of sense. The quest for God in "sensible emptiness" was charted by seventeenth-century mystical poet and Anglican clergyman Thomas Trahern. Wilbur calls his own soul back from Trahern's disembodied "camels of the spirit" plodding toward arid bliss. He seeks instead the embodied spirit fully present to the senses, "shaped and borne" like Bethlehem's " light incarnate."

A World Without Objects Is A Sensible Emptiness Richard Wilbur

The tall camels of the spirit
 Steer for their deserts, passing the last groves loud
With the sawmill shrill of the locust, to the whole honey of the arid
 Sun. They are slow, proud,

And move with a stilted stride
 To the land of sheer horizon, hunting Trahern's
Sensible emptiness, there where the brain's lantern-slide
 Revels in vast returns.

O connoisseurs of thirst,
 Beasts of my soul who long to learn to drink
Of pure mirage, those prosperous islands are accurst
 That shimmer on the brink

Of absence; auras, lustres,
 And all shinings need to be shaped and borne.

Think of those painted saints, capped by the early masters
    With bright, jauntily-worn

    Aureate plates, or even
  Merry-go-round rings. Turn, O turn
From the fine sleights of the sand, from the long empty oven
    Where flames in flamings burn

    Back to the trees arrayed
  In bursts of glare, to the halo-dialing run
Of the country creeks, and the hills' bracken tiaras made
    Gold in the sunken sun.

    Wisely watch for the sight
  Of the supernova burgeoning over the barn,
Lampshine blurred in the steam of beasts, the spirit's right
    Oasis, light incarnate.

The Glass Man Scott Cairns

> *He is the transparence of the place in which He is...*

This is where he washed to shore
during rough weather in November.
We found him in a nest of kelp,

salt bladders, other sea wrack—
all but invisible through
that lavish debris—and we might

have passed him by altogether
had he not held so perfectly
still, composed, so incoherently

fixed among the general
blowziness of the pile.
Unlikely is what he was,

what he remains—brilliant,
immutable, and of speech
quite incapable, if revealing

nonetheless. Under his foot,
the landscape grows acute, so that it seems
to tremble, thereafter to dissolve,

thereafter to deliver to the witness
a suspicion of the roiling
confusion which brought him here.

---

*Christian poets of a postmodern age with its polished case for aporia,
"degree-zero" of spirit, risk outright ridicule by confessing, or refusing to
rationalize away, their personal experience of Presence. Yet the speaker
of Annie Dillard's "Thanksgiving—Christmas II," recklessly admits to
the Christian mystic's guiltiest pleasure, a sensuous Presence held in inti-
mate, even erotic relation. She presents the object of her heart's desire as
expressly christic, protesting to "the girl in the courtyard," like Peter
denying Christ, "I never saw him before in my life." Throughout her
stormy affair, spiritual distractions come and go. The "springtime lamb"
of the poem's refrain carries an obvious Christian charge.*

---

from **Feast Days: Thanksgiving—Christmas II** Annie Dillard

> *Woman, why weepest thou?*
> *Whom seekest thou?*
> > *—John*

December, and all its dark rains.
The apples in the cellar
are black, and dying inside their skins.
They pray all night in their bins,
but nobody listens;
they will be neither food nor trees....

God send us the springtime lamb
minted and tied in thyme
and call us home, and bid us eat
and praise your name.

God am I smug when they talk about Belsen—
I've never killed anyone in my life!
I simply betray:

let the phone ring,
seal a typed letter,
say to the girl in the courtyard,
"I never saw him before in my life,"
call a cab, pull on gloves,
and leave. And leave you,
and leave you with the bill....

Today you hurt your hand
on the fireplace.
Tonight a Chinook
rose up from the south.
And my mouth
stuck shut,
my belly shook,
my eyes blinked hot,
and I went to the window.

There, stalking the lawn,
white tipis, wraith-like, ranged.
A smell of blood burned up.
The moon bruised down.
Antlers hung in the trees.
A thousand tipi doors lashed back,
void, like riven graves....

I remember reading
in my room, just reading,

and shutting the book,
and looking up,
and missing you, missing you,
and reading the paper again.
There's no freedom in it
or in fear;
my heart's not mine.
Once I went to the door,
and an old black woman was there,
in a clown suit
and a clown's peaked hat,
and she carried a brown cloth bag.
Once an ape trailed through the hall
in my nightgown.
Once I surprised in the bathroom
the last of the Inca kings,
tall Atahualpa,
in his hand-stitched bat-skin robe.

"Don't worry," I said.
"It's all right," I said,
and ducked.

Oh, I've been here and there
around the heart—
a few night spots, really,
the kind that call themselves "Rathskellers,"
dim-lit, always changing hands,
and frequented on Sundays
by the regulars....
and you,
variously:
weeping at the piano,
eating fly-brown meat with a spoon,
swirling a beer, and saying,
"Marry me"; or
"I read your letter

(diary, palm)"; or
"You don't understand."
And then always
"Good-bye"
(So long, Take care)—
Remember?
And then I leave.
I'm always the one who leaves.

God send us the springtime lamb
minted and tied in thyme
and call us home, and bid us eat
and praise your name.

In moments of tranquility experienced by poets Levertov and Cairns,
Presence abides.

Midnight Gladness Denise Levertov

> *"Peace be upon each thing my eye takes in,*
> *Upon each thing my mouth takes in."*
> *—Carmina Gadelica*

The pleated lampshade, slightly askew,
dust a silverish muting of the lamp's fake brass.
My sock-monkey on the pillow, tail and limbs asprawl,
weary after a day of watching sunlight
      prowl the house like a wolf.
Gleams of water in my bedside glass.
Miraculous water, so peaccfully
waiting to be consumed.

The day's crowding arrived
at this abundant stillness. Each thing
given to the eye before sleep, and water
at my lips before darkness. Gift after gift.

Waking Here Scott Cairns

This night, one of those clouded
nights that glue the sheets
to your legs and drain the hope
of sleep from you, so that even the woman
tossing beside you becomes nothing more
than an irritation. So, the two of you
grow slowly stupid in the dark,
being for the most part awake, but numbed
by heat and darkness. At such a time,
you might believe you'll go on
like this forever; but the night above you
clears, your borrowed room
cools by slow degrees, and the moment
arrives when you startle to the fact
of having slept.
If, at this moment, you would lift
yourself to one elbow to witness
the moonlit room, you would know
that there is waking in this house
a word, simple as *blood,* whose sound spoken
clearly enough might make things right,
a word like *water,* or *light,* a word
clean and honest as *dirt,* or a woman
you wake to clear autumn nights, the odd light
of the moon on her, a quiet word that tells you
all that it is you're in the world to learn.

In "The Presence of God" and "The Apprentice Sees Himself in the Sunset," David Craig employs the plain diction and vernacular imagery of the street mystic to describe epiphany: the seeing of God in the moment, from pigeons to the sunset, to the core identity of the self. Craig's vision of mystical unity is born of contemplation, and his spiritual apprentice concludes with an offbeat restatement of a contemplative teaching, the observance of silence as a discipline for engaging Presence in the "fragile instrument" of the physical world.

The Presence of God David Craig

He spoke in a thimble
a choir of pigeons necking about
long peals rakes of ice railroad tracks
in front of toothless buildings hollow
corridor smiles and the
bite in frozen grass

up they flew
and over
me and every spider wire

a cold hissing soft
under the flap
and feather of muscled wings

The Apprentice Sees Himself in the Sunset David Craig

The lepers grew excited
beneath my window this morning,
danced like Carmen Miranda,
or a band at the Holiday Inn.

115

Almost immediately,
I had vision on Third Street, a pietá:
Mother Teresa held Jimmy Swaggert.
Some kids, off to the side, were laughing,
and I heard the sound of a basketball settling,
for a second, in the chain net while the sky
seemed like some fragile instrument
made entirely of glass.

Break it
whenever you can. The slivers
stuck in your throat
might save you from speaking.

Pentecost David Craig

What is this Holy Spirit?
And what is it doing in the eggplant?

---

*When the first disciples gathered fifty days after Christ's death for the
Jewish Shavuot, or feast of Pentecost, a "holy spirit" is said to have de-
scended on them in tongues of fire accompanied by a powerful wind.
Wind, or breath, is the other meaning of* pneuma, *the ungendered word
for spirit in the original Greek used to describe the event. The account
provides an image of Presence communicated directly to sense experi-
ence. The assemblage broke into a glossolalia or "speaking-in-tongues"
that was mysteriously intelligible across all language barriers. The term
Holy Spirit has since been understood by Christians as a mystery of
Christ's presence, which in turn is a mystery of God's presence, which in
turn is Spirit. For David Craig and practitioners of Christian spiritual-
ity, this endless ring or so-called trinity of God in Christ in Spirit is the
cosmic breath that breathes even in eggplant.*

*"And Also from the Son" is Scott Cairns's hesitant account of a pen-
tecostal moment while sitting in his garden—or should he just write it*

off as a trick of the light? He draws the title of his poem from the ancient Christian Nicene Creed, which describes the Spirit as God's self-communication, expressed by the Latin formula Cairns uses for the poem's epigraph, usually translated "who proceeds from the Father and the Son."

And Also from the Son Scott Cairns

—qui ex Patre filioque

As you might expect, my momentary vision barely
qualifies: you know, sensation something like the merest
swoon, some uncertainty about why all of a sudden
the back garden, its bamboo and rose, the reaching pecans
(one's apparent field contracting to a field of vision)
took to trembling, as well as other accompanying
uncanniness. I mean, *was* the garden trembling or had
it suddenly, unnaturally stopped? Was the disturbing
motion something I was seeing or something I was
seeing with? And why am I asking you?

Perhaps I'm not. Probably, the most I'm doing is one
kind of homage to a moment and a form, a rhetoric
disclaiming what the habitual senses can't make much of.
This is what I can vouch for: I was at rest in a still,
restful corner of our back garden. I had expected
even to doze, but instead found my attention fixing
all the more alertly on the narrow scene, and then I
wasn't seeing anything at all, which is why I'm less
than eager to call this business exactly a vision.
Does one ever *sink* into a vision?

Let's suppose one might. Once interred, what does one come to
    find?
I found the semblance of a swoon, and began to suspect
ongoing trouble at the heart, a fullness in the throat,
an expanding, treble note whose voice was neither mine alone

117

nor completely separate. I know enough to know you
cannot believe this, not if I were carelessly intent
on saying it was *so*. It was a fiction which I chanced
upon as evening overtook our walled back garden—
whether by virtue of light's ebbing or the fortunate
influx of approaching shade, who would say?

---

*In "The Man With the Hoe," Les Murray identifies the Spirit as love,
present in "decay," in the margins of the human and natural landscape
like Christ, the marginal Nazarene. As the poem's speaker works his
potato field, jets flying overhead remind him how this "Lord of love" has
been chilled by technology and commerce, how nuclear arms have ex-
propriated "the love that ignites stars." Pitting warmth against cold, the
poem ends on the "holey paddock" with an affirmation of Presence in
the "bantering pauses" of simple human encounter, the "Christ in
everyone" Saint Benedict saw.*

The Man with the Hoe Les Murray

1

Thinking about air conditioning's Willis Carrier
who also won the West, I am turning
earth in on a long potato drill,
which is like folding history down on trench lines

of unnumbered mild faces. The day
is overcast, with rain pricking the air
and us to hurry, plying our hoes along this promontory
above Horses Creek. The channel-billed cuckoo

shouts, flying, and the drug squad helicopter
comes singing *I'll spot it, your pot plot*.
O Lord of love, look from above,
sang the churches, but what looks down

from beyond the sky now's the television
of a spy satellite, feeding the coordinates
of today's cloud nations into spinning
tapes for the updating screens of judgement.

The Lord of love is in decay. Relievedly.
He's in worn flanks of stonework, in weathering
garden posts, in the survival of horses,
in humans' long survival after mating, in ticky-tacky

buildings that mean the builders were paid properly
and not always by magnates. He is more apparent
in the idea, verandas and visitings of a hospital
than the stunning theatre. More in surrounds than the center

where he is ground against, love versus love, he lives
in the bantering pauses. The pattern of love's also
behind our continuing to cover these potatoes
which, by her mercy, also look like potatoes.

2

Warmth makes cool. The mystery of refrigeration—
but now three fighter aircraft distil out
of the north hills, fast, ahead of their enormous
collapse of sound. Cloud resorbs them. As in the bra ad

the heart lifts and separates, shrivelled with exultation
that is the angel of history: a boy bored rigid
with farmwork sights along a noble light-draining
sword blade held at the level of his mouth.

Cold. Burning cold. The old tremendous imagery
of the Judgement recycles cold, in a bitter age
where love is passion and passion is the action.
Who could trust a God of love, now we have seen

the love that ignites stars, and ourselves possess such ignition?
Who would trust a god on heat nearer than the stars?
Who can trust heat, that may now freeze the planet?
Who can trust coldness, matrix of utter heat?

We cry for cool, because we long for warmth.
When the fighters grown obsolete, and their pipes cool,
warmth reinvests them. It seems a reversing cycle.
Let the Lord be warm and cool, and judgement be

a flower I'm not good enough to unfold yet,
as I stitch down this earth, and my uncle comes driving
his skittish young tractor over our holey paddock,
my uncle the ex-smoker—not pot: we're older than the pot lot—

who starts the conversation with a ruminative ahaanh,
not *aha! I've caught you!* A shyer reconnecting ahaanh
warm from past meetings. This is among my people
whom I do understand, but not before they speak.

---

*Maura Eichner delights in the world's particulars, the properties of
"common things." She provides a good example of how, for the Christ-
ian poet generally, tangible phenomena define not a limit of knowing
but a horizon where knowing and mystery converge. The concrete sin-
gular, like Eichner's "white enamel bucket" in her poem "Summer,"
points meaningfully to itself, but it addresses more than a congregation
of atoms. In "A Woman Is Waiting for a Bus," a familiar scene res-
onates for Eichner in much the same way. The woman pelted by rain at
the bus stop reminds the poet of biblical narrative: of the life-sustaining
providence of Noah's Ark awaiting the refuge of Mount Ararat, and of
the life-engendering powers of Eve.*

Summer Maura Eichner

fills the white enamel bucket, overflows
its red rim with black-eyed susans.

Light has poured into
the brilliant petals hugging

purple-black, cone-shaped discs.
Hairy leaves, thick stems

gulp water in the bucket.
From a sunny meadow, I carry it

into the house pioneering backward:
decades ago, wagons from the west

loaded with hay and sweet clover
carried the seed of black-eyed susans

—the blessing on common things—from
Massachusetts to Georgia

so that Walt Whitman could say:
. . . every hour of light and dark,

every cubic inch of space
is a miracle.

A Woman is Waiting for a Bus Maura Eichner

In the rain, in Baltimore.
Even her big red umbrella
is speechless about courage,
journey's end, the door

of home. Two buses (not
her transfer) pass. She stands
in flooding rain, bulky as
an ark waiting for ararat.

The third bus has come
—gone. She huddles
into rain. Wind sloshes
wetness across her numb

flesh. Open to receive
bitter weather and give back
warmth, she waits—black
ancient beautiful eve.

---

*It may be hard for the non-Christian to grasp the full extent of the
pathos of Denise Levertov's "Flickering Mind" and "Variation and Re-
flection on a Theme by Rilke." The poet yearns for Christ-consciousness
yet despairs of attaining it. What Levertov seeks is complete absorption
in the Now, contemplative union with the ground of her being, with the
"unchanging presence" in "the stream, the fish, the light, / the pulsing
shadow." But a flickering mind betrays her. Prisoners of time and de-
sire, she is saying, we hold ourselves present to Presence fitfully at best.*

Flickering Mind Denise Levertov

Lord, not you,
it is I who am absent.
At first
belief was a joy I kept in secret,
stealing alone
into sacred places;
a quick glance, and away—and back,
circling.
I have long since uttered your name

but now
I elude your presence.
I stop to think about you, and my mind
at once
like a minnow darts away,
darts
into the shadows, into gleams that fret
unceasing over
the river's purling and passing.
Not for one second
will my self hold still, but wanders
anywhere,
everywhere it can turn. Not you,
it is I am absent.
You are the stream, the fish, the light,
the pulsing shadow,
you the unchanging presence, in whom all
moves and changes.
How can I focus my flickering, perceive
at the fountain's heart
the sapphire I know is there?

The poetic sequence The Book of Hours *by German poet Rainer Maria
Rilke (1875–1926) is spoken by a monk, who shares with the reader his
struggle to engage ultimate mystery.*

Variation and Reflection on A Theme By Rilke
(The Book of Hours, Book I, Poem 7) Denise Levertov

1

If just for once the swing of cause and effect,
                                        cause and effect,
would come to rest; if casual events would halt,
and the machine that supplies meaningless laughter
ran down, and my bustling senses, taking a deep breath

fell silent
and left my attention free at last . . .

then my thought, single and multifold,
could think you into itself
until it filled with you to the very brim,
bounding the whole flood of your boundlessness:

and at that timeless moment of possession,
fleeting as a smile, surrender you
and let you flow back into all creation.

2

There will never be that stillness.
Within the pulse of flesh,
in the dust of being, where we trudge,
    turning our hungry gaze this way and that,
the wings of the morning
brush through our blood
as cloud-shadows brush the land.
What we desire travels with us.
We must breathe time as fishes breathe water.
God's flight circles us.

---

*Fullness of Presence fails poet Andrew Hudgins too, certainly of the kind
known to Christ's friend and disciple in "Mary Magdalene's Left Foot."
David Citino investigates radical estrangement from Presence in his es-
say-poem "The Tribe with No Myth."*

Mary Magdalene's Left Foot Andrew Hudgins

I saw the picture in *Newsweek* or *Time*
and couldn't believe who was back in the news.
But there it sat, encased in antique gold
and pedestrian prose, apart from the rest

of her imaginably lush lost body,
which it recalls with false synecdoche.

The news is littered with the bodies of women
—whores, some—who have returned to minerals,
a pile of iron and zinc and calcium
that wouldn't even fill a shoe. We glimpse
of Mary Magdalene a golden whole
that never ached for flesh or grew hair coarse
enough to scrub mud from a traveler's foot.

But gold is meretricious flattery
for the whore who washed Christ's feet with tears,
who rubbed sweet oil into his sores, then kissed
each suppurating wound that swelled his flesh,
knowing that it was God's clear flesh beneath
its human dying. And that is more than you or I
will ever know of where we place our lips.

Letter from the Shaman: The Tribe with No Myth David Citino

In their territory there lived
no gods or consorts, seraphim or trolls,
no sky-father or earth-mother.
Snakes were snakes, women women
and men no more or less.
Rivers, tors and groves were mere features
of topography. Those few who cared
to gaze into the sky at night
would do so, no questions asked.
They understood that the moon
waxed and waned for no apparent reason
but science, and the stars
spinning at random formed
quite by accident what other tribes
in their frenzied stupors

swore were signs, prey and hunter,
lovers, haters, daughters and sons.
The earth perhaps was flat,
perhaps not. What did it matter
in the end? Folk without lore,
no one could remember. They recognized
no grandparents among the beasts and birds:
some were good to eat; some not;
while others were to be feared
purely for practical reasons,
poison, talon, crush and fang,
They made no distinction between raw, cooked.
Time didn't count. Dreams never meant.
Coming of age was precisely when
the night before the hairless young
couldn't bleed or grow erect as spears,
couldn't conceive, while the day after
they could. Their fires burned slowly,
with no stories to feed the flames.
When it came time for them to go
there was no talk of planting,
no songs of fear or yearning
they would rise to walk again
among the living. Their dead were dead.
In this land lovers loved
because it seemed a good idea,
all things being equal.
Patternless, drifting from one fire
to the next, one coupling,
the tribe came apart, each woman and man
rational as hell, creatures
of wandering. And their children
wander among us still today,
drifting, missing but not quite lost.

In "Poetry and Religion," Les Murray likens the incommensurable Presence "caught" in religious experience to the indwelling of poetry within a poem. Both praying and poeing (a Murray verb form for his stock-in-trade) are activities of the same kind of truth. For Murray, as for other Christians, works of imagination mediate the transcendent through the human spirit. As he writes elsewhere, "Art...has joined creation from our side, / entered Nature, become a fact / and acquired presence." Art at its best, Murray goes on to say, is "a standing miracle...an anomaly, finite but inexhaustible, / unaltered after analysis / as an ancient face."

Poetry and Religion Les Murray

Religions are poems. The concert
our daylight and dreaming mind, our
emotions, instinct, breath and native gesture

into the only whole thinking: poetry.
Nothing's said till it's dremed out in words
and nothing's true that figures in words only.

A poem, compared with an arrayed religion,
may be like a soldier's one short marriage night
to die and live by. But that is a small religion.

Full religion is the large poem flowing in repetition;
like any poem, it must be inexhaustible and complete
with turns where we ask Now why did the poet do that?

You can't pray a lie, said Huckleberry Finn;
you can't poe one either. It is the same mirror:
mobile, glancing, we call it poetry,

fixed centrally, we call it a religion,
and God is the poetry caught in any religion,
caught, not imprisoned. Caught as in a mirror

that he attracted, being in the world as poetry
is in the poem, a law against its closure.
There'll always be religion around while there is poetry

or a lack of it. Both are given, and intermittent,
as the action of those birds—crested pigeon, rosella parrot—
who fly with wings shut, then beating, and again shut.

Denise Levertov writes of the Presence caught in the poetry and life of Caedmon. The Venerable Bede's Ecclesiastical History of the English Nation, *completed in* A.D. *734, tells how this illiterate herdsman living a generation earlier miraculously received the gift of song and went on to compose the "Hymn of Creation," England's first poem in the vernacular. Denise Levertov's monologue retells Caedmon's story in his own words. The alliterations at the moment of Caedmon's epiphany pay homage to the genius of Anglo-Saxon poetry: "affrighted... effacing... feeble... forest... feathers... flame... upflying." Caedmon's surrender to the mystery of Presence joins him creatively to the "ring of the dance," the energies of transcendence. Like so many Christian poets, Levertov associates the power of language with the power of Spirit. "Torches, feathers of flame" are images of Pentecost, where flaming tongues of Spirit fired the apostles' tongues into ethereal speech. Caedmon's interpersonal communion with transcendence comes closest, for many Christians, to what is meant by "salvation."*

Caedmon Denise Levertov

All the others talked as if
talk were a dance.
Clodhopper I, with clumsy feet
would break the gliding ring.
Early I learned to
hunch myself
close by the door:
then when the talk began

I'd wipe my
mouth and wend
unnoticed back to the barn
to be with the warm beasts,
dumb among body sounds
of the simple ones.
I'd see by a twist
of lit rush the motes
of gold moving
from shadow to shadow
slow in the wake
of deep untroubled sighs.
The cows
munched or stirred or were still. I
was at home and lonely,
both in good measure. Until
the sudden angel affrighted me—effacing
my feeble beam,
a forest of torches, feathers of flame, sparks upflying:
but the cows as before
were calm, and nothing was burning,
    nothing but I, as that hand of fire
touched my lips and scorched my tongue
and pulled my voice
                    into the ring of the dance.

God's Body

*T*heologian Sallie McFague has given the name "God's Body" to nature, to the vast cosmic organism of which the human organism is a part. Hers is a radical expression of the idea of Incarnation as spirit becomes flesh. In a "numinous" spirit-revealing nature, the mystical traditions of East and West tread much the same sacred ground, from Amerindian and animist religions to Judaism and Christianity, Hinduism, Buddhism, Shinto, and New Age eco-spirituality. Even the secular romantic shares in the experience of nature's glory, power and mystery.

In a poetry like Wendell Berry's, the concept of God's Body seems particularly apt. Berry is a farmer, working his Kentucky hillside with a team of horses. His empathy with the land runs deep. Not only does his verse celebrate God's immanence in nature, but it sees there an exemplum of Christian ideals.

Sabbaths: 1985 III Wendell Berry

Awaked from the persistent dream
Of human chaos come again,
I walk in the lamed woods, the light
Brought down by the felling of great trees,
And in the rising thicket where
The shadow of old grace returns.
Leaf shadows tremble on light leaves,
A lighter foliage of song,
Among them, the wind's thousand tongues,
And songs of birds. Beams reaching down
Into the shadow swirl and swarm
With gleaming traffic of the air,
Bright grains of generative dust
And winged intelligences. Among
High maple leaves a spider's wheel
Shines, work of finest making made
Touchingly in the dark.
                      The dark
Again has prayed the light to come
Down into it, to animate
And move it in its heaviness.
So what was still and dark wakes up,
Becomes intelligent, moves, names
Itself by hunger and by kind,
Walks, swims, flies, cries, speaks, or sings.
We are all praising, praying to
The light we are, but cannot know.

Independence Day Wendell Berry

Between painting a roof yesterday and the hay
harvest tomorrow, a holiday in the woods
under the grooved trunks and branches, the roof
of leaves lighted and shadowed by the sky.
As America from England, the woods stands free
from politics and anthems. So in the woods I stand
free, knowing my land. My country, 'tis of the
drying pools along Camp Branch I sing
where the water striders walk like Christ,
all sons of God, and of the woods grown old
on the stony hill where the thrush's song rises
in the light like a curling vine and the bobwhite's
whistle opens in the air, broad and pointed as a leaf.

Sabbaths: 1985 I Wendell Berry

Not again in this flesh will I see
the old trees stand here as they did,
weighty creatures made of light, delight
of their making straight in them and well,
whatever blight our blindness was or made,
however thought or act might fail.

The burden of absence grows, and I pay
daily the grief I owe to love
for women and men, days and trees
I will not know again. Pray
for the world's light thus borne away.
Pray for the little songs that wake and move.

For comfort as these lights depart,
recall again the angels of the thicket,
columbine aerial in the whelming tangle,
song drifting down, light rain, day

returning in song, the lordly Art
piercing out its humble way.

Though blindness may yet detonate in light,
ruining all, after all the years, great right
subsumed finally in paltry wrong,
what do we know? Still
the Presence that we come into with song
is here, shaping the seasons of His wild will.

To the Unseeable Animal Wendell Berry

> *My daughter:*   "*I hope there's an animal*
> *somewhere that nobody has ever seen.*
> *And I hope nobody ever sees it.*"

Being, whose flesh dissolves
at our glance, knower
of the secret sums and measures,
you are always here,
dwelling in the oldest sycamores,
visiting the faithful springs
when they are dark and the foxes
have crept to their edges.
I have come upon pools
in streams, places overgrown
with the woods' shadow,
where I knew you had rested,
watching the little fish
hang still in the flow;
as I approached they seemed
particles of your clear mind
disappearing among the rocks.
I have walked deep in the woods
in the early morning, sure
that while I slept
your gaze passed over me.

That we do not know you
is your perfection
and our hope. The darkness
keeps us near you.

from **Window Poems: 19–20** Wendell Berry

Peace. Let men, who cannot be brothers
to themselves, be brothers
to mulleins and daisies
that have learned to live on the earth.
Let them understand the pride
of sycamores and thrushes
that receive the light gladly, and do not
think to illuminate themselves.
Let them know that the foxes and the owls
are joyous in their lives,
and their gayety is praise to the heavens,
and they do not raven with their minds.
In the night the devourer,
and in the morning all things
find the light a comfort.
Peace.... If we, who have killed
our brothers and hated ourselves,
are made in the image of God,
then surely the bloodroot,
wild phlox, trillium and mayapple
are more truly made
in God's image, for they have desired
to be no more than they are,
and they have spared each other....

David Brendan Hopes has written, "If I love nature it is not because it's beautiful, though it is, but because it bears witness. Even the witness it bears is terrible and uncompromising. For every discrete fact that you can make a wise saying about, it will announce a thousand times that you will never know, never know.... Consistency is a concept at odds with the true continuity of things, which is a pattern of change too vast and radiant for human theory to compass. Rocks battered by fire were battered there by flood. Yesterday's immutable atom is today's fleeting quantum. God does not say the same thing on Sinai as He does in Galilee. Yet the universe is not random. There is a consistent message. It is not understand but see; not know but love."

Hopes's view of creation is more visionary and at the same time more austere than Berry's. For Hopes, the "light" and "love" of God are not aboriginal properties of nature. In "Under the Drumlin," an inventory of the earth's crust beneath a drumlin or mound of glacial drift, God is seen to enter nature as something distinct: "Saints discovered in old times / that a ladder leads down from God" through the tiers of angels ("Powers, Thrones, Dominions"), after which "Earth drops the stairway into herself." A kind of partnership has been forged: "The Hand open at the top to give / is open at the bottom to receive. / The gestures are forever complete and indistinguishable."

Under The Drumlin David Brendan Hopes

> I will tell you what lies under this hill
>   worked and hammered by the old ice.
> First: roots, bleached hairs and thumbs,
> grass roots woven to a floor the mice walk on,
>   cocks of wild carrot, pushing down, begetting,
>   the weathered apple with burnt child's arms
>   for roots, tingling at the tips
> like nerves stung over and over.
>   Roots cross and kiss. There is no way.

Under roots—rock: agate, sulphur, turquoise.
These are lizards and moths that die before the cold.
Quartz where the moon was frozen.
Marble, veined, bone-white where monsters,
Titans, ground sloths, rebel angels fell to die.
If you think this is a fancy, dig a deep trench
in fall and watch what forces up in April:
flowers like claws of gryphons,
lichen like eyes on blind rock,

stems reaching and groping, gnawing the turf,
crest-shaped, nape-color, green and watchful.
Under them: black water.
Hill floats on water as sailboat rides the quiver of a lake.
It does not, like surface pools, reflect.
It sheds a blackness from its heart.
Its light draws roots down.
Water stirs the jewels and bones.
It is blown to vapor by the sucking vortex of the grass.

Saints discovered in old times
that a ladder leads down from God.
It soars through Powers, Thrones, Dominions,
sleeps in the sedge.
Earth drops the stairway down into herself,
the inverse, the secret circumference,
Holy the Burning braced by Holy the Black
The Hand open at the top to give
is open at the bottom to receive.

The gestures are forever complete and indistinguishable.
Tiny joints of springtales creak
like fireplace cats'.
Beasts on their cilia dance at morning.
Rock moves its deep thighs in the water.
Think of water that stood in rainbow while
the wind shook rain on one side, diamond,

and the sun the heavens on the other, gold.
This is the sea that sleeps here.

From the breast, the silence
it is forced only by more water pouring down,
longing to lie unmoved with the weight of the hill
on its face like the breath of a lover.
Dance if we rise and dance if we sink.
It is how the world is made.
There are creatures stalking in the dark.
Their names, like true names of stars, are hidden.
They are the suns that called us in the common night.

---

*In "Job from His Mountain," human kinship extends to the hills, trees,
the wind, birds, and wildflowers like False Solomon's Seal—all the one
body of "the old earth." For Hopes, the "blessing" of Job is authoritative
because it flows from Job's radical encounter with God and God's rela-
tionship to creation, where "sow-thistle in a limestone cup is Covenant."
Job's post-Edenic innocence opens to the same vision of sacred wholeness
that Hopes considers in "The Swimmer," appearing in the chapter "In-
justice."*

---

from **Job from His Mountain** David Brendan Hopes

And Job from his mountain sees
how the foundations were laid sly and dark,
the battlements of ice above them.
He knows the measure, the spring, the fastening.
How the water sings behind its doors!
O, how in his seasons Mazzaroth climbs
the ranges shining, and the child crows
cry in the wilderness and are filled,
each one of them.

Job from his mountains blesses the sweet hills.
They are proof by their presence.
    They shall answer in the Consummation
        and only the sea's voice will speak after them.
    They bore the ice and for their anger
bear the flowers. We are not speaking
    of likelihood now, but of the hills.
        The work of the hills is watch, wait.
    The why of the hills is where they lead.

Job from his mountain blesses the trees
    who clap their hands in the heights.
        They climb the hills by resting on them.
    They receive their ornament of birds by waiting.
When the ice left they walked back
    generation by generation till it was earth again.
        They wed water and wind and make themselves.
    They ascend upon their own deaths, dead wood
upon dead wood in the stars of morning.

Job from his mountain blesses the wind
    and the limbs and waters and
sticks and stalks in the wind.
Wind is music when it strikes.
    All things have roots to resist it,
        wings to ride it. Birds cling with claw,
    ascend with feather; tree roots and leaves;
Earth has her heart to anchor her,
    her hills to lift her up....

Job from his mountain blesses False Solomon's Seal.
It is a two-thirds arch,
    a parabola broken by a spray of berries.
        Its curve is not completed in a space
    of dirt floor, but in
promissory seeds, in generations.
    Job from his mountain blesses

our old selves who follow through the dust,
who come to withered hills for bread of stone

and honey of the hawk's slant fading home
   by early night. Where there is nothing
      sow-thistle in a limestone cup is Covenant.
   There is always something green against the season.
Job merry on the unlooked-for hills,
   bless who bore me, grass, beast, woman.
      Hold me in them for a little while
   as the old earth holds her brood
till they are her again, green, forgetting.

"The Glacier's Daughters" traces a lyric history of the origin and prolif-
eration of vegetative life forms. Hopes enlarges his notion of cosmic
synergy by granting creative initiative to nature, to the weeds who are
the botanical "daughters" of earth. It is they who appropriate, rather
than receive, the dynamic of sacred life: "God howls and we suck him
down."

The Glacier's Daughters David Brendan Hopes

Mother plasma. Father fire.
   He thundered and she sucked him down.
      See yourself in blue light on the water,
   the live heat, the heirloom of a trillion generations.
We are the bolt-born, lightened from the sleep.
   We are the horrible stirring, the wriggle out,
      Out, rising on the corpses of the first hour.
   The sea was eaten and the land was eaten
and it is not enough.

   We are an imperial family.
      Hill, cleft, we have them,
   sun, shade, sea-deep. Divide us,

we flow back. Burn us, we blacken
and take root. Drown us, we fin, we gill.
Starve us and we gnaw. Tiny teeth.
Slivers of nails, burrowing back-paws.
We have cousins who uphold the roof.
We have cousins who gambol in fire.

First mother, Terra, the crone
takes us for ornament gladly, that her face
alone is memorable among the drone stars.
We are the flight which is repose between two dances.
We are the weavers. Our eyes are on our legs.
We bore with our tap root. We whiten the sea
when we breach above her to the moon's face.
We hugged the pointless hills to ourselves,
lance-leaved, multi-petaled, made them.

Under our black eye-spotted whirring backs,
under the hooves that buoy us over cousin grass,
we have changed everything.
It was deep and we dug.
It was lofty and we lifted.
It was many and we multiplied.
It was lovely and we took shapes to us
that are the single loveliness forever.
It was winter and we died.

It was cold in the world and we waited.
The glacier was the night.
It bore its ghosts and stars.
It was the strange time when our mother
turned her head and slept, and wept
in her sleep tears that hardened
in the moon and crushed us.
We would not leave her. We dreamed
what we might be when the bad time left us.

Cliffbrake, birch, red cedar, saxifrage,
    wolf's claw, moonwort, bleeding heart,
bloodroot, bloodroot.
We are the glacier's daughters.
    We rip the rock.
        We grow fingers where our hearts would be.
    We work down, gripping, grinding stone to soil,
squeezing green from dark where nothing
    moved since mountain danced up from the sea.

    Two fists hammer her, the sleeping mother.
    Father is night and fury. We are the second.
We are fire in green gloves, wind in a cup of flowers,
    bulging where the snow beat flat.
        Green, the glacier's daughters, giving back,
    atoning for our father, for the sins of God.
Rock wears us in its nakedness.
    Its shame is turned to forests.
        Its wounds run green and frill.

    Climb this battleground, this withered rock,
among your sisters who have labored longer;
    toothwort, ironwood, hart's tongue, bracken.
        We are first-born at the task, recovering,
    amending all with sinew where our hearts were.
We fight for the garden lost by God's turned back,
    against sleet, snow, the intolerable solstice,
        ever the ice-hill looming with its bastinade of stars.
    We have made ourselves from nothing.

We cling to the cliffs and pity them,
    pity the brief oaks their beauty, how they
        out-grip God and how the least wears them away.
    We sigh to the hurt hills, "Pilgrim. . . ."
We are the foundation. Trees taste and stay,
    lavish trees heavy from south with their clouds of flowers,
        their arms rising to the sun as if they planned

to climb forever, the roots
forgetting as they pour toward heaven.

We come first in spring before they shade us.
    We are green through winter, remembering
cold beside which this cold is a needle
in a sea of ice. We are the glacier's daughters.
    Grandfather fire is in us. Grandmother, the abiding.
      We reach out and take. We have
turned winter into world again.
We fetch this hill from nothing.
    God howls and we suck him down.

---

*Hopes and Berry are by no means alone in their response to nature as a
sacred organism of creation. Many Christian poets, with them, sense
Wordsworth's "something far more deeply interfused" in the natural
world.*

Back Porch Fundamentalist Maura Eichner

In the afternoon
he chose the corner in the sun.
Then he set his porch rocker
facing the mimosa
where gold wires
of light tapped
the leaves, and he, himself,
by a simple act of seeing
observed a miracle.
If anything is, he said,
them pods
on this tree is the keys
of the kingdom.

Sister Mary Appassionata Proves to the Entomology Class That Woman and Man Descended from the Cricket David Citino

Our mother and fathers,
sojourners in bogs, architects
of prairie clods, perennials
strewn over mountainsides,
forders of roiling creeks, herds,
loving under thatch and star,
each word together a bellows
heartening the flame, sang
to summer rain and generation,
feared only the sudden shrill bird
of fire or wind. Where they fell
cities were raised. We lost our ear
to concrete and brick, thick rivers
stagnant under iron spans, tug
and barge contending with siren,
horn, raucous hell of press, mill,
forge. Tonight just beyond
the bedroom wall our parents and the wind
will return to soothe earth's
August fever with a cool hand,
remind us of love's sympathetic magic,
leaping and creaking from clump
and bush, thick weedy field,
chanting the history of the world.

October Maples, Portland Richard Wilbur

The leaves, though little time they have to live,
Were never so unfallen as today,
And seem to yield us through a rustled sieve
The very light from which time fell away.

A showered fire we thought forever lost
Redeems the air. Where friends in passing meet,
They parley in the tongues of Pentecost.
Gold ranks of temples flank the dazzled street.

It is a light of maples, and will go;
But not before it washes eye and brain
With such a tincture, such a sanguine glow
As cannot fail to leave a lasting stain.

So Mary's laundered mantle (in the tale
Which, like all pretty tales, may still be true),
Spread on the rosemary-bush, so drenched the pale
Slight blooms in its irradiated hue,

They could not choose but to return in blue.

from **Feast Days: Thanksgiving—Christmas III** Annie Dillard

> *And the captain of the Lord's host said unto Joshua,*
> *Loose thy shoe from off thy foot; for the place*
> *whereon thou standest is holy.*   *—Joshua*

I kick through a forest of hands
by Tinker Creek. The sassafras hands
wear mittens; the tulip tree hands
demand money; "Wait!" cry the fraying hands
of a frivolous silver maple,
"I love you!"
A cottonwood hand floats down the creek
on its back, like Ophelia.

And deep on the banks of the creek
some hands uncurl;
some hands unleaf, and damply become
rich water,
wild and bitter perfume,

and loam, where bluets will bloom.
So your hand, asleep in my hair,
takes root, and flowers there.

Let me mention
one or two things about Christmas.
Of course you've all heard
that the animals talk
at midnight:
a particular elk, for instance,
kneeling at night to drink,
leaning tall to pull leaves
with his soft lips,
says, alleluia.

That the soul and fresh-water lakes
also rejoice,
as do products
such as sweaters
(nor are plastics excluded
from grace),
is less well known.
Further:
the reason
for some silly-looking fishes,
for the bizarre mating
of certain adult insects,
or the sprouting, say,
in a snow tire
of a Rocky Mountain grass,
is that the universal
loves the particular,
that freedom loves to live
and live fleshed full,
intricate,
and in detail.

God empties himself
into the earth like a cloud.
God takes the substance, contours
of a man, and keeps them,
dying, rising, walking,
and still walking
wherever there is motion.

At night in the ocean
the sponges are secretly building;
by day in a pharmacy drawer
capsules stir in their jars.
Once, on the Musselshell,
I regenerated an arm!
Shake hands. When I stand
the blood runs up.
On what bright wind
did God walk down?
Swaying under the snow,
reeling minutely,
revels the star-moss,
pleased....

Mollusc Les Murray

By its nobship sailing upside down,
by its inner sexes, by the crystalline
pimplings of its skirts, by the sucked-on
lifelong kiss of its toppling motion,
by the viscose optics now extruded
now wizened instantaneously, by the
ridges grating up a food-path, by
the pop shell in its nick of dry,
by excretion, the earthworm coils, the glibbing,
by the gilt slipway, and by pointing
perhaps as far back into time as

ahead, a shore being folded interior,
by boiling on salt, by coming uncut over
a razor's edge, by hiding the Oligocene
underleaf may this and every snail sense
itself ornament the weave of presence.

"The Craze Field" is inspired by the dried riverbeds and wadies of Western Australia. Murray renders the ancient lagoon basin as a living physiology of palate, membrane, meniscus—the "primal tissue" of creation from which life sprang and continues to be recapitulated in "a kind of fire." Artifacts found in the craze field, bearing traces of Latin, obscurely postulate the light: "corr lux." Another archeological fragment begins with the words of English author G. K. Chesterton, "who lose belief in God will not only believe / in anything..." The closing phrase of the inscription is Murray's.

The Craze Field Les Murray

These lagoons, these watercourses,
streets of the underworld.
Their water has become the trees that stand along them.

Below root-revetments, in the circles of the water's recession
the ravines seem thronged with a legacy of lily pads.
Earth curls and faintly glistens, scumbled painterly and peeling.

Palates of drought-stilled assonance,
they are cupped flakes of grit, crisps of bottom, dried meniscus
lifted at the edges.

Abstracts realized in slime. Shards of bubble, shrivelled viscose
of clay and stopped life:
the scales of the water snake have gone to grey on this channel.

.   .   .

Exfoliate bark of the rain tree, all the outer
plaques have a jostling average size.
It is a kind of fire, the invention of networks.

Water's return, however gradual (and it won't be)
however gentle (it wont be) would not re-lay all seamless
this basal membrane;
it has borne excess of clarity.

This is the lush sheet that overlay the first cities,
the mother-goddess towns, but underlay them first;
this they had for mortar.

Laminar, half detached, these cusps are primal tissue,
foreshadowings of leaf, pottery, palimpsest,
the Dead Lagoon Scrolls.

In this hollow season
everything is perhaps to be recapitulated,
hurriedly, approximately. It is a kind of fire.
Saturate calm is all sprung, in the mother country.

•   •   •

The lagoon-bed museums meanwhile have a dizzy stillness
that will reduce, with all the steps that are coming,
to meal, grist, morsels.
Dewfall and birds' feet have nipped, blind noon have nibbled
this mineral matzoth.

The warlike peace-talking young, pacing this dominion
in the beautiful flesh that outdoes their own creations,
might read gnomic fragments:

   corr lux Romant irit

or fragmentary texts:

who lose belief in God will not only believe
in anything. They will bring blood offerings to it

Bones, snags, seed capsules
intrinsic in the Martian central pan,
are hidden, in the craze, under small pagoda eaves.

---

*"The Craze Field" and David Citino's "The Sea of Kansas, Ohio Tun-
dra, Time Still Running Out" are both poems that associate an aspect of
nature with Christianity's sacrament of communion, or eucharist. The
"mineral matzoth" of Murray's poem recalls the transformed eucharis-
tic bread (historically the Jewish unleavened matzoth) that many Chris-
tians witness as the sacramental medium of "God's body," the flesh of
Christ. The spiritualizing of bread and wine experienced in faith at
communion has been given the name "transubstantiation" by some tra-
ditional theologies. David Citino applies the term to photosynthesis, the
natural transformation of carbon dioxide into life-giving oxygen. His
poem decries the human insult to God's Body, and by the power of pho-
tosynthesis, Citino is saying, nature's many forms of plant-life serve as
"green Christs" to redeem the air and save us from our sins of ecological
abuse, at least for a time. In "Our Lost Angels," Scott Cairns mourns
the passing of this sacramental sense of nature, as the scientific para-
digm replaces the mythic and spiritual in natural discourse.*

The Sea of Kansas, Ohio Tundra, Time Still
Running Out David Citino

Kansas one million centuries ago, a tropical sea
streaming buoyantly enough to float the ichthyosaur
while mammoths hunting stunted shrubs thunder over
Ohio's rutted tundra, their breath eternal winter.
We're born to new topography, but still this earth
spins us between trajectories of ice and burning,
apogee and perigee of the perilous trek. On Venus
there's heat enough to melt lead, cook the heart.

On Mars, blood would shatter into crimson snow.
There's no place else we can be, in truth, creatures
lusting for moderation, drifting above
the temperate wrack and barm of uterine seas, struggling
up generation's beach to reach solid ground, each fist
an eon of weather, each corpse a tangle of roots.
Passing those who couldn't catch their breath, faces
blue as mountain sky, we know we're not home free.
Burning our histories by barrel and ton, exhaling
our every greed, we've filled the air with CO_2, 23% more
than our parents' parents knew. The very rain corrodes.
How much longer can the children hold their breath?
Plants have saved us so far, green Christs to eat
our sin. Miracles of transubstantiation.
All up and down the street oak and elm, elder and ash
rise to full height, breathing, breathing, nettle and shrub,
redbud and shagbark, weed-blades thrusting up
to shatter concrete, each leap from root to seed
to bloom to fruit our diastole, systole,
each green plot our Eden, time still running out.

Our Lost Angels Scott Cairns

Ages ago, clouds brought them near
    and rain brought them to our lips;
        they swam in every vase, every cupped palm.
    We took them into ourselves
    and were refreshed.
For those luckier generations, angels
    were the sweet, quickening substance
        in all light, all water, every morsel of food.
Until the day the sun changed some, as it had,
    took them skyward, but thereafter
        the clouds failed to restore them.
In time, streams gave up
    every spirit, and the sea, unreplenished,

152

finally became the void we had feared
it would become, the void we had imagined.
And, as now, clouds brought only rain,
    and the emptied rain
    brought only the chill in which
we must now be wrapped.

Between them, Andrew Hudgins's "Consider" and David Craig's "Francis Helps a Brother Who Is in Sin" summarize the Christian incarnational response to nature. Saint Francis of Assisi (1182–1226) is one of Christianity's best-known defenders of the earth and its creatures as a sacred community.

Consider Andrew Hudgins

You have considered the lilies of the field,
how they do nothing for their splendor
and how they shine like moons upon their stalks,
arrayed in the exacting glory of the sun.
Consider now the mosses of the cypress swamp,
the great droop-headed grasses of the salt marsh,
and how, beneath the shadowed pastels
of the wetland flowers, there lingers a hint of violet
that fades in full light, whitens and dies
like a sin you are especially partial to
because it makes your life more intricate
and somehow better. Consider, too, the various lights
that outlast the last, hard leg of the pilgrimage
through leaf and branch, moss, mist, haze, and gnats,
are rare and changed, softened with impurities,
and should be blessed each with a proper name.
In the sun-bright fields it's just called light
because it's known there only in its scouring brightness.
Consider the dream I dreamt last night of Christ
glowing in holiness, as metal in a forge

153

will pulsate red, yellow, and finally white
before it starts to lose its this-world shape.
He asked me to bathe his burning face
and soften the radiance that was killing him,
and I led him to the marsh and immersed him,
almost vanishing in the stream, that rose around us.
Consider: from the reeds close at hand the marsh hen lunges,
a blast of stubby wings and dangling legs,
so awkward she soon relinquishes the sky,
flashing the patch of white beneath her tail
as she bolts between the tassels of marsh grass.
And down the random corridor of water oaks
beckons the hollow, two-note fluting of an owl.

Francis Helps a Brother Who Is in Sin David Craig

Francis walked in silence
a step ahead of his brother
The sun was setting and the bark on the trees
turned orange

They sat on a hill
first Francis then the brother
They sat watching the moon rise
shed a column of light on the water

Walking back
Francis stooped
picked up a dead branch
"Did you know," he asked
"that the forest has bones?"

He broke the branch over his knee
The sound echoed through the trees
in the twilight

Fools

Christians often seem obsessed with "doing good" and "being good." Their intimate encounter with Presence, however ecstatic, is not an end in itself. Grasped in the light of Christian spirituality and scripture, Presence implants in them the idea of living in the imitation of Christ. The desire to give oneself away for the sake of others, to be a "fool for Christ" in Saint Paul's words, carries on a tradition of the moral life that goes back four thousand years to the ancient Hebrews, to the imperatives of the good they called *mitzvoth*. The Ten Commandments and the so-called Sermon on the Mount are obvious mainstays of this legacy. But the lived pattern of Christ's life remains the archetype, a mix of sacrifice and subversion targeting the world's attractive doctrines of self-interest.

The Translation of Raimundo Luz: My Imitation Scott Cairns

I sold my possessions, even the colorful pencils.
I gave all my money to the dull. I gave my poverty
to the president. I became a child again, naked
and relatively innocent. I let the president have my guilt.

I found a virgin and asked her to be my mother.
She held me very sweetly.

I watched father build beautiful shapes with wood.
He too had a gentle way.

I made conversation in holy places with the chosen.
Their theater was grim.

I suggested they cheer up. Many repented,
albeit elaborately.

I floated the wide river on a raft.
I set Jim free.

I revised every word.

One morning, very early, I was taken by brutes and beaten.
I was nailed to a cross so sturdy I thought
father himself might have shaped it.

I gestured for a cool drink and was mocked.
I took on the sins of the world and regretted my extravagance.
I gave up and died. I descended into hell
and spoke briefly with the president.

I rose again, bloodless and feeling pretty good.

I forgave everything.

The mental patient making a fool of himself in Denise Levertov's "Man Wearing Bird" also imitates Christ, "a pillar of / righteousness, uphold-ing / mystery," and is fated like Christ to endure "foolish grins" and "awestruck staring." The dead pigeon on his head stands in, or flops in, for the ancient symbol of the Holy Spirit "that spoke and continues to speak." As the bird's prophet, the patient will raise it like "the Host" of communion, the wafer of ceremonial bread that manifests the presence of Christ, in symbol or in substance, to the communicant.

Man Wearing Bird Denise Levertov

> *One afternoon, I saw a patient standing in the middle of the drive-*
> *way.... Something was moving on his head. Suddenly, two large wings*
> *flapped over his head in the light breeze... He had rolled his pants up*
> *to his knobby knees and wore an opened leather jacket over a T-shirt*
> *with a large number 17.... The mesmerized motorists slowed to a crawl*
> *for a longer look. ... The patient later told his therapist he had ...*
> *realized that people were startled by his appearance. In fact, he had*
> *relished it. ...*
>   —Boston Globe, December 1983

I could be stone,
a live bird on my civic head.
They would not look twice.

This is my pigeon
and I its prophet.
No one but I

found it. It died
for me to find,
to lift like the Host

and place aloft, a soft
weight on my naked scalp,
where one more time

flailing wings can
contest with the wind.
I am a column, a pillar of

righteousness, upholding
mystery, a dead pigeon that spoke
and continues to speak, that told

no one but me what to do,
told me to hold still under its
cold flutterings, told me

to relish the foolish grins, the awestruck
staring of passing, passing,
tenuous motorists, stand

barelegged in the winter day, display—
with the same wind beating
upon it—the number life and its warders

assign me, inscribed on my thin shirt
over my heart:

I the prophet,
chosen from all, ennobled, singular,
by this unique
unfathomable death.

---

*The freedom and spontaneity of Christian fools like Wendell Berry's
mad farmer reflect Christ's own image of the liberation of his followers,
whom he assured would "have life and have it to the full."*

So, friends, every day do something
that won't compute. Love the Lord.
Love the world. Work for nothing.
Take all that you have and be poor.
Love someone who does not deserve it.
Denounce the government and embrace
the flag. Hope to live in that free
republic for which it stands.
Give your approval to all you cannot
understand. Praise ignorance, for what man
has not encountered he has not destroyed.
Ask the questions that have no answers.
Invest in the millennium. Plant sequoias....
Listen to carrion—put your ear
close, and hear the faint chattering
of the songs that are to come.
Expect the end of the world. Laugh.
Laughter is immeasurable. Be joyful
though you have considered all the facts....
Go with your love to the fields.
Lie easy in the shade. Rest your head
in her lap. Swear allegiance
To what is nighest in your thoughts.
As soon as the generals and the politicos
can predict the motions of your mind,
lose it. Leave it as a sign
to mark the false trail, the way
you didn't go. Be like the fox
who makes more tracks than necessary,
some in the wrong direction.
Practice resurrection.

from **Prayers and Sayings of the Mad Farmer** Wendell Berry

I

It is presumptuous and irresponsible to pray for other people. A good man would pray only for himself—that he have as much good as he deserves, that he not receive more good or more evil than he deserves, that he bother nobody, that he not be bothered, that he want less. Praying thus for himself, he should prepare to live with the consequences.

II

At night make me one with the darkness.
In the morning make me one with the light.

III

If a man finds it necessary to eat garbage, he should resist the temptation to call it a delicacy.

V

Don't own so much clutter that you will be relieved to see your house catch fire.

VI

Beware of the machinery of longevity. When a man's life is over the decent thing is for him to die. The forest does not withhold itself from death. What it gives up it takes back.

VII

Put your hands into the mire.
They will learn the kinship
of the shaped and the unshapen,
the living and the dead.

VIII

When I rise up
let me rise up joyful
like a bird

When I fall
let me fall without regret
like a leaf.

XI

By the excellence of his work the workman is a neighbor. By selling only what he would not despise to own the salesman is a neighbor. By selling what is good his character survives his market.

XII

Let me wake in the night
and hear it raining
and go back to sleep.

XIII

Don't worry and fret about the crops. After you have done all you can for them, let them stand in the weather on their own.

If the crop of any one year was all, a man would have to cut his throat every time it hailed.

But the *real* products of any year's work are the farmer's mind and the cropland itself.

If he raises a good crop at the cost of belittling himself and diminishing the ground, he has gained nothing. He will have to begin over again the next spring, worse off than before.

Let him receive the season's increment into his mind. Let him work it into the soil.

The finest growth that farmland can produce is a careful farmer.

Make the human race a better head. Make the world a better piece of ground.

What My Teachers Taught Me I Try to Teach My Students Maura Eichner

A bird in the hand
is not to be desired.
In writing, nothing
is too much trouble.

Culture is nourished, not
by fact, but by myth.
Continually think of those
who were truly great
who in their lives fought
for life, who wore
at their hearts, the fire's
center. Feel the meanings
the words hide. Make routine
a stimulus. Remember
it can cease. Forge
hosannahs from doubt.
Hammer on doors with the heart.
All occasions invite God's
mercies and all times
are his seasons.

from **Out of Cana** Maura Eichner

Eat bread. Drink wine. Try to sing the song
of Christ. Live life. If you can dance, dance.
Everywhere grace awaits. Desire to love to love.

**Sister Mary Appassionata Lectures the Science Class:
Fossils, Physics, Apple, Heart** David Citino

Fossil bones, splintered bits of pelvis,
jawbone, tooth and skull aren't
of early apes and men
but of fallen angels made by greed too gross
to fly, who shattered when they hit the ground.

We know from physics every clock
winds down, each woman and man lies down
one more time than necessary for sleep or love.

Every movement culminates in stone,
each light and life in the ocean of night.

Drowned bodies, drunkards, heroes, saviors
surface always on the third day.

Virgin wool cures the deepest ache or burn.

Girls with big breasts and too much heart won't
fit into heaven. The boy who can unclasp
a girl's brassiere with one hand
knows too much for his own good
and all his life will have his hands full,
his mouth open at the wrong time.

The key to happiness? Knowing every second
of every day what to do with the hands,
when to loose or hold the tongue.

The holiest creatures are those that fly. God
Himself's part falcon, cuckoo, pelican, dove.

The girl who indulges herself
by climbing spiked fences, riding a horse
with too much passion, stooping too often
to pick mushroom or orchid
or dreaming of lovers who feel as she does
will from the wedding night on
be too easy on her husband.

Man's the only animal dumb enough to try
to cry back the dead, take
another's life only out of spite,
give his life for love.

Those whose eyebrows meet can never be trusted.

Women named Agnes always go mad.

No hunger justifies eating an apple
without first bringing it to life by breathing
on it, filling it with beauty
by rubbing it across the heart.

In "The Quality of Sprawl," Les Murray works up a kind of Christian personality profile. Sprawl is reckless charity, easy benevolence, a "loose-limbed" freedom from convention, lack of pretense, a "rough" uncompli-cated faith. Wendell Berry's mad farmer is clearly a man of sprawl.

from **The Quality of Sprawl** Les Murray

Sprawl is the quality
of the man who cut down his Rolls-Royce
into a farm utility truck, and sprawl
is what the company lacked when it made repeated efforts
to buy the vehicle back and repair its image.

Sprawl is doing your farming by aeroplane, roughly,
or driving a hitchhiker that extra hundred miles home.
It is the rococo of being your own still center.
It is never lighting cigars with ten-dollar notes:
that's idiot ostentation and murder of starving people.
Nor can it be bought with the ash of million-dollar deeds.

Sprawl lengthens the legs; it trains greyhounds on liver and beer.
Sprawl almost never says Why not? with palms comically raised
nor can it be dressed for, not even in running shoes worn
with mink and a nose ring. That is Society. That's Style.
Sprawl is more like the thirteenth banana in a dozen
or anyway the fourteenth....

Sprawl is really classless, though. It's John Christopher Frederick
    Murray
asleep in his neighbors' best bed in spurs and oilskins
but not having thrown up:
sprawl is never Calum who, drunk, along the hallways of our
    house,
reinvented the Festoon. Rather
it's Beatrice Miles going twelve hundred ditto in a taxi,

No Lewd Advances, No Hitting Animals, No Speeding,
on the proceeds of her two-bob-a-sonnet Shakespeare readings.
An image of my country. And would that it were more so.

No, sprawl is full-gloss murals on a council-house wall.
Sprawl leans on things. It is loose-limbed in its mind.
Reprimanded and dismissed
it listens with a grin and one boot up on the rail
of possibility. It may have to leave the Earth.
Being roughly Christian, it scratches the other cheek
and thinks it unlikely. Though people have been shot for sprawl.

---

*The speaker in "The Liar's Psalm" by Andrew Hudgins evaluates the
Christian ethic of love against the ethic of "truth." He decides, like a
Christian fool, he would rather lie than hurt someone he loves, a strategy
of the heart opposing "the actual." But Christians are fools for truth, as
well, so tensions arise. In his apologetic last line, the poem's speaker, like
doubting Thomas the apostle, probes love's wound for truth's assurance.*

The Liar's Psalm: Repentance Andrew Hudgins

I repent the actual. It has never got me anywhere.
It is nothing against principalities, against powers.
My father will die and I will carry on. I dread his death

more than mine because it will come sooner—knowledge I
    repent. In lies
he will outlive the liar. And that's me. The lie itself
will carry on, is itself a child, a separate life, a blow

against the gods of objects. Who are not happy with me
or with their densities. They are not worth their flawed kingdoms.
And neither do I love them. They are dangerous. They are too

stupid to be insignificant, too proud of their ability
to blister my hands and make them raw. I repent letting them,
and I repent logic, which has no god: it will do

anything, it will go anywhere. Tell it your destination
and it will take you there. A taxi. *This* is the nature
of evidence: how could you prove the meat you ate last night

wasn't horse meat, goat flesh,
or something I had, the night before, sliced from my thighs?
Or that it was meat at all? Or that you ate? There is no

bottom to what we will believe, and no top.
So I have made this vow.
Never again will I insult you with the actual, something

that has no birthday, while lies are born
six times a second and each with a festival. They are the gifts
we give ourselves, like morphine, a change of clothes, a piece

of apple pie, a black chrysanthemum, a job—I could go on.
I am ashamed when I remember whom I have attacked
with actuality. My mother with her stinginess. My wife

with her black and purple dress—you should have seen it!—
and her infidelities. My friend who steals ashtrays. My brother's
avoirdupois. I repent that blade and I repent

my skill with it. When blessed with falsehoods, I will tell them.
When told a lie, I will believe it. I will not doubt
a word you say. Forgive me now my finger in the wound, and
knuckle deep.

---

*The speaker of "The Eye" by Richard Wilbur also strives for a less judg-
mental way of being. For inspiration he turns to Lucy, the fourth-cen-
tury saint from Sicily and the subject of the popular Italian song "Santa*

---

from **The Eye** Richard Wilbur

> *". . . all this beastly seeing"* —*D. H. Lawrence*

II

Preserve us, Lucy,
From the eye's nonsense, you by whom
Benighted Dante was beheld,
To whom he was beholden.

If the salesman's head
Rolls on the seat-back of the bus
In ugly sleep, his open mouth
Banjo-strung with spittle,

Forbid my vision
To take itself for a curious angel.
Remind me that I am here in body,
A passenger, and rumpled.

Charge me to see
In all bodies the beat of spirit,
Not merely in the *tout en l'air*
Or double pike with layout

But in the strong,
Shouldering gait of the legless man,

168

The calm walk of the blind young woman
Whose cane touches the curbstone.

Correct my view
That the far mountain is much diminished,
That the fovea is prime composer,
That the lid's closure frees me.

Let me be touched
By the alien hands of love forever,
That this eye not be folly's loophole
But giver of due regard.

Christians are often not satisfied with just being good. Scripture exhorts them to be perfect. The result is constant, sometimes feverish moral scrutiny, of the kind David Citino, Daniel Berrigan, and Andrew Hudgins consider below. The Christian concept of "sin," revisited by Scott Cairns, is the calculus of such a pursuit of the moral ideal. The nature of it is revealed in the Greek word that sin translates, hamartía, *an archery term for "missing the mark." In their examinations of personal and communal missings of the mark of perfection, Richard Wilbur and David Brendan Hopes capture a distinctive melancholy of the fool for Christ.*

Situation No. 7: The Poison Lover David Citino

One night
deep in middle age
as your lecherous spirit
bucks and wings you into pleasure,
you discover
that your young lover's long body
harbors a bouquet of snakes,
that she or he's been bred
by your worst enemy

169

for the sole purpose
of congealing you
into the cold meat of age,
that in your limp nakedness
you're without amulet,
scapular, mojo, prayer.

What do you do?

Situation No. 13: City Hall David Citino

Tall in a top hat,
the mayor, who minutes before
was gunned down by urban terrorists,
hands you the key to a city
where no one can live.

You make no acceptance speech,
but grateful and bright
before the cameras
you place a long hard kiss
on the corpse's lips, pledge
your political patronage,
borrow his hat.

Having invested heavily in real estate
and social love, you set fire
to your own obsolete foundries,
open a chain of carry-outs
in marginal neighborhoods,
make plans to take your family
away to the suburbs.

You become the target
of random acts of inhumanity.
Even you no longer believe

your speeches. You notice
one morning in the mirror
a hint of corruption, the birth
of insolvency, blight and decay.

What's your next move?

---

*In "We Will Now Hear the Word of God," Daniel Berrigan shows little
patience for a pair of chaplains who ministered during the poet's im-
prisonment for civil disobedience. One chaplain's asperges, his sprin-
kling of the prisoners with holy water, is reciprocated with a blessing of
an altogether different kind.*

We Will Now Hear the Word Of God from Each
of Our Beloved Chaplains Daniel Berrigan

1.

Rev Stump is   believe it or not   for real
as a stump to a grown tree
so he to the verdant gospel
this corpulent burgher   this fictitious
rubbery stamp   Stump
a huckster's   a hack's gospel
Stump   wormwood   miles of smiles

2.

the priest   an irish caricature   wheels up
in his cadillac each a.m. an alderman
to a cobbler's funeral   we   the dead faces
his asperges hisses on   have yet
like Lazarus in hell
one cold Christian curse
bestowal, blessing

Andrew Hudgins seems pleased that his behavior can sometimes "satisfy the light" of scrutiny in "Beneath Searchlights."

Beneath Searchlights Andrew Hudgins

Shop windows glow like fish tanks. Even in town
the sky's so full of stars I can imagine
sun beyond sun until there seems no darkness
in the dark—a trick the mind plays against midnight.
But just a trick. It doesn't change the darkness:
cats yowl, my dog's hair bristles in response.
He's snuffling at a bush when suddenly
harsh light explodes around me. And then I hear
the *whup, whup, whup* of helicopter blades
above and slightly to the left—the spot,
though higher, where I imagine my soul drifts
and watches me. The searchlight lingers.
The taut leash makes my hand point toward the dog.
Come here, I hiss. He's busy. I haul him, choking,
into the light. Now that my alibi
stands growling at my side, I dance a jig,
then bow — but upward, blindly. As if applauding,
the spotlight dips once, veers off, scraping hard
light over houses, trees. The choked dog whimpers.
He jerks, I pull, and we compose one linked
uneasy beast that seesaws through the dark streets,
this way and that, toward home, sleep, food, and work—
repeat, repeat, repeat until we die.
But that's untrue. Too stark. Sometimes—tonight—
I satisfy the light that questions me.

A Recuperation of Sin Scott Cairns

I suppose we might do away with words like *sin*.
They are at least archaic, not to mention rude,
and late generations have been pretty well schooled

against the presumption of holding *anything*
to be absolutely so, universally
applicable, especially anything like

sin which is, to put it more neatly, unpleasant,
not the sort of thing one brings up. Besides, so much
of what ignorance may have once attributed

to *sin* has been more justly shown to be the end
result of bad information, genetic flaw,
or, most often, an honest misunderstanding.

And I suppose *sin's* old usefulness may have paled
somewhat through many centuries of overuse
by corrupt clergy pointing fingers, by faithless

men and women who have longed more than anything
for a more rigid tyranny over their wives
and husbands, over their somnambulant children.

In fact, we could probably forget the idea
of sin altogether if it were not for those
periodic eruptions one is quite likely

to picture in the papers, or on the TV—
troubling episodes in which, inexplicably,
some giddy power rises up to occasion

once more the spectacle of the innocent's blood.

In "Another Voice," Richard Wilbur concedes that what the "patient voice" of Christ urges upon his followers is just, but at the same time, "the soul knows what it knows." The Greek soul, for example, knew Corcyra, an island savaged by revolution during the Peloponnesian War. In Wilbur's soul, the "giddy ghost" of the Holy Spirit contends with "atrocious fact." "The Proof" is Wilbur's sigh of relief that the patient voice apears to be indicative of a patient God.

Another Voice Richard Wilbur

The sword bites for peace,
Yet how should that be said
Now or in howling Greece
Above the sorry dead?
Corcyra! cry the crows,
And blacken all the sky.
The soul knows what it knows,
But may not make reply.

From a good face gone mad,
From false or hissing tongue,
What comfort's to be had,
What sweetness can be wrung?
It is the human thing
To reckon pain as pain.
If soul in quiet sing,
Better not to explain.

Great martyrs mocked their pain
And sang that wrong was right;
Great doctors proved them sane
By logic's drier light;
Yet in those I love the most
Some anger, love, or tact

Hushes the giddy ghost
Before atrocious fact.

Forgive me, patient voice
Whose word I little doubt,
Who stubbornly rejoice
When all but beaten out,
If I equivocate,
And will not yet unlearn
Anxiety and hate,
Sorrow and dear concern.

The Proof Richard Wilbur

Shall I love God for causing me to be?
I was mere utterance; shall these words love me?

Yet when I caused his work to jar and stammer,
And one free subject loosened all his grammar,

I love him that he did not in a rage
Once and forever rule me off the page,

But, thinking I might come to please him yet,
Crossed out *delete* and wrote his patient *stet*.

---

*David Brendan Hopes's "On the Feast of Saint John the Evangelist" pre-
sents a moral sensibility wounded by the world's deafness to the song of
the holy. The feast of John, the gospel writer and the apostle Jesus loved,
falls in the week following the winter solstice.*

175

On the Feast of Saint John the Evangelist David Brendan Hopes

The solstice moon rides within a ring of ice
gleaming blue silver, blood silver, silver, mist silver.
The snow is blue; cobalt silver on the moon-struck mountain.
In the corner of the porch roof, against the moon,
a spider spins a warped web. She is dazed with cold. Hunger.
She stops. She starts again, spinning badly,
past her time, utterly hopeless and beyond help.
I cannot decide if this is beautiful or horrible.
Either way, it cannot be looked at very long.
The ice halo spreads and pales, swallowing the sky.

In a dream the spider came down off the moonlit
porch, to my bedside. I tried to explain it to her.
This is the world. Many spirits of many kinds dwell in it
and do not permit it to be pure. What called you?
Tell me what you hungered for. There was nothing alive
in the snowfields. Nothing to eat.
Was it the beauty of the moon, the blue mouth of the ices,
singing? The saints sing to themselves.
The saints eat their own hearts,
then cannot show us how it's done.

In the dream neither of us was afraid.
In the dream I cupped my hand and carried her.
In the dream she rode out to tell it to the frozen moon.

The so-called corporal acts of mercy provide a Christian checklist of
mitzvoth, *good done in the Jewish senses of the word as a response to*
God's will and, equally, out of heartfelt love for neighbor. The seven
acts are feeding the hungry, giving drink to the thirsty, clothing the
naked, sheltering the homeless, visiting the sick and the imprisoned, and
burying the dead. In "Nursing Home," David Craig narrates a personal
experience of corporal service. But Andrew Hudgins suggests, in

"Colonel," that such works of mercy, acts of complete self-giving, may be an infused rather than a native human impulse.

Nursing Home, 3rd Shift David Craig

(after C. K. Williams)

This one guy who had recently been brought in,
having had his first heart attack. Feisty. He'd
slug you when you tried to change his diaper, ("Depends"
they called them), as you tried to remove the mound
of shit, the smear, wipe his ass, the back of his
balls.
    And Horace. Stately, small,
a former factory worker. He'd cry out "Pee-pee, pee-pee"
whenever you passed him, making rounds. How
when you took him to the bathroom, you'd have
to shuffle along side of him, your hands under his elbows
(I'd sometimes make noises like a train).
Mornings he dressed easy, but you wondered if he'd just
be sitting on that couch all day, waiting for meals,
movement.
        Charlie was ambulatory, loved
the Tigers, his old Japanese transistor radio
pressed to his ear, in front of the TV,
catching the late game from the coast.
He could only mumble, but was happy.
That year they won the pennant.
            There was an old lady
who used to talk non-stop whenever you potted her.
She talked about the town's long gone Heinz plant,
about her family's history. All in one long
continuous monologue. The two other women:
                Joanie,
too old to talk, with a little girl's smile.
She had been a teacher, liked her sock doll
with her when, in the mornings, I'd strap

177

her into her all-day chair. The straps were soft, padded,
and the early morning women workers, cheerful.
                        The other one, Mary,
was the owner's mother, and loved it when I, a man, dressed her.

I quit though. Work hours cut in half
without notice, tired of going home, smelling
of urine. It struck me, how much
they were like most people, living because,
ultimately, they liked it. Maybe they
were an unusual bunch. But it seemed good for
them. Babies again, in diapers.
Getting changed and touched a lot. People digging them,
not because of what they brought to the conversation,
but because they were alive.

                        And for me,
no matter what I'm doing now, it always seems the same:
trying to learn to do the little thing well,
trying to, as the Moslems say, remember;
to learn how to be there, serve, each time, maybe,
getting a little closer to where
I want to be.

---

*Hudgins concludes "Colonel" with a reference to the famous hymn
"Onward Christian Soldiers."*

Colonel Andrew Hudgins

My father lifts the crippled airman's body
and jokes about how light he is and how
we need some rain. He holds him while the man's
young wife strips off the yellowed linen, cracks
white sheets above the bed and lets them drift
across the mattress. She smooths them, tucks the corner.

My father lays the shriveled Christian down.
Three times one week, four times the next. A job
he shares with someone from another church.
He comes home ashen. And every single time,
before he leaves the house he turns to me,
false casually, "You want to come along?"
"Do you need help?" I ask, and he says no.
He leaves. I watch teevee. I'm sixteen, shit!
And I don't want to be a soldier yet.

---

*The greatest fool of them all, asserts Kathleen Norris in "Luke 14: A
Commentary," is Christ himself. She compares him to the popular film
character Inspector Clouseau, a bungling naif who cuts to the heart of
mystery through sheer, uncalculated pluck and the disarming force of
his simplicity. The poem's title cites the passage where Christ appeals to
his disciples to take the lowliest place at the table, and to invite only
strangers when they give a party, ones who are poor, crippled, lame, or
blind, "for they have no means of repaying you."*

Luke 14: A Commentary Kathleen Norris

He is there, like Clouseau,
at the odd moment,
just right: when he climbs
out of the fish pond
into which he has spectacularly
fallen, and says condescendingly
to his hosts, the owners
of the estate: "I fail
where others succeed." You know
this is truth. You know
he'll solve the mystery,

unprepossessing
as he is, the last

of the great detectives.
He'll blend again into the scenery, and
more than once, be taken
for the gardener. "Come

now," he says, taking us
for all we're worth: "sit
in the low place."
Why not? we ask, so easy
to fall for a man
who makes us laugh. "Invite those
you do not know, people

you'd hardly notice." He puts
us on, we put him on; another
of his jokes. "There's
room," he says. The meal is
good, absurdly
salty, but delicious. Charlie
Chaplin put it this way: "I want to play
the role of Jesus. I look the part.
I'm a Jew.
And I'm a comedian."

Wayfarers

C hrist described himself as having "no place to lay his head." So too does the contemporary Christian feel "in" but not "of" the present age. The spiritual life is a pilgrimage, a quest whose final destination, says Denise Levertov, is a mysterious "unknown place / where we shall know / what it is to arrive." On the way, pilgrims traverse an alien land at odds with their foolishness, though in that land is everything they have loved and known.

I Learned That Her Name Was Proverb Denise Levertov

And the secret names
of all we meet who lead us deeper
into our labyrinth
of valleys and mountains, twisting valleys
and steeper mountains—
their hidden names are always,
like Proverb, promises:
Rune, Omen, Fable, Parable,
those we meet for only
one crucial moment, gaze to gaze,
or for years know and don't recognize

but of whom later a word
sings back to us
as if from high among leaves,
still near but beyond sight

drawing us from tree to tree
toward the time and the unknown place
where we shall know
what it is to arrive

Levertov once again invokes poet Rainer Maria Rilke. Called the eter-
nal beginner, Rilke brought monastic zeal to the "needful journey" of
spiritual enlightenment. The "imperative mystery" drawing both the
older poet and Levertov in "To Rilke" is identified in "The Calvary
Path" with the way of the cross. Levertov's pilgrim feet, like Christ's,
lead her up the hill just outside Jerusalem where Christ was crucified.

To **Rilke** Denise Levertov

Once, in dream,
                         the boat
pushed off from the shore.
You at the prow were the man—
all voice, though silent—who bound
rowers and voyagers to the needful journey,
the veiled distance, imperative mystery.

All the crouched effort,
              creak of oarlocks, odor of sweat,
              sound of waters
              running against us
was transcended: your gaze
held as we crossed. Its dragonfly blue
restored to us
                         a shimmering destination.

I had not read yet of your Nile journey,
the enabling voice
drawing that boat upstream in your parable.
Strange that I knew
your silence was just such a song.

A Calvary Path Denise Levertov

Where the stone steps
falter and come to an end
but the hillside rises
yet more steeply,
obtruded roots of the pines
have braided themselves
across the path to continue
the zigzag staircase.
In times past the non-human—

plants, animals—
often, with such gestures,
intervened in our lives,
and so our forebears
believed when all lives were seen
as travellings-forth of souls.
One can perceive
few come here now—
it's nothing special,
not even very old,
a naive piety,
artless, narrow. And yet
this ladder of roots
draws one onward, coaxing
feet to become
pilgrim feet, that climb
(silenced by layers
of fallen needles,
but step by step
held from sliding)
up to the last
cross of the calvary.

---

*Andrew Hudgins's narrative, "Loose Change," documents the alienation
of the Christian wayfarer. The speaker in Hudgins's "How Shall We
Sing the Lord's Song in a Strange Land?" voices the Christian's ambiva-
lence toward the world. Like Christ to the cross, he is nailed "irretriev-
ably" by love to the home that is not home. Hudgins takes the poem's
title from Psalm 137, which begins, "By the waters of Babylon we sat
down and wept."*

Loose Change Andrew Hudgins

We'd sip our water and wait till supper came,
then he'd return thanks. It was never quick

or done by rote. It was heartfelt—and loud—
while everybody in the truckstop watched.
They tried to do it secretly, the way
you look at cripples, retards, droolers, freaks.
I'd raise my head and watch them watching us,
and once, seeing my head unbowed, he said,
Elizabeth, Marie, please close your eyes.
He says that we are strangers here on earth
and it is true I've never felt at home.
In Denver, once, a man asked me the way
to Mile High Stadium, and though I'd been
in town almost two years and had a job
I said, *I'm a stranger here myself,*
amazed at what was coming from my lips.
Are you okay? he asked. How could I say
that I'd been talking bad theology?
But it was worse for Daddy, I suspect.
At least I watched the world and tried to make
accommodation. Since he wouldn't tip
I lifted loose change from the offering plate
to slip onto the table as we left.
Staring right at the waitress, I would think,
Take this you slut, I've stolen it for you.

How Shall We Sing the Lord's Song in
a Strange Land? Andrew Hudgins

We crept up, watched a black
man shovel dry bursts of dirt
into the air. Engrossed,
he didn't see me till
my friend hawked hard and then
stepped out of sight. The man
jerked back, convinced I'd come
to spit on him. Held there
by guilt that wasn't fairly mine,

I braced for what he'd say.
Instead, he smiled, forgave
the sin I hadn't sinned,
and turned back to his work.
I stumbled off and yelled,
Goddamn you! at my friend,
who laughed. Behind us, sand
exploded from the hole, caught wind,
and drifted slowly down
past headstones. Within a month
two boys found the black man hanging
from a hickory, his face
vague in a mist of gnats.
And every time they told the story
the gnats grew thicker, fiercer.
But I believed. I ached
the guiltless ache of dreams
and shuddered. A family that
I never saw mourned him.
Their lives changed and that change
spread out past my small-boy
imagining—though I
tried hard to follow it,
at twelve already remembering
how, ten years old, I'd stand
before the mirror and aim
a flashlight in my mouth.
White cheeks glowed red. I knew
that when I flicked the switch
I would no longer shine
with bloodlight, like stained glass.
I would return to the flesh
I'd always been. Back then,
I thought that if I could
I'd forgive nothing—I'd
change everything. But that's
before I learned how we

get trapped inside the haunts
and habits of this world.
While we drink coffee, gossip,
my cousin's daughter pounds on
the piano. It drives me nuts.
But Ellen's used to it.
The child plays till she drops,
and then we lug her
—elongated and limp—to bed.
My cousin tucks her in,
chooses one music box
from dozens on a shelf, winds it,
and sets it by her child's
damp head. The girl hums, drifts
from one world she creates
into another. A dark
circle of drool surrounds her head.
My cousin loves her with
the tenderness we save
for something that will ruin
our lives, break us, nail
us irretrievably
into this world, which we,
like good philosophers,
had meant to hate. This world,
this world is home. But it
will never feel like home.

---

*The idea of human love nailing us to a transient world is further devel-
oped in poems by Annie Dillard and Richard Wilbur. In "The Man
Who Wishes to Feed on Mahogany," Dillard presents the idea literally,
our loves fixed like crosses in the landscape of earth. In "Love Calls Us
to the Things of This World," the movement of laundry drying on the
line suggests for Richard Wilbur the purity and angelic joy of the soul
freed from its earthly bonds. At first the soul "shrinks" at the prospect of
reentering another human day. Yet soon, drawn back by "bitter love," it*

*puts on the garment of the body as it must, just as the body in turn puts
on the garments hauled down from the "ruddy gallows" of the clothes-
line.*

The Man Who Wishes to Feed on Mahogany Annie Dillard

*Chesterton tells us that if someone wished to feed exclusively on
mahogany, poetry would not be able to express this. Instead, if a man
happens to love and not be loved in return, or if he mourns the absence
or loss of someone, then poetry is able to express these feelings precisely
because they are commonplace.*
— *Borges, interview in* Encounter, *April, 1969*

Not the man who wishes to feed on mahogany
and who happens to love and not be loved in return;
not mourning in autumn the absence or loss of someone,
remembering how, in a yellow dress, she leaned
light-shouldered, lanky, over a platter of pears—
no; no tricks. Just the man and his wish, alone.

That there should be mahogany, real, in the world,
instead of no mahogany, rings in his mind
like a gong—that in humid Haitian forests are trees,
hard trees, not holes in air, not nothing, no Haiti,
no zone for trees nor time for wood to grow:
reality rounds his mind like rings in a tree.

Love is the factor, love is the type, and the poem.
Is love a trick, to make him commonplace?
He wishes, cool in his windy rooms. He thinks:
of all earth's shapes, her coils, rays and nets,
mahogany I love, this sunburnt red,
this close-grained, scented slab, my fellow creature.

He knows he can't feed on the wood he loves, and he won't.
But desire walks on lean legs down the halls of his sleep,
desire to drink and sup at mahogany's mass.

His wishes weight his belly. Love holds him here,
love nails him to the world, this windy wood,
as to a cross. Oh, this lanky, sunburnt cross!

Is he sympathetic? Do you care?
And you, sir; perhaps you wish to feed
on your bright-eyed daughter, on your baseball glove,
on your outboard motor's pattern in the water.
Some love weights your walking in the world;
some love molds you heavier than air.

Look at the world, where vegetation spreads
and peoples air with weights of green desire.
Crosses grow as trees and grasses everywhere,
waiting in wood and leaf and flower and spore,
marking the map, "Some man loved here;
and one loved something here; and here; and here."

Love Calls Us to the Things of This World Richard Wilbur

　　The eyes open to a cry of pulleys,
And spirited from sleep, the astounded soul
Hangs for a moment bodiless and simple
As false dawn.
　　　　　　　Outside the open window
The morning air is all awash with angels.

　　Some are in bed-sheets, some are in blouses,
Some are in smocks; but truly there they are.
Now they are rising together in calm swells
Of halcyon feeling, filling whatever they wear
With the deep joy of their impersonal breathing;

　　Now they are flying in place, conveying
The terrible speed of their omnipresence, moving
And staying like white water; and now of a sudden

They swoon down into so rapt a quiet
That nobody seems to be there.

                            The soul shrinks

   From all that it is about to remember,
From the punctual rape of every blessèd day,
And cries,
          "Oh, let there be nothing on earth but laundry,
Nothing but rosy hands in the rising steam
And clear dances done in the sight of heaven."

   Yet, as the sun acknowledges
With a warm look the world's hunks and colors,
The soul descends once more in bitter love
To accept the waking body, saying now
In a changed voice as the man yawns and rises,

   "Bring them down from their ruddy gallows;
Let there be clean linen for the backs of thieves;
Let lovers go fresh and sweet to be undone,
And the heaviest nuns walk in a pure floating
Of dark habits,
              keeping their difficult balance."

In "Advice to a Prophet," Wilbur argues that whatever can be said in truth about the violent uses we make of earthly life, the identity of the world and of ourselves is inseparable. We know ourselves, says the poet, only by analogy and resemblance to nature. And it may well be that nature knows itself only by us, and without us may forget itself, confounding its forms and reflexes, its watercourses burning like Homer's wild river Xanthus, set aflame by the god Hephaestus to force it back to its banks.

Advice to a Prophet Richard Wilbur

When you come, as you soon must, to the streets of our city,
Mad-eyed from stating the obvious,
Not proclaiming our fall but begging us
In God's name to have self-pity,

Spare us all word of the weapons, their force and range,
The long numbers that rocket the mind;
Our slow, unreckoning hearts will be left behind,
Unable to fear what is too strange.

Nor shall you scare us with talk of the death of the race.
How should we dream of this place without us?—
The sun mere fire, the leaves untroubled about us,
A stone look on the stone's face?

Speak of the world's own change. Though we cannot conceive
Of an undreamt thing, we know to our cost
How the dreamt cloud crumbles, the vines are blackened by frost,
How the view alters. We could believe,

If you told us so, that the white-tailed deer will slip
Into perfect shade, grown perfectly shy,
The lark avoid the reaches of our eye,
The jack-pine lose its knuckled grip

On the cold ledge, and every torrent burn
As Xanthus once, its gliding trout
Stunned in a twinkling. What should we be without
The dolphin's arc, the dove's return,

These things in which we have seen ourselves and spoken?
Ask us, prophet, how we shall call
Our natures forth when that live tongue is all
Dispelled, that glass obscured or broken

In which we have said the rose of our love and the clean
Horse of our courage, in which beheld
The singing locust of the soul unshelled,
And all we mean or wish to mean.

Ask us, ask us whether the worldless rose
Our hearts shall fail us; come demanding
Whether there shall be lofty or long standing
When the bronze annals of the oak-tree close.

---

*Talk of attachments and bitter love only magnifies Wilbur's guiding
awareness, as his "voyage" goes on, of the world's impermanence. In
"Objects," the artistry of Dutch genre painter Pieter de Hooch
(1629–1684) may seem to exist in an "intransitive" relation to what it
creates, not acting upon objects but letting them speak in a kind of en-
during sufficiency for and of themselves. But Wilbur cannot rest in the
illusion, for in all objects lurks the smile of Alice-in-Wonderland's
Cheshire cat, a "tragic / fading away." Wilbur experiences in this the
freedom of the Christian wayfarer, "fearful" in its wonder and mystery
but also in the existential responsibility to an ephemeral world it calls
forth from the believer. In his meditation on entropy, "Principles of
Scarcity, Doctrines of Growth," David Citino exposes the Cheshire smile
in our battle for earthly mastery.*

---

from **Objects** Richard Wilbur

There's classic and there's quaint,
And then there is that devout intransitive eye
Of Pieter de Hooch: see feinting from his plot of paint
The trench of light on boards, the much-mended dry

Courtyard wall of brick,
And sun submerged in beer, and streaming in glasses,
The weave of a sleeve, the careful and undulant tile. A quick
Change of the eye, and all this calmly passes

Into a day, into magic.
For is there any end to true textures, to true
Integuments; do they ever desist from tacit, tragic
Fading away? Oh maculate, cracked, askew,

Gay-pocked and potsherd world
I voyage, where in every tangible tree
I see afloat among the leaves, all calm and curled,
The Cheshire smile which sets me fearfully free.

Principles of Scarcity, Doctrines of Growth David Citino

Research shows that for each discovery
of alternative sources of energy, every breakthrough
in the necessary technology,
countless mechanical things go haywire or quit,
valves and gears rusting open or shut
like mouths of palsied old men
wetting their trousers on benches in a city park,
needles of meters dancing like charismatics,
ticking into danger zones, silicon chips struck
senseless, forgetting their binary creed,
not knowing bit from byte, tapes erased,
screens dark. It's estimated by official sources
high in the Secretariat of the U.N. that rates
of global cruelty and rage continue
to grow geometrically while understanding
plods along in the achingly slow human way,
one plus one means two.
We've got incontrovertible proof
that for every candle matched to stay
night's Ice Age a power grid goes down
along some seaboard, the albino squirrel
it took all time to make
blasted to ash in the great transformer,
a galaxy trembling like a gypsy moth in hail

that speaks one last time its perfect colors
then falls, every dawn the awful fatal wound.

from **Scenes with Harlequins** Geoffrey Hill

Even now one is amazed
by transience: how it
outlasts us all.
Motley of shadow

dabbles the earth,
the malachite bronze
nymphs and sea gods, the pear tree's
motionless wooden leaves.

In this light, constrained spirit,
be a lord of your age.
Rejoice; let the strange
legends begin.

In a sonnet from Hill's "Funeral Music," one of the damned, leaving life, speaks to his body, "my little son," remembering his days in the passing kingdom of enfleshment.

---

from **Funeral Music** Geoffrey Hill

My little son, when you could command marvels
Without mercy, outstare the wearisome
Dragon of sleep, I rejoiced above all—
A stranger well-received in your kingdom.
In those pristine fields I saw humankind
As it was named by the Father; fabulous
Beasts rearing in stillness to be blessed.
The world's real cries reached there, turbulence

195

From remote storms, rumor of solitudes,
A composed mystery. And so it ends.
Some parch for what they were; others are made
Blind to all but one vision, their necessity
To be reconciled. I believe in my
Abandonment, since it is what I have.

---

*In Scott Cairns's "My Amusing Despair," fictive Portuguese poet and
wayfarer Raimundo Luz confesses to feeling "a little detached," as if he
had "somewhere else to go."*

The Translation of Raimundo Luz:
My Amusing Despair Scott Cairns

I confess that I am not
a modern man. As a modern man
I am a little flawed.
Raimundo is much too happy.

Many times, more times
than I would care to admit to you,
I have suffered from this
unforgivable lack, this absence.

All around me, poets
tearing at their bright blouses, tearing
at their own bare flesh.
All night long—their tortured singing.

And still I have suffered
an acute lack of despair. Why is that?
Is Raimundo stupid?
Am I unfeeling? Doesn't the bleak

weight of the north ever
pinch my shoulders? Well, no, not often.
And when it does—which is
not very often—I can't help feeling

a little detached. As if
I had somewhere else to go. As if
I were a spectator,
a dayworker watching the slow clock.
I have an interest in the outcome,
but not a strong interest.

Exile Scott Cairns

Here *exactly*—a little elbow room. Here, in this margin of poor
housing, harsh climate, and unreliable municipal services—
something of a breathing space.

Have you *seen* the faces of the wanderers? Even in the midst of
lamentation (especially then), they are radiant, wide-eyed and
weeping, open-mouthed, keening at the tops of their lungs, and
delirious with joy and purpose.

Even as the familiar supplications for delivery ascend alongside
the fragrance of the sensors, even as their voices rise to aston-
ishing volume, and a number of garments—for emphasis—are
torn beyond repair, even as the ritual of despair attains unbear-
able pathos, the blesséd appear to be taking some pleasure in
the whole affair.

They have *their* etymologies too, after all—Holiness finding at
its root a taste for separateness, fragmentation, periodic dis-
ruption in the status quo. Of course they are wandering *toward*
something, but not in any great hurry.

Soon enough, they will come upon a day when the journey is fully behind them, when their colorful tents will be rolled up for good and left to rot in some outbuilding. Soon enough, the carts and litters will decay, the herds grow fat and unused to travel. Soon enough, the land will pull them in to stay.

And of their exile? nothing will remain except the memory—fading even so—of a journey and a life with few oppressive properties, a daily jaunt unparceled by boundaries or taxes—in short, an excursion expressed for a season between the demands of heathen kings and their last, conclusive embrace.

A Third Possibility Wendell Berry

I fired the brush pile by the creek
and leaping gargoyles of flame
fled over it, fed on it, roaring,
and made one flame that stood
tall in its own wind, snapping off
points of itself that raved and vanished.

The creek kept coming down, filling
above the rocks, folding
over them, its blank face dividing
in gargles and going on, mum
under the ice, for the day was cold,
the wind stinging as the flame stung.

Unable to live either life, I stood
between the two, and liked them both.

Love

*F*rom the pulpit to the soapbox to the papal encyclical, the Christian theme of choice is love. "God is love," says the Gospel of John, which is close to saying "Love is God," which is close to an altogether different religion. But if the Christian love affair is to be understood, "God is love" must be confronted not as a mere sentiment but somehow literally as a binding theological definition. Hence, Christ's foundational commandment for a Godly life: "Love one another."

British writer C. S. Lewis identified the "four loves" of the Christian as affection, friendship, *eros,* and charity. Christian poets enlarge on each of these dimensions of love, the first three loves being "natural," occurring in spite of ourselves. But the selections begin with the fourth love, *caritas* in the Latin, *agapé* in the Greek, which is love existentially, unconditionally given as a gift, the way Christians conceive that God loves humankind.

from **Embracing the Multipede** Denise Levertov

On the dream sidewalk
moving towards you
a caterpillar, shiny, hairless, not cute.
Move it
out of harm's way!
It's ringed like an earthworm,
repulsively fecal in color,
with snail-eyes searching about.
Rescue it!
Footsteps will crush it!
It's not so much
like nothing you've ever seen before
as it is a mixture
of millipede and scorpion.
It's moving towards you,
not cute.
Offer it
your help! It looks
hostile, it may sting you,
but it's small,
each of the multiple feet
the size of an eyelash,
wavering eyes like pinheads.
It's hairless, shiny, repulsive,
scoop it carefully
into your hands,
take it to safety! Not cute, not cute,
it shrinks as you move to meet it,
don't let it vanish before you have time
to give it your heart, a work of mercy.

Unconditional love of the stranger elicits a personal testament from Wendell Berry in "The Guest." Inevitably, as a Christian, Berry invokes the example of the "Good Samaritan," the socially outcast traveler in Christ's parable who tended to the victim of a wayside mugging at great personal effort and expense. Berry wonders if the money and cigarettes he gives the homeless man at his door is such an act of charity, or an evasion of it.

The Guest Wendell Berry

Washed into the doorway
by the wake of the traffic,
he wears humanity
like a third-hand shirt
—blackened with enough
of Manhattan's dirt to sprout
a tree, or poison one.
His empty hand has led him
where he has come to.
Our differences claim us.
He holds out his hand,
in need of all that's mine.

And so we're joined, as deep
as son and father. His life
is offered me to choose.

*Shall I begin servitude
to him? Let this cup pass.
Who am I?* But charity must
suppose, knowing no better,
that this is a man fallen
among thieves, or come
to this strait by no fault
—that our difference

is not a judgment,
though I can afford to eat
and am made his judge.

I am, I nearly believe,
the Samaritan who fell
into the ambush of his heart
on the way to another place.
My stranger waits, his hand
held out like something to read,
as though its emptiness
is an accomplishment.
I give him a smoke and the price
of a meal, no more

—not sufficient kindness
or believable sham.
I paid him to remain strange
to my threshold and table,
to permit me to forget him—
knowing I won't. He's the guest
of my knowing, though not asked.

David Brendan Hopes contends that no one in the community lies beyond the reach of agapic love, not even the crusty old woman in his "Invalid of Park Street." Noting the doomed beauty of the lovers who meet, pair up, and grow old on the street below her window, how "doves and lions become cows and crows," Hopes's invalid knows that she, like the brash little chickadee at her bird feeder, and like the lovers on Park Street, are the same in want, "want not in proportion to any need, / want unreasonable and overflowing, / our days and nights overshadowed with desire." She challenges the breadth of the lovers' charity, and ours: "would you come in / as readily as you tend my flowers / to kiss this sick wreck in its dreams?"

The Invalid of Park Street David Brendan Hopes

Like stitches in a gown, holding sleeve to bodice,
lace to hem, crossed, close and tight,
these lovers walk forever knuckle to joint,
palm to palm.
God builds them half,
makes them find a friend to arch them,
shore them, finish them.
The first day they stroll by
touching elbows when they dare.

The second day they twine from shoulder to fingertip,
walking, stopping, shocking the street
with their pose when they halt
like carvings of lovers who know they'll die alone.
The third day and after
it is just the hands,
the whole rush circled there,
the surety that ten hooked fingers are enough.
There is nothing that would not break them if it could.

One thing can.
You may have seen me
through my window that looks north onto Park Street.
You may have seen one hand at rest
atop the yellow blanket,
its satin border tucked in carefully
where my wrist hits fabric.
You may have seen the rock garden
someone put in underneath my window

so the alyssum, the assertive live-forever
might taunt until the snow avenges me.
You may have seen the bird feeder
against the window I can reach
by leaning on two canes. They said birds

would take my mind from me
and they were right.
    Consider the sunflower hull
        out of which a chickadee ate.

    It is small and dry, its striped pattern
torn where she held it in one claw,
    hammered with her head until
        the meat stood bare.
    Consider the care, the caution of its making,
compact, enduring, praiseworthy in all parts,
    lacking no quality that should mark
        a fire-colored tree-sized blossom
    bound in a dish for a winter bird.

It does not yield up too soon,
    does not hold niggardly, but is free, full.
        It does not change the treasure in the dark of the hull.
    What was food at the opening
is food at the consummation.
    Without it, chickadee snuffs out.
        When I hobble to the window, the brash bird
    kicks, scatters seeds, shells,
shrills for more and waits on the rail

    while more is brought. She swoops
        against the lace of my cuff in her anxiety
    to be there first. She holds her ground against me.
She tells me if I linger too long
    with my shadow on the fresh seed.
        Her impertinence, like a soul's before God,
    is blessed. She flutes her whole-tone
from the mound of empties, taking the richness
    that is her right, scolding the mere bearer away.

    Chickadee, hook-hand passers-by, and I—
we are of one ambition and one lineage:

Want. Want not in proportion to any need,
    want unreasonable and overflowing,
        our days and nights overshadowed with desire,
    and as we eat the hunger's keener,
as we embrace, the distance worse,
    as we clutch out hands are too small
        and the wind steals it away.

    You may have seen the fireman's "I"
on the front door, the "I" decal
    for invalid, that they might know
        what bones burnt here,
    wren bones that stopped bearing me,
sticks, stalks, tinder.
    If you missed the useless fingers on the blanket,
        that would tell you, the great red "I."
    Hurry. Let me burn.

You guess right that I watch as you
    pride past yoked and doubled, your bones
        like beeches laughing when the wind comes up.
    From the liver-spotted parchment ivory
of the hand in the window you guess right
    that I watched your mothers
        in their willow-time with smitten boy-hands
    at their waists, and watched at last
black hair unwoman their upper lips,

    watched dugs like scout cows wobble out
        before them, keeping the world at udder's length
    Doves and lions become cows and crows.
It may surprise you to learn it makes me sad
    to lie here and see you beautiful
        at the brink of all your loss.
  Your men will raise their fists
against the sows that swallowed up their loves.
    You'll circle like weasels afraid to strike.

Yet each April you are hand in hand
and stupid with love.
Look at me. Would you come in
as readily as you tend my flowers
to kiss this sick wreck in its dreams?
I used to think of the moon and stars
when they stooped low and in the north.
They are the same distance from us all. I think of warnings
to paste on your window when the fire goes out.

Affection among family members, which the Greeks called storgé, *and
the bond between friends they called* philía *differ from* agapé *in that
they arise from personal feeling, whereas* agapé *generally has its origin
in the mandates of conscience. Their basis in spontaneous instinct gives
affection and friendship no less stature for Christians, who see in any
loving connection between people the activity of God. Wendell Berry
writes with affection to and of his spouse; David Craig pens a benedic-
tion to his brother; and the deceased speaker of a Scott Cairns poem re-
minds his friends of the dearness of* philía.

To Tanya at Christmas Wendell Berry

Forgive me, my delight,
that grief and loneliness
have kept me. Though I come
to you in darkness, you are
companion of the light
that rises on all I know.

In the long night of the year
and of the spirit, God's birth
is met with simple noise.
Deaf and blind in division,
I reach, and do not find.
You show the gentler way:

We come to good by love;
our words must be made flesh.

And flesh must be made word
at last, our lives rise
in speech to our children's tongues.
They will tell us how we once stood
together here, two trees
whose lives in annual sheddings
made their way into this ground,
whose bodies turned to earth
and song. The song will tell
how old love sweetens the fields.

The Wild Rose Wendell Berry

Sometimes hidden from me
in daily custom and in trust,
so that I live by you unaware
as by the beating of my heart,

suddenly you flare in my sight,
a wild rose blooming at the edge
of thicket, grace and light
where yesterday was only shade,

and once more I am blessed, choosing
again what I chose before.

from **Prothalamion** David Craig

> III.   *"No, not I, but Christ*
> *who liveth in me."*   —*St. Paul*

Brother we are like weeds growing
in the fields. Our arms,

lettuce for the bees.
As a child I used to watch you
ride your bike standing on the seat,
into a fallen telephone pole.
We have grown through the friends
and powers that have peopled our days.
And now Ragtime another turning.
May it bring you peace and children,
realization that we are not here for
ourselves but for the laying down:
hands to wood feet to wood
And may the years that brought you
keep you and the love that yearns
coal the fires of your handlebar dreams.

After the Last Words Scott Cairns

By now I'm dead. Make what you will of that.
But granted you are alive, you will need
to be making something more as well. Prayers
have been made, for instance, but (trust me)

the dead are oblivious to such sessions.
Settle instead for food, nice meals (thick soup);
invite your friends. Make lively conversation
among steaming bowls, lifting heavy spoons.

If there is bread (there really should be bread),
tear it coarsely and hand each guest his share.
for intinction in the soup. Something to say?
Say it now. Let the napkins fall and stay.

Kiss each guest when time comes for leaving.
They may be embarrassed, caught without wit
or custom. (See them shifting from foot to
foot at the open door?) Could be you will

repeat your farewells a time or two more
than seems fit. But had you not embraced them
at such common departures prayers will
fall dry as crumbs, nor will they comfort you.

Romantic or sexual love is arguably the most popular subject of world poetry. Judeo-Christian precedent for it is the Bible's Song of Songs from the third century B.C., *the work of a poet, quite possibly female, whose experience of God was so passionate that only erotic imagery would do to characterize it. More than just a metaphor, Christian poets through the history of verse have perceived in sensual love, to use Sister Mary Appassionata's phrase, "the lineaments of God." For both the Christian and non-Christian poet, eros is the mode of human connection most vulnerable to the extremes of ecstasy and anguish.*

---

from **Sister Mary Appassionata Lectures
the Pre-Med Class** David Citino

6. The Nature of Love
Because God couldn't figure how to be
everywhere He invented mothers. Women and men

are the only animals that drink when there's no
thirst, love in and out of season, recognize
the lineaments of God beneath a lover's clothes.
God made us pupils, gave us rods and cones so we

could really see. Billions have gone, millions
today are on the way because they can't know love.

The paramecium, which needs no other to work
its history, still seeks out others like
itself, powerless to couple yet groping, clumping
through life's utter night toward love. Every fossil

solves for us part of love's puzzle, stones
and bones that bore us all the way from sea and tree

to now. Lovers wind like strands of protein,
dance of the double helix, Eve and Adam every time
again. It wounds and heals, drum of heart's systole
and diastole, urgent peristalsis of flesh and soul.

Sister Mary Appassionata Lectures the Eighth Grade Boys and Girls: The Family Jewels David Citino

In the beginning He put man's parts
of love where today you find the nose,
and woman's where her mouth is now.
But she grew too lean and hungry;
he couldn't stop sneezing. Loving,
they couldn't catch their breath.
Neither could get a word in edgewise.

So He put them where today you find
the hands, but it became too hard
to separate the gestures of friends
and lovers. An embrace came to mean
too little, a handshake much too much.
The tribes couldn't discern work from play,
war from peace, itch from scratch. So

He put the instruments of love where
they belong, mouth for ardor, zeal
and pleas, nose for scents, hands
to make or break, give and take, things
of passion closer to the heart than
brain, veiled as all great beauty
must be. Hidden from the greedy

and profane, the family jewels.

211

*Both David Brendan Hopes and Andrew Hudgins resign themselves to
the inexorable demands of eros. Hopes's fatalism about love in "Winter
Birds" is tempered by the bittersweet irony that passion and spirit seem
to lay siege together, are perphaps indistinguishable. By his radical in-
carnational formula, "flesh follows soul / sucking the salt sweat from the
breast." The poem's division into stanzas of sonnet length, each with an
interlocking rhyme scheme, subtly mocks the polite conventions of the
love lyric.*

*Hudgins's contemporary Gothic narrative, "Heat Lightning in Time
of Drought," frames a haunting vision of sexuality with compassion and
humor. Desires of the heart are "like a mine / where fire still burns, a
century underground, / following the veins of black coal, rearing up / to
take a barn, a house, a pasture."*

from **Winter Birds** David Brendan Hopes

1

Don't think the stars and moon are all
that set out sailing over Thornden Hill
this last August night.
I have never said what is in my heart.
I have pointed to the birds
and let them have the summarizing words
as their wintery lives are blown apart.
Now listen. That is the compassing call
of a nighthawk filling his belly for the long flight.
He is doing what we all soon will.
He finds his way by voices. They touch
roof and wall. By his cries
he knows how distant and how much.
He fills up heaven till the echo dies.

2

Do you think because you suffered for love
nothing more will be asked of you?

Do you think because your beauty was besieged
an hour, an afternoon, a week or two,
that all the high dead lovers are appeased?
Because your bones ride stark in your cheeks for love
do you think one cord of the net is eased?
I say there are nine hells for every one
you bawled away behind you.
You think you have endured. You have not begun.
If you saw where the road was you went not in love.
If it is gentle, it is through.
Do you suppose that what you gave, and lost, and missed
will keep you from knotting the blankets in your fist?

3

A lover taken in winter is an ice-bound harbor,
a she-wolf, a bolted door.
A lover taken in winter is a lock
and a well-stocked house
and a guarded door.
She will not give. She will not lose.
A lover taken in winter is amaranth.
She is a high wall and a black door.
A lover taken in winter
is a ruby, a shelter, a knife,
a golden door.
Love begun in winter is a fox
and a prophet and a blind door.
He closes. He survives.

5

Pure as the note of a bird, sometimes,
the sound of bark scraped on bark,
wood bowing wood.
There are strings in oaks, reeds in pines,
percussion in the cedar dark
below the cliffs, where trees that withstood
are struck by trees that were defeated

by winter and relaxing rock.
All work to bring silence from their noise.
Shaft smooths trunk; the brush repeated
planes the gnarl; the wind-blown shock
flattens, dies. Uneasy with their own voice,
the solitary outlast all the rest..
They've seen the weasel led by singing to the nest.

6

There is something rhetorical, of course,
in repenting love for its perversity
after it has been loved out,
after drawing the tingle of tongue and snout
as far as the night will let them go.
I did not know what roads could be
except the one that wound to me;
I did not see how time rolls us about
until all the rose-sweet lovers go
bud to briar and bloom to stump, their course.
It is not yet so late that I'll extol
the suitable over what hurt best,
nor forget how flesh follows soul
sucking the salt sweat from the breast.

Heat Lightning in Time of Drought Andrew Hudgins

My neighbor, drunk, stood on his lawn and yelled,
Want some! Want some! He bellowed it as cops
cuffed him, shoved him in their back seat—*Want some!*—
and drove away. Now I lie here awake,
not by choice, listening to the crickets' high
electric trill, urgent with lust. Heat lightning flashes.
The crickets will not, will not stop. I wish
that I could shut the window, pull the curtain, sleep.
But it's too hot. *Want some!* He screamed it till
I was afraid I'd made him up to scream

what I knew better than to say out loud
although it's August-hot and every move
bathes me in sweat and we are careless,
careless, careless, every one of us,
and when my neighbor screams out in his yard
like one dog howling for another dog,
I call the cops, then lie in my own sweat,
remembering the woman
who, at a party on a night this hot,
walked up to me, propped her chin on my chest,
and sighed. She was a little drunk, the love-light
unshielded in her eyes. We fell in love.
One day at supper the light fixture dropped,
exploded on the table. Glass flew around us,
a low, slow-motion blossoming of razors.
She was unhurt till I reached out my hand
—left hand—to brush glass from her face.
Two drops of blood ran down her cheek.
On TV, I'd seen a teacher dip a rose
in liquid nitrogen. When he withdrew it,
it smoked, frozen solid. He snapped one petal, frail
as isinglass, and then, against the table,
he shattered it. The whole rose blew apart.
Like us. And then one day the doorbell rang.
A salesman said, *Watch this!* He stripped my bed
and vacuumed it. The nozzle sucked up two
full, measured cups of light gray flakes. He said,
That's human skin. I stood, refusing the purchase,
stood staring at her flesh and mine commingled
inside the measuring cup, stood there and thought,
*She's been gone two years, she's married, and all this time
her flesh has been in bed with me.* Don't laugh.
Don't laugh. That's what the Little Moron says
when he arrives home early from a trip
and finds his wife in bed with someone else.
The man runs off. The Little Moron puts
a pistol to his own head, cocks the hammer.

His wife, in bed, sheets pulled up to her breasts,
starts laughing. *Don't you laugh!* he screams. *Don't laugh—*
you're next. It is the wisest joke I know because
the heart's a violent muscle, opening
and closing. Who knows what we might do:
by night, the craziness of dreams; by day,
the craziness of logic. Listen!
My brother told me of a man wheeled, screaming,
into the ward, a large Coke bottle rammed
up his ass. I was awed: there is no telling
what we'll do in our fierce drive to come together.
The heart keeps opening and closing like a mine
where fire still burns, a century underground,
following the veins of black coal, rearing up
to take a barn, a house, a pasture. Although
I wish that it would rain tonight, I fret
about the heat lightning that flicks and glitters
on the horizon as if it promised rain.
It can't. But I walk outside, stand on parched grass,
and watch it hungrily—all light, all dazzle—
remembering how we'd drive out past the town's light,
sit on the hood, and watch great thunderheads
huge as a state—say, Delaware—sail past. Branched
lightning jagged, burst the dark from zenith to horizon.
We stared at almost nothing: some live oaks,
the waist-high corn. Slow raindrops smacked the corn,
plopped in the dirt around us, drummed the roof,
and finally reached out, tapped us on the shoulders.
We drove home in the downpour, laughed, made love
—still wet with rain—and slept. But why stop there?
Each happy memory leads me to a sad one:
the friend who helped me through my grief by drinking
all of my liquor. And when, at last, we reached
the wretched mescal, he carefully sliced off
the worm's black face, ate its white body, staggered
onto this very lawn, and racked and heaved
until I helped him up. *You're okay, John.*

You've puked it out. "No man—you're wrong. That worm
ain't ever coming out." Heat lightning flashes.
No rain falls and no thunder cracks the heat.
No first concussion dwindles to a long
low rolling growl. I go in the house, lie down,
pray, masturbate, drift to the edge of sleep.
I wish my soul were larger than it is.

---

*For Richard Wilbur in "Loves of the Puppets," eros fails unless it
grounds itself in the emotional needs of "each other's lack."*

Loves of the Puppets Richard Wilbur

Meeting when all the world was in the bud,
Drawn each to each by instinct's wooden face,
These lovers, heedful of the mystic blood,
Fell glassy-eyed into a hot embrace.

April, unready to be so intense,
Marked time while these outstripped the gentle weather,
Yielded their natures to insensate sense,
And flew apart the more they came together.

Where did they fly? Why, each through such a storm
As may be conjured in a globe of glass
Drove on the colder as the flesh grew warm,
In breathless haste to be at lust's impasse,

To cross the little bridge and sink to rest
In visions of the snow-occluded house
Where languishes, unfound by any quest,
The perfect, small, asphyxiated spouse.

That blizzard ended, and their eyes grew clear,
And there they lay exhausted yet unsated;

Why did their features run with tear on tear,
Until their looks were individuated?

Once peace implies another, and they cried
For want of love as if their souls would crack,
Till, in despair of being satisfied,
They vowed at least to share each other's lack.

Then maladroitly they embraced once more,
And hollow rang to hollow with a sound
That tuned the brooks more sweetly than before,
And made the birds explode for miles around.

As Wilbur suggests, the force of desire can isolate as much as bond. Four poets mourn the afflictions of eros.

The Adulterer Scott Cairns

In my shadow world, no one
ever quite wakes up, slow eyes,
forever red from rubbing, fall
vacantly from one vague form to the next.

Some days, a sun might shine, but its light
bumps against everything like a wash
of tepid water, and even then does nothing
to illuminate the place. Understand,

the problem doesn't rest
in a simple lack of light, but in an abundance
of light that does no good. In my world,
leaves are barely green, faces remain

confused with darkness. We have stories
full of unclear language, whole volumes

218

of wrong names. Each time we find the place
where we can stand our vague mistakes no longer,

we settle into what will pass as sleep.

---

*Sister Mary Appassionata lectures on Onan, the figure in the Book of
Genesis who refused his legal obligation to mate with his brother's wid-
ow and instead "wasted his seed on the ground." Geoffrey Hill, also
reaching back to an ancient story, offers an image of pagan eros in "The
Re-birth of Venus."*

Sister Mary Appassionata Lectures the
Bible Study Class: Homage to Onan David Citino

Resurrection man, father
of the race and genocide,
puppeteer playing God,

you're empty gesture,
open hand a blessing, fist
a curse. As powerful

nearly as the one who
waits with finger on button
poised to end it all

with the biggest bang.
Impossible as the needle
through the camel's eye,

love born dying at your feet.
What's the sentence to fit
such crime? As part of

your passion, to endure
whenever alone desire's
shivering frictions until

you're worn out, to bear
the unbearable weight,
gravity of humanity, to

stumble down streets
thronged with lovers fit
for one another, those who

didn't fail, to move to death.

from **Metamorphoses** Geoffrey Hill

The Re-birth of Venus

And now the sea-scoured temptress, having failed
To scoop out of horizons what birds herald:
Tufts of fresh soil: shakes off an entire sea,
Though not as the dove, harried. Rather, she,

A shark hurricaned to estuary-water,
(The lesser hunter almost by a greater
Devoured) but unflurried, lies, approaches all
Stayers, and searchers of the fanged pool.

New Year's Eve in Bismarck, North Dakota Kathleen Norris

Flying in
Before snow closed the airport,
Waiting
For a way out,
Drinking at the Patterson,

Peppermint schnapps
For the season,
The town,
The storm.
The bartender joins in.
He's old, and wears a black
String tie.

A cowboy, drunk, says
"You're lookin' good.
Got a figure like a bombshell.
Like an angel. An angel from outer space.
Some guys'd up n' say,
'C'mon, you're gonna have some.' I believe in God.
I'd never say that to a girl."

It's ten below in Bismarck. They say it's colder
In outer space.
The Ecclesiastes
In my hotel room
Is uncharacteristically hopeful.
"Better is the end of a thing,"
He says, loosening his loincloth,
"Than the beginning thereof."

---

*Among the more arduous projects of Christian love is reconciliation, best summed up in Christ's parable of "the prodigal son." The account notes a father's unconditional forgiveness of a younger son as much as an older son's resentment of his forgiven brother. In her retelling of the story in "The Father," Maura Eichner deploys variations of a sequence of six words—*journey dark water light fire wind—*to end the lines of her sestina, divided into six stanzas of six lines each and a final triplet.* Fire *appears three additional times in the internal text. These words shape for Eichner the Christian drama that each act of forgiveness recapitulates. They trace a journey from darkness through waters of rebirth into light by the pentecostal fire of* pneuma, Spirit-wind.

The Father Maura Eichner

Luke 15:11–32

Never had the old man made such a journey.
His robes enfolded him like driving wind.
No one remembered the old man running. Even fire
had never moved him. His estates were the light
of the town. Yet, there he was, running to a dark
figure huddling the road. Love was flood-water

carrying him forward. Some tried to dike the water;
nothing could hold him. Love loosed a wind
of words: "My son is coming home." Dark
grief behind, the father ran, arms open as light.
He had to lift the boy before his son's fire
of sorrow burned the father's sandals. Journey?

The old man could remember no other journey
but this homecoming: he held his son in the fire
of his arms, remembering his birth: water
and fire. Servants ran along thrusting at the wind
of excitement: what shall we do? what torchlight
prepare? "Bathe away the pig-pen-slopping-dark

that cloaks my son. Prepare a banquet. Jewel the dark
with fires. My son was dead. My son is afire
with life. The land is fruitful. Joy is its water.
Where is my eldest son? The end of the journey
is ours. My son, do you grieve? turn from the light
to say you are unrewarded? Son, is the wind

from the south closer to you than me? is the wind
of your doubt stronger than my love for you? Water
your hardness, my son. Be a brother to the dark
of your brother's sorrow. Be a season of light
to his coming home. You will make many a journey
through cities, up mountains, over abysses of fire,

but for tonight and tomorrow, my eldest, fire
your heart, strike at its stone. Let it journey
toward dawning, be a thrust at the dark
your brother will never forget. Find a woman of water
and fire, seed her with sons for my name and wind-
supple daughters for bearing daughters and sons of light.

I am a father of journeys. I remind you the dark
can be conquered by love-blasting fire. I made air and wind
a compassionate homeland. Be at home in the light."

---

*Kathleen Norris attests that the irreconcilable is reconciled by the power
of "True Love." For Scott Cairns in "On Slow Learning," reconciliation
lies in the forgiving of our differences, which by nature are here to stay.*

True Love Kathleen Norris

binds all wounds,
wounds all heels,
whatever. You can tell.
William Buckley,
Gore Vidal, Sampson
and Delilah. Paul
and the Corinthians.
You can tell.

It makes us fight
and bleed, takes us to the heights,
the deeps, where we don't
want to go. Adam and Eve. Noah
and Mrs., David,
Bathsheba, Ruth,
Naomi. You can tell.

The way light surges
out of nothing. The Magdalene,
the gardener. God help us,
we are God's chosen now.

On Slow Learning Scott Cairns

If you've ever owned
a tortoise, you know
how terribly difficult
paper training can be
for some pets.

Even if you get so far
as to instill in your tortoise
the value of achieving the paper,
there remains one obstacle—
your tortoise's intrinsic sloth.

Even a well-intentioned tortoise
may find himself in his journeys
to be painfully far from the mark.

Failing, your tortoise may shy away
for weeks within his shell, utterly ashamed,
or, looking up with tiny, wet eyes, might offer
an honest shrug. Forgive him.

The Dark

E vil is love absent. For Saint Augustine, evil was absence absolute, a naught of being, the abyss of non-God and non-good. Yet the Christian imagination seems to have belied him. Through the ages it has conjured evil as something that most emphatically *is*, and engaged it as a presence, a charisma, as sentient and discriminating as a person. The Judeo-Christian personification of evil, beginning with the Evil One, appeals to the facts of human history with its roster of torturers, murderers, tyrants, and our own secret pathologies. Personification suits poetry well, and many a Christian poet, scouting for images, has glimpsed our shadow in the company of the dark.

Louise Erdrich is of part-German, part-Chippewa descent, and in "Christ's Twin" her Native American and Christian inheritances darkly converge in an icon of the mystery of evil. Is her poem's twin the Native American Trickster, or the Book of Revelation's Anti-Christ, or modern psychology's shadow side? Erdrich places him at the flight of the infant Jesus and his parents into Egypt; he was present when Christ cast the demons into a herd of swine; he appears to have taken part in the diaspora at Babel; somehow he participated in Christ's burial and resurrection. Erdrich gives no comfort, to Christians especially, by insisting he is neither the devil nor a fallen angel.

Christ's Twin Louise Erdrich

He was formed of chicken blood and lightning.
He was what fell out when the jug tipped.
He was waiting at the bottom
of the cliff when the swine plunged over.
He tore out their lungs with a sound like ripping silk.
He hacked the pink carcasses apart, so that the ribs spread
like a terrible butterfly, and there was darkness.
It was he who turned the handle and let the dogs
rush from the basements. He shoved the crust
of the volcano into his roaring mouth.
He showed one empty hand. The other gripped
a crowbar, a monkey wrench, a crop
which was the tail of the ass that bore them to Egypt,
one in each saddlebag, sucking twists
of honeyed goatskin, arguing
already over a woman's breasts.
He understood the prayers that rose
in every language, for he had split the human tongue.
He was not the Devil nor among the Fallen—
it was just that he was clumsy, and curious,
and liked to play with knives. He was the dove
hypnotized by boredom and betrayed by light.

227

He was the pearl in the mouth, the tangible
emptiness that saints seek at the center of their prayers.
He leaped into a shadow when the massive stone
rolled across the entrance, sealing him with brother
in the dark as in the beginning.
 Only this time he emerged first, bearing the self-
inflicted wound, both brass halos
tacked to the back of his skull.
He raised two crooked fingers; the extra die
tumbled from his lips when he preached
but no one noticed. They were too busy
clawing at the hem of his robe and planning
how to sell him to the world.
They were too busy drinking
at the fountain.
They were drunk.
They would drown for love.

---

*From the same weave of traditions, Erdrich creates the magic realist
Leonard trilogy, the tale of an eccentric loner possessed of "ingenious"
powers. Deaf and half blind, Leonard menaces a small town of the
American West similar to the Wahpeton, North Dakota, of Erdrich's
childhood. "Leonard" is the name given to a sorcerer or a teller of lies.*

Portrait of the Town Leonard Louise Erdrich

I thought I saw him look my way and crossed
my breast before I could contain myself.
Beneath those glasses, thick as lead-barred windows,
his eyes ran through his head, the double-barrels
of an old gun, sick on its load, the trigger held
in place by one thin metal bow.

Going toward the Catholic church, whose twin
white dunce caps speared the clouds for offering,

we had to pass him on the poured stone bridge.
For nickels we could act as though we'd not
been offered stories. How those all turned out
we knew, each one, just how the river eats
within its course the line of reasoning.

He went, each morning, to the first confession.
The sulking curtains bit their lips behind him.
Still those in closer pews could hear the sweet
and limber sins he'd made up on the spot.
I saw a few consider, and take note—
procedural. They'd try them out at home.

And once, a windless August, when the sun
released its weight and all the crops were burned,
he kept watch as the river thickened. Land
grew visibly and reeked to either side,
till windowed hulks, forgotten death cars reared
where dark fish leapt, and gaped, and snatched the air.

Leonard Commits Redeeming Adulteries
with All the Women in Town Louise Erdrich

When I take off my glasses, these eyes are dark magnets
that draw the world into my reach.
First the needles, as I walk the quiet streets,
work their way from their cushions of dust.
The nails in the rafters twist laboriously out
and the oven doors drop
an inch open.
The sleep-smell of yesterday's baking
rises in the mouth.
A good thing.

The streetlamps wink off just at dawn,
still they bend their stiff necks like geese drinking.

My vision is drinking in the star-littered lawn.
When the porch ivy weaves to me—
Now is the time.
Women put down their coffee cups, all over town.
Men drift down the sidewalks, thinking.
What did she want?
But it is too late for husbands.
Their wives do not question
what it is that dissolves
all reserve. Why they suddenly think of cracked Leonard.

They uncross themselves, forsaking
all protection. They long to be opened and known
because the secret is perishable, kept, and desire
in love with its private ruin.
I open my hands and they come to me, now.
In our palms dark instructions that cannot be erased,
only followed, only known along the way.

And it is right, oh women of the town, it is *right*.
Your mouths, like the seals of important documents
break for me, destroying the ring's raised signature,
the cracked edges melting to mine.

Leonard Refuses to Atone Louise Erdrich

The moon comes up, a white cow
grazing on limbo.
Today in the confessional I yelled,
Father, I am the deaf one, absolve me
in a voice I can hear.
But as usual, he mumbled in the curtain
and the saints cast their eyes
past me, into the cold space of the loft
when I knelt at their feet.

What sins have I done
that you should forsake me?
Again, I asked loudly.
The saints are far deafer than I.
Their ears, curls of plaster,
have grown closed from listening
to the organ's unceasing low sobs.

I sit where the moon rides up,
swollen and tender,
the beast of my burdens. Her back is broad
enough to carry my penance and yours.
When she moans, the whole sky
falls open.
My weight has done this,
My life an act of contrition
for the sins of a whole town.

But now, when I let the weight fall,
she arches, a slender thing
shot from a quiver.
Oh white deer hunted into a cloud,
I was your child, now I leap down,
relaxed into purpose,
my body cleaves through the air like a star.

Make your wishes, small children.
You others, make vows,
quickly, before I snuff myself out
and become the dark thing
that walks among you,
pure, deaf, and full
of my own ingenious sins.

Like Erdrich, David Citino in "Possession in Iowa" draws from child-hood to ruminate on the unseen powers of the dark. Andrew Hudgins in "The Liar's Psalm" draws from the venerable romance of Reynard the Fox, paying mock tribute to a natural virtuoso of deceit. For perfecting the art of the ruthless, the poet praises his hero with a tip of the hat to Torquemada, cruelest of the Inquisitors in fifteenth-century Spain.

Sitting in the Sixth Grade at Ascension of Our Lord School in Cleveland, Ohio, Reading a Pamphlet Entitled "Possession In Iowa"   David Citino

This was a new catechism, a new testament.
I looked at the page and saw the farm girl soar
above the disordered brass bed, agile as a fly,
cling naked to the ceiling while in the doorway
her mother, shapeless as bread dough in a sad print dress,
sobbed noiselessly into a ruffled apron, father
having long before fled to the barn to hammer something
heavy and loud. Where did the girl learn
the good church Latin she used to curse
the pudgy German pastor come to purge her?
Who taught her to revile his shiny pants and black shoes
in a sow's squeal that raised the hackles
under the soiled collar, taught her the very thing
to say about his mother and a host of beasts,
to stare at a point below his belt and wet her lips
until he squirmed, and ran to call the Jesuits?
I read on, the rows of bean and corn
filling with weeds on all four horizons beyond
the weathered wooden house, the windmill gone mad,
neighbors clustered in the yard among clucking hens,
praying softly to hear every word, crows
chuckling above. Who made this? Why? And the girl,
when it was over was she another Dorothy back
in Kansas, bored with tiresome farmhands

232

and going nowhere? And at forty, harsh blond hair
beehived on her head, breasts supported by wires,
wearing clothes too girlish, running to fat and prone
to cry for no reason? I wondered about her,
and all the things that might be without being seen.

from **The Liar's Psalm: Homage to the Fox** Andrew Hudgins

> *He that cannot wimple false hood in truth's kerchief,*
> *hath neither art nor cunning; but he that can do it,*
> *and deliver error without stammering, he may do wonders....*
> —Reynard the Fox

Let us make homage to the fox, for his tail is as lush
as Babylon. His eyes, all glitter and distrust,
are cruel as a Spanish crucifixion, and his paws so subtle
they can empty your refrigerator without the light
coming on. But these virtues
aren't why we praise the fox. Let us make homage
for he's a liar nonpareil and there is none as ruthless.
His gorgeous tongue is more lush than
his tail, sharper than his eyes, quicker than his paws.
Magnificent instrument! Equal parts oil and sugar, grease and candy,
and there is no truth in it — praise the fox. Everything is intricately
untrue, Byzantine, consistent unto its own rules, easier said
than done, because there are lies ad infinitum and one truth, and that
monk-drab to him who wears sport coats by Calder
and iridescent pants. His tongue is honed on glass. The rabbit
he shreds like confetti and the feathers of the duck
are pasted to his grin, which is tighter
than Torquemada's and would make opposing counsel weep.
The fox—praise him in parts and praise him whole—makes no
bones about it. The truth is lack of courage,
failure of imagination, low stakes, high dudgeon, middle passage,
and there is no profit in it. Praise him for deceit.
We have business to conduct with him and we don't stand a chance.
Praise him. His tongue will cleanse our bones. Praise the fox.

233

Hudgins's fox lives in perfect accord with his nature, but David Brendan Hopes's Jack Rhymer is at war with his. He inhabits the dark as a figure of pathos. His history reflects elements of one of the major themes of Christian anthropology, humanity's essentially "fallen" state. Once he was Jack of Eden, living in perfect grace, and Jack Galahad, seeker of the light and worthy to drink from the holy grail of Christ's last supper. But he fell to his nature, and abandoned the holy quest. Jack has turned to his shadow side in a kind of self-defense. Plying the streets, he remembers the light and sings to be vanquished by it. The poet cloaks his subject in the tattered bravado of a rhymed ballad whose rhythms every so often tear apart, weary as Jack himself.

Jack Rhymer David Brendan Hopes

Who am I? A tramp, I guess,
booting the road among the moons,
sleeping by the stars and wandering
the wildernesses of strange rooms.

Jack the fix-it-man and Jack the pimp,
Jack driver, Jack snow-man, Jack racketeer,
Jack of the dim street where
I answer to most any name I hear.

Jack scholar I am, Jack of the books.
I have forgotten what they say,
but how they say it sticks with me
that I might twist it around my way.

Jack Rhymer at last,
son of desperate fathers for sure,
making high talk to put them in
so some of their voices may endure.

I've walked out and I have seen
the raree show and fraud.
By empty doors and neon signs
I cry the travesties of God.

I turned my heart toward the town,
seeing how its children cry
solitary, unlovable, and afraid
with their backs against the floating sky.

I put myself in peril of the night
seeking a god to bear their blame.
I put myself in danger of the street
to see shame walking unashamed.

Jack of Eden I was called
till hunger broke the spell;
Jack Galahad my name before
the Christ-cup sat on the shelves of hell.

Jack mystery you call me now.
Unlike the hallows of the emerald age,
I prophesy unto the world
the dispensation of rage.

Jack of lovers, king of hearts,
crazy in the wounded town,
waiting for glad day to come
and lay our midnight down.

I set myself to war with God
till God confronts the hopeless street,
sing in cul-de-sacs and bars
hosannas for my own defeat.

Holy Thursday Geoffrey Hill

Naked, he climbed to the wolf's lair;
He beheld Eden without fear,
Finding no ambush offered there
But sleep under the harboring fur.

He said: "They are decoyed by love
Who, tarrying through the hollow grove,
Neglect the seasons' sad remove.
Child and nurse walk hand in glove

As unaware of Time's betrayal,
Weaving their innocence with guile.
But they must cleave the fire's peril
And suffer innocence to fall.

I have been touched with that fire,
And have fronted the she-wolf's lair.
Lo, she lies gentle and innocent of desire
Who was my constant myth and terror."

Holy Innocents David Brendan Hopes

Some horror routed them from their homes.
Their fathers were dead.
Their mothers ran wild in the hills, forgetting them.
All night the children were herded in a line
toward the Dreadful City.
When they reached a certain crook in the road, robed figures
seized them and ripped their hearts out with tongs heated
in a fire of coals.
The coals were made of books of love rendered down
to sorrowing red suns, that the fire would be hotter,
and that no one would write of love again.
What they put in the empty chests is secret,
but I have seen it happen: I saw them slip devices
in between the ribs, whirring machines,
some with a gleam of gold
some with a gleam of steel
some with the matte of dust and rubble.
The children stumbled and trembled, caught each other,
and miraculously went on.
They came to the Dreadful City. It recognized them
as its own, its towers gleaming gold and steel,
its dark streets dust and rubble.
Henceforth
gold would follow those who shone with gold.
Steel would bolster those who glinted steel.
Dust would hide the deeds of those who
hid in dust and rubble.

I went and stood over the hearts strewn at the roadside.
I bade them turn to flowers,
to fly like red birds to their owners, awakening
remembrance.
But crows had come to finish them.
The crows said, *Ha!*
The crows said, "This is not a story."

The hearts would not get up. The hearts
fed themselves into the beaks of crows.
Inside the Dreadful City the machines whirred and clicked.
The children were making their way amid cheering crowds.
Everything had gone right—
gold and steel, the concealment of the dust.
Even where I stood the accolades were louder
than the keen of mothers crying in the hills
for their children who were no more.

---

*The power that grips Jack Rhymer and engulfs the Holy Innocents, the
allure of the dark, is the subject of Scott Cairns's "Regarding the Monu-
ment." A statue undergoes eerie metamorphosis, changing in semblance
but remaining ever the same. "In Praise of Darkness" couches the
metaphor in terms of human paradox. Cairns implicates the reader in
a turbulent, deeply ambiguous encounter with nihilism. He sets the
"you" of his poem against the sympathetic personage of Jorge Luis
Borges, the distinguished twentieth-century Argentine writer for whom
space, time, the self, and God were fictions in a labyrinth. The person-
age of Cairns's third poem, "Lucifer's Epistle to the Fallen," exudes the
unction and solicitude befitting the Prince himself.*

Regarding the Monument Scott Cairns

> *But roughly but adequately it can shelter*
> *what is within (which after all*
> *cannot have been intended to be seen).*
> >   —Elizabeth Bishop

Of course it is made of *would*, and *want*,
the threads and piecework of *desire*. Its shape
is various, always changing but always
insufficient, soliciting revision.

> I thought you said it was made of *wood*.
> You said it was made of wood.

Never mind what I may have said; I might
have said anything to bring you this close
to the monument. As far as that goes,
parts of it *are* wood, parts are less, more.

      Some kind of puzzle? What can it do?
      If the wind lifts again we're in trouble.

Certain of its features endure—its more
sepulchral qualities—whether it gestures
ahead or back, the monument
is always in some sense memorial.

      Is it safe? It looks so unstable.
      Do you think it's safe to come so close?

I don't think it's safe, but I don't think safe matters.
It's changing. Even now. Watch how it turns
into its new form, taking something
of what it was, taking something else.

      I don't feel well. Does it have to do that?
      Is it growing? Still? Something must be wrong.

The monument is growing still, even if
diminishment must be a frequent stage
of its progress. If we return tomorrow
it may appear much less; it may seem gone.

      I don't see the point. What is the point?
      I'm leaving now; you stay if you want.

But the part that lies buried, its foundation,
will forge its machinery ever and again,
and the wind will return it to motion
if more powerfully, and more horribly.

In Praise of Darkness Scott Cairns

Here, behind this attic door is Borges,
waiting in a straight chair, bound there
by thin wire and by rags. Soon you will
ask him the questions again, and soon

he will say his answers, his insane
and foolish words, smiling as if he had said
enough, as if he had answered what you've asked.
And you will hit him again, and split

his skin; you'll invent pain and slowly
let him know what it is you've made.
But, as before, nothing will have changed.
If he speaks at all he'll only say his

nonsense to the air until you must
hit again to make him stop. So you
come to hate the hand that pulls open
the attic door, that gives you Borges,

waiting in a straight chair, looking out
from the corner of an attic room. There is
a wash of light from the window, and it warms
his face, his arms; he feels it pouring

through the neat, dark suit he wears.
You believe he is mad. He is too old
for this and nearly blind, and the light
on his face makes him beautiful.

When you enter the room, he sees
an angel enter; he turns his head
toward your noise, his face expectant.
You have never been so loved.

Lucifer's Epistle to the Fallen Scott Cairns

Lucifer, Son of the Morning, Pretty Boy,
Rose Colored Satan of Your Dreams, Good as Gold,
you know, God of this World, Shadow in the Tree.

Gorgeous like you don't know! Me, Sweet Snake, jeweled
like your momma's throat, her trembling wrist. Tender
as my kiss! Angel of Darkness! Angel

of Light! Listen, you might try telling *me*
your troubles; I promise to do what I can.
Which is plenty. Understand, I can kill

anyone. And if I want, I can pick
a dead man up and make him walk. I can
make him dance. Any dance. Angels don't

get in my way; they know too much.
God, I love theater! But listen, I know
the sorry world He walks you through.

Him! Showboat with the Heavy Thumbs! Pretender
at Creation! Maker of Possibilities!
Please! I know why you keep walking—you're skittish

as sheep, and life isn't easy. Besides,
the truth is bent to keep you dumb to death.
Imagine! The ignorance you're dressed in!

The way you wear it! And His foot tickling
your neck. Don't miss my meaning; I know none
of this is your doing. The game is fixed.

Dishonest, if you ask me. So ask. God
knows how I love you! My Beauty, My Most
Serious Feelings are for you, My Heart turns

upon your happiness, your ultimate
wisdom, the worlds we will share. Me, *Lucifer.*
How can such a word carry fear? *Lucifer,*

like love, like song, a lovely music lifting
to the spinning stars! And you, my cooing
pigeons, my darlings, my tender lambs, come, ask

anything, and it will be added to your
account. Nothing will be beyond us; nothing
dares touch my imagining.

The Bibliographers Geoffrey Hill

Lucifer blazing in superb effigies
Among the world's ambitious tragedies,
Heaven-sent gift to the dark ages,

Now, in the finest-possible light,
We approach you; can estimate
Your not unnatural height.

Though the discrete progeny,
Out of their swim, go deflated and dry,
We know the feel of you, archaic beauty,

Between the tombs, where the tombs still extrude,
Overshadowing the sun-struck world:
(The shadow-god envisaged in no cloud.)

---

*Richard Wilbur's encounter with one Corporal Lloyd Tywater during
wartime provides him, in "Tywater," with an image of the elegant mas-
tery of negation. The Gadarenes who address Jesus as Rabbi in Wilbur's
"Matthew VIII, 28 ff" are the two demoniacs whom Christ exorcised by
driving their possessing devils into a nearby herd of swine.*

Tywater Richard Wilbur

Death of Sir Nihil, book the *nth,*
Upon the charred and clotted sward,
Lacking the lily of our Lord,
Alases of the hyacinth.

Could flicker from behind his ear
A whistling silver throwing knife
And with a holler punch the life
Out of a swallow in the air.

Behind the lariat's butterfly
Shuttled his white and gritted grin,
And cuts of sky would roll within
The noose-hole, when he spun it high.

The violent, neat and practiced skill
Was all he loved and all he learned;
When he was hit, his body turned
To clumsy dirt before it fell.

And what to say of him, God knows.
Such violence. And such repose.

Matthew VIII, 28 ff Richard Wilbur

Rabbi, we Gadarenes
Are not ascetics; we are fond of wealth and possessions.
Love, as you call it, we obviate by means
Of the planned release of aggressions.

We have deep faith in prosperity.
Soon, it is hoped, we will reach our full potential.
In the light of our gross product, the practice of charity
Is palpably inessential.

It is true that we go insane;
That for no good reason we are possessed by devils;
That we suffer, despite the amenities which obtain
At all but the lowest levels.

We shall not, however, resign
Our trust in the high-heaped table and the full trough.
If you cannot cure us without destroying our swine,
We had rather you shoved off.

---

*In "An Immortal," Les Murray imports a classical lexicon to personify
warlust, human history's perennial darkness. Unlike his ancient prac-
tice, the "Warrior" god refuses to strip the modern dead of their hi-tech
gear gleaming in the colors of "duco" metallic paint. Nor does he any
longer show his brute likeness on the field of battle. He still incites us to
carnage but appears more obscurely now, perhaps as the enemy "boy," or
"the bookie," or "the expert craftsman" whom warfare enriches. Like the
military conscripts in the poem who would rather listen to music than
"storm the house of meaning," we will never know the Warrior truly till
we meet him in death. But meantime "the glory of the wheeled blade,"
our immortal death wish, brings condemnation to us all. Murray in-
duces a headlong, clashing impetus with a six-beat line, the Alexandrine,
associated with "heroic" verse like that of George Chapman's Elizabethan
translations of Homer.*

An Immortal Les Murray

Beckoner of hotheads, brag-tester, lord of the demi-suicides,
in only one way since far before Homer have you altered:
when now, on wry wheels still revolving, the tall dust showers back
and tongue-numbing Death stills a screaming among the jagged
      images,
you disdain to strip your victims' costly armour, bright with fire and
      duco,
or even to step forth, visible briefly in your delusive harness,

glass cubes whirling at your tread, the kinked spear of frenzy in your
   hand.

Do you appear, though, bodily to your vanquished challengers
with the bare face of the boy who was large and quickest at it,
the hard face of the boss and the bookie, strangely run together,
the face of the expert craftsman, smiling privately, shaking his head?
Are you sometimes the Beloved, approaching and receding through
   the glaze?
Or is this all merely cinema? Are your final interviews wholly
   personal
and the bolt eyes disjunct teeth blood-vomit all a kind of mask lent
   by physics?

We will never find out, living. The volunteers, wavering and firm,
and the many conscripted to storm the house of meaning
have stayed inside, listening to music. Or else they are ourselves,
sheepish, reminiscent, unsure how we made it past the Warrior
into our lives—which the glory of his wheeled blade has infected,
so that, on vacant evenings, we may burn with the mystery of his
   face,
his speed, his streetlight pointing every way, his unbelief in joking.

---

*The Immortal has been stalking us, says Murray, "since far before
Homer." His handiwork during England's Wars of the Roses is remem-
bered by Geoffrey Hill in a sonnet from "Funeral Music."*

---

from **Funeral Music** Geoffrey Hill

They bespoke doomsday and they meant it by
God, their curved metal rimming the low ridge.
But few appearances are like this. Once
Every five hundred years a comet's
Over-riding stillness might reveal men
In such array, livid and featureless,

With England crouched beastwise beneath it all.
"Oh, that old northern business. . ." A field
After battle utters its own sound
Which is like nothing on earth, but is earth.
Blindly the questing snail, vulnerable
Mole emerge, blindly we lie down, blindly
Among carnage the most delicate souls
Tup in their marriage-blood, gasping "Jesus."

Angels Louise Erdrich

The cats wind together in the barn.
Their weightless bodies fly across the field like scarves,
Draped on a woodpile, vibrating
in a patch of sun,
their eyes are frozen glass.
Their mouths,
lined with rose petals,
shirred with bloody silks
and bone needles,
open with the delicate interest
of the very old angels, the first ones,
in whose eyes burned the great showers of the damned.

Grace

G race is the Christian experience of God's love and favor. But grace amazes Christians because it seems so freely given. It can happen to anybody, they say, regardless of who desires or deserves it. Christians can explain this, if at all, only as a gratuitous behavior of the perfect love that is God. Many of the poems in this chapter mirror the way the experience of grace is reported, since grace often seems to occur, like a poem, as a moment of radical awareness. The most commonplace of things—household objects, a conversation, the time of the day—are cherished in their newness and singularity as if the observer were continuously being born into existence. Les Murray develops the broader Christian testimony of grace, how it breaks in on the unfolding of history.

Apple Fools David Craig

Apple fools we are
Ripe as cups of cider and the horse's
clodded wake

let the wet mornings come ring out
green beans beneath the leaves pumpkin
piping on the vine
Speckled corn aloft Indian feathered
high on the door

Squash squats on the rafters
pot belly bent legged Buddha stove
boots and coveralls
Give us this grace and all this day
the crowded table the
pinions' fold

The Apprentice Is Amazed David Craig

Oh, for the holiness which is a needle
and all the space it leaves in a wine glass;
Glass! Clear and fragile as cement mixers
—a topic for discussions!
Everything transient, like Reeboks,
the holes in your jeans.

Everywhere in my life, people are leaving.
Except in the crowded department stores,
chandeliers glistening near the ceiling.
This is what there is!
Salami, a cold orange with its incredible juices.
Who would have thought life
was going to contain that!

*The sentences comprising another of Annie Dillard's found poems,
"Dash It," are lifted intact from* Nature's Diary *by Mikhail Prishvin
(1925), translated by L. Navrosov.*

Dash It Annie Dillard

How wonderfully it was all arranged that each
Of us had not too long to live. This is one
Of the main snags—the shortness of the day.
The whole wood was whispering, "Dash it, dash it..."

What joy—to walk along that path! The snow
Was so fragrant in the sun! What a fish!
Whenever I think of death, the same stupid
Question arises: "What's to be done?"

As for myself, I can only speak of what
Made me marvel when I saw it for the first time.
I remember my own youth when I was in love.
I remember a puddle rippling, the insects aroused.

I remember our own springtime when my lady told me:
You have taken my best. And then I remember
How many evenings I have waited, how much
I have been through for this one evening on earth.

Imperative Scott Cairns

The thing to remember
is how tentative all of this
really is. You could wake up dead.

Or the woman you love
could decide you're ugly.

Maybe she'll finally give up
trying to ignore the way you
floss your teeth when
you watch television.
All I'm saying is that
there are no sure things here.

I mean, you'll probably wake up alive,
and she'll probably keep putting off
any actual decision about your looks.
Could be she'll be glad your teeth
are so clean. The morning could be
full of all the love and kindness
you need. Just don't go thinking
you deserve any of it.

Cairns does not question the essential worth of those whom grace has favored but merely voices the conviction that grace cannot be earned, the Christian "amazement" that grace so often happens without obliging our own ideals of equity. He goes on in "Salvation" to note the "annoyance" of the persistence of grace in the comedy of the human landscape. "Another Song" sounds what is often described as the "ground bass of joy," the expression of grace in the interior life of the Christian.

Salvation Scott Cairns

—after Jonathan Holden

Granted, the choir
is an embarrassment. Those faces
are too simple to be true. Take
Mrs. Beamon, our soprano, whose
perfect smile might warm some
into admiration, if they can forget
how she daily cows her skinny
alto daughter into tears.

The choir master himself
is ridiculous; the way he stands
tells everyone how short he thinks
he is. That alone could help you
like him, but when he takes every solo
like a general at war, you'll
probably change your mind.
Those two alone can make forgiveness
a nearly impossible thing. And each
of these singers has a similar story,
a sad quirk that tries each week to shape
those smiles into something lovely.
If you glance over this scene
too quickly, or without enough
real humor, you might write off every other scene
it touches, every kindness
that allows such comic abuse
to abound. You might see
those hilarious faces and believe
they are the whole show; you could miss
the real act. The comedy
is this: despite the annoyance
of grace, and this tired music
of salvation, it is what we all expect.

Another Song Scott Cairns

Most mornings I wake up slowly. That's just
the way I am. I wake up slow as I can, listening first
to one thing, then another. The milk bottles chiming

just outside the door, then the milktruck idling in the street.
If I'm lucky, the girl through the wall will be singing
and I'll hear her next, singing while she dresses. Maybe

she's brushing her hair, or tying the ribbon for her stocking
—that would be nice. And out in the hall, some man will
probably kiss Miss Weitz good-bye again—yes, I believe

those are their lowered voices now, and that is his cough.
Others are coming out now, their doors opening and closing so
variously, too many to sort out. Why sort them out? And now

the factory whistle is telling the night shift that enough is enough.
Now I hear myself humming along, joining in this little chorus
of good intentions. When everything is ready, I'll go out.

---

*In "Imagist at Coney Island," part of her cycle on literary figures,
Maura Eichner renders an account of a graced meeting between Ameri-
can poet Ezra Pound (1885–1972) and painter John Butler Yeats, father
of Irish poet William Butler Yeats. Eichner interposes a few phrases
from Pound's own version of the encounter. Besides capturing the grace
of the moment itself, the poem hints at a relationship between grace and
the creative process.*

Imagist at Coney Island Maura Eichner

One decade into the 20th century,
Pound, with his back

to Brooklyn, pointed his beard
to the Atlantic. Simply

to receive the kingdom, Ezra
linked arms with John Butler Yeats.

Their shoes filled with sand. Pleasure
rode the water, solid as Staten Island Ferry.

At dusk, lights rose like a fever chart.
Coney Island "marvelous against the night."

In the amusement park Yeats
rode an elephant on the merry-go-round,

"smiling Elijah in the beatific vision."
Pound leaned against a railing

pouring sand from each shoe,
words ripening in him in August heat.

---

*In "The Chimes of Neverwhere," Les Murray muses on the action of
grace in the human story. His whimsical realm of Neverwhere is popu-
lated by that which is no more, or never was. The noble edifices of Eu-
rope annihilated by Hitler's war are in Neverwhere. The "happiness of
Armenia" is there too, for it certainly is nowhere else in the torment of
Armenia's past. Peter and Heloise Abelard's children are in Neverwhere
because in fact these star-crossed lovers of the Middle Ages had only one
son, Astrolabe. Soon afterwards, Heloise's parents had Peter castrated
for secretly marrying their daughter, and the lovers fled into separate ex-
ile, sharing the rest of their days only through letters. The Manchu dy-
nasty returns in Neverwhere because it never returned anywhere else,
and the grammar book of the Picts can be perused only in Neverwhere
because the closest the ancient folk of Scotland ever came to written lan-
guage was the tattoo.*

*But Neverwhere is also the repository of all the horrors that never
were, the "enslavements, tortures, rapes, despair" that grace has "deflect-
ed... from the actual." Among these is the Cold War apocalypse, World
War III, whose not-having-happened spared a Third Australian Imper-
ial Force from being called up and suffering the tragic fate of its two pre-
decessors in the wars of the first half of the century. Of course we can
never have a precise inventory of these works of a favoring Providence.
Murray is content to speculate that because of grace, and its abiding
presence among us collectively (which for Murray is symbolized by
"Church"), our good fortune has been the more.*

The Chimes of Neverwhere Les Murray

How many times did the Church prevent war?
Who knows? Those wars did not occur.
How many numbers don't count before ten?
Treasures of the Devil in Neverwhere.

The neither state of Neverwhere
is hard to place as near or far
since all things that didn't take place are there
and things that have lost the place they took:

Herr Hitler's buildings, King James' cigar,
the happiness of Armenia,
the Abelard children, the Manchu's return
are there with the Pictish Grammar Book.

The girl who returned your dazzled look
and the mornings you might have woke to her
are your waterbed in Neverwhere.
There shine the dukes of Australia

and all the great poems that never were
quite written, and every balked invention.
There too are the Third AIF and its war
in which I and boys my age were killed

more pointlessly with each passing year.
There too half the works of sainthood are
enslavements, tortures, rapes, despair
deflected by them from the actual

to beat on the human-sacrifice drum
that billions need not die to hear
since Christ's love of them struck it dumb
and his agony keeps it in Neverwhere.

How many times did the Church bring peace?
More times than it happened. Leave it back there:
the children we didn't let out of there need it,
for the Devil's at home in Neverwhere.

The Throne of Grace Kathleen Norris

First their car broke down, then Darlene and Kaylee drank up all the butterscotch schnapps in Newcastle, Wyoming. That night they had a chew in the motel hot tub, on the theory that chlorine, heat, and nicotine would steam the alcohol out. "I had to wear my sweat suit," Darlene explained, "and in the morning it was still soaking wet. I had a pair of jeans, but nothing for on top. I figured I could wear my jacket if I remembered to keep it zipped." But when she and Kaylee went across Main Street for breakfast and Kaylee took her jacket off, Darlene forgot and did the same. "I'm standing there in my bra at seven in the morning," she said, "and this one old coot looked up from his bowl of cereal, his face lit up like a kid on Christmas morning. Then he shook his head and went back to eating."

Juggler Richard Wilbur

A ball will bounce, but less and less. It's not
A light-hearted thing, resents its own resilience.
Falling is what it loves, and the earth falls
So in our hearts from brilliance,
Settles and is forgot.
It takes a sky-blue juggler with five red balls

To shake our gravity up. Whee, in the air
The balls roll round, wheel on his wheeling hands,
Learning the ways of lightness, alter to spheres
Grazing his finger ends,

Cling to their courses there,
Swinging a small heaven about his ears.

But a heaven is easier made of nothing at all
Than the earth regained, and still and sole within
The spin of worlds, with a gesture sure and noble
He reels that heaven in,
Landing it ball by ball,
And trades it all for a broom, a plate, a table.

Oh, on his toe the table is turning, the broom's
Balancing up on his nose, and the plate whirls
On the tip of his broom! Damn, what a show, we cry:
The boys stamp, and the girls
Shriek, and the drum booms
And all comes down, and he bows and says goodbye.

If the juggler is tired now, if the broom stands
In the dust again, if the table starts to drop
Through the daily dark again, and though the plate
Lies flat on the table top,
For him we batter our hands
Who has won for once over the world's weight

The Apprentice Prophecies David Craig

It's the wreath you don't come upon
in a snowy field some gray morning,
the few remaining strands
of tinsel, moving in the cold.
And days later, the cabin nearer
the horizon, light through the shades,
a chilly sky before dawn.

It's your steel porch rail in sunlight
beneath the mailboxes; bright, flat black,

the brick behind. You'll be struck dumb
by the ordinary, and everything
will start to matter:
what shirt you put on,
how to pronounce your name.

You'll start helping dogs across the street,
be careful not to cycle over worms
after rain. You and the whole neighborhood,
everyone with quick, uncertain wheels.
Hand brakes and balance. You'll come home hours later,
muddy, but happy.

You'll keep waiting for it to end.

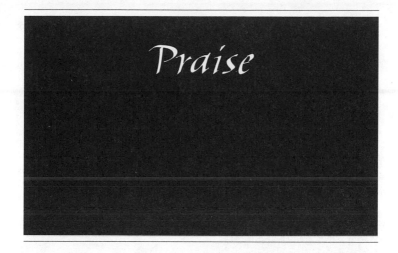

Praise

*P*raising God could be considered the Christian response to grace, the bearing of perfect love back to its source. Like the Jewish tradition it builds on, Christianity has evolved innumerable ways to address ultimate mystery. Praise is foremost of these, and either constitutes the central thrust of prayer, as in the Psalms, or holds a place of honor in almost all other prayer forms. Christian theology characterizes praise as the basic stance of nature, whose glories mutely give to their creator the praise we utter consciously as nature's mouthpiece. Whatever form it takes, praise of a Creator God nakedly marks the full Judeo-Christian distance from a cosmology of chance grandeur.

Les Murray presents an archetypal Sabbath assembly in "The Gaelic Long Tunes," the Christian voice raised in familiar celebration. Murray evokes the vintage of his subject with the rhythms and alliterative techniques of Old English poetry, as well as with archaic terms like "tauten" (make taut), "gig" (a small whaling boat), and "precentor" (a leader of the choir). The reference to "circuit days" establishes the poem's locale as a place too small or remote for resident clergy, requiring instead the services of a minister circulating among several towns. Murray likens the community's "God-paean" to features of its experience in the long boat, the vessel of its livelihood.

The Gaelic Long Tunes Les Murray

On Sabbath days, on circuit days,
the Free Church assembled from boats and gigs
and between sermons they would tauten
and, exercising all they allowed of art,
haul on the long lines of the Psalms.

The seated precentor, touching text,
would start alone, lifting up his whale-long tune
and at the right quaver, the rest set sail
after him, swaying, through eerie and lorn.
No unison of breaths-in gapped their sound.

In disdain of all theatrics, they raised
straight ahead, from plank rows, their beatless God-paean,
their giving like enduring. And in rise
and undulation, in Earth-conquest mourned
as loss, all tragedy drowned, and that weird
music impelled them, singing, like solar wind.

The Pastor Praises the Creator David Citino

Dearly beloved, I mean today
to praise the God who gave the tribes
wine, the crisp flesh of suckling pig,
then told them "Thou must not."

Who gave them swords and ploughshares,
lambs and lions, demons and redeemers.
Who made half of them like pestles,
half like mortars, then told them

in themselves they were complete.
Cool soothing fingers and fevers
between the legs. Reason and gooseflesh,
curtains and candles, lightning and oak,

seven days to live and as many sins,
lungs and mold, books and blind men, veins
and age. Who fashioned them a harvest home,
then created wanderlust and roads.

Our Father David Craig

Glory to the Father
Who guideth His children with a tender hand,
Who watches over the hay-bailers,
and to Whom the cricket sings.
He is like the stars and the broad rivers
that move beneath them.
He is like Paris or Rome.
He is like taxes.

He forgeth the metal in the fire,
the birds fly from His singing,
glows at the end of the day.

262

Who is there to visit Him?
Who to bring Him mirrors?

Hyperbole David Craig

Praise the Lord
Who loveth the fat man,
for he is jocund.
Who loveth the beetle and the amoeba
for they are universes
unto themselves.
Who maketh the round ball
and the skinny hole.

He is the milk and sap
of our dispositions, the red arm,
the other shoe. We walk
for hours behind Him,
losing our way,
losing our way.

---

*"Glory Glory / Psalm 19" and "But God Is Silent / Psalm 114" are two
of Daniel Berrigan's paraphrases from the Book of Psalms, a collection
of religious songs in the Bible, some dating as far back as the fifth cen-
tury* B.C. *The content of "But God Is Silent" is suggested by both Psalms
114 and 115. These were presented as a single psalm in Saint Jerome's
Latin version of scripture, with which Berrigan as a Jesuit would be fa-
miliar. They also provide the traditional setting for the* Hallel *or
"Praise," of the Jewish Passover meal.*

Glory Glory / Psalm 19 Daniel Berrigan

The heavens bespeak the glory of God.
The firmament ablaze, a text of his works.

Dawn whispers to sunset
Dark to dark the word passes; glory glory.

All in a great silence,
no tongue's clamor—
yet the web of the world trembles
conscious, as of great winds passing.

The bridegroom's tent is raised,
acry goes up: He comes! a radiant sun
rejoicing, presiding, his wedding day.
From end to end of the universe his progress—
No creature, no least being but catches fire from him.

But God Is Silent / Psalm 114 Daniel Berrigan

     Sotto voce
cynics pass the word—
Let's hear from your god
How many legions has he?

But god is silent
the creator of splendors
earth and heaven, a dazzle of stars
all creatures that fly, swim, walk
breathe and blossom
yes and simple unblinking stones
sun and moon, splendid beyond telling
and the squat toad
the owl's myopic stare

This panoply, this outspread
banquet of sight and mind
and its silent
Maker

our momentous Friend
our androgynous Lover!

---

*Berrigan's endearments reveal the "I-Thou" intimacy that Christians,
and Jews before them, have always presumed when conversing with
their God. Andrew Hudgins illustrates this as well in "Praying Drunk,"
a chatty monologue during which the poet freely puts in for "a lot of
money and a woman." Hudgins recognizes the primacy of praise ("I
ought to start with praise"), but for him, as for many Christians at
prayer, it comes less readily to the lips than thanks, supplication, even
confession. This may be why scripture rates praise as a sacrifice. Hud-
gins grapples with his praise demons at length in "Psalm Against
Psalms."*

Praying Drunk Andrew Hudgins

Our father who art in heaven, I am drunk.
Again. Red wine. For which I offer thanks.
I ought to start with praise, but praise
comes hard to me. I stutter. Did I tell you
about the woman whom I taught, in bed,
this prayer? It starts with praise; the simple form
keeps things in order. I hear from her sometimes.
Do you? And after love, when I was hungry,
I said, *Make me something to eat.* She yelled,
Poof! You're a casserole!—and laughed so hard
she fell out of the bed. Take care of her.

Next, confession—the dreary part. At night
deer drift from the dark woods and eat my garden.
They're like enormous rats on stilts except,
of course, they're beautiful. But why? What *makes*
them beautiful? I haven't shot one yet.
I might. When I was twelve, I'd ride my bike
out to the dump and shoot the rats. It's hard

to kill your rats, our Father. You have to use
a hollow point and hit them solidly.
A leg is not enough. The rat won't pause.
Yeep! Yeep! it screams, and scrabbles, three-legged, back
into the trash, and I would feel a little bad
to kill something that wants to live
more savagely than I do, even if
it's just a rat. My garden's vanishing.
Perhaps I'll merely plant more beans, though that
might mean more beautiful and hungry deer.
Who knows?

      I'm sorry for the times I've driven
home past a black, enormous, twilight ridge.
Crested with mist, it looked like a giant wave
about to break and sweep across the valley,
and in my loneliness and fear I've thought,
O let it come and wash the whole world clean.
Forgive me. This is my favorite sin: despair—
whose love I celebrate with wine and prayer.

Our Father, thank you for all the birds and trees,
that nature stuff. I'm grateful for good health,
food, air, some laughs, and all the other things
I'm grateful that I've never had to do
without. I have confused myself. I'm glad
there's not a rattrap large enough for deer.
While at the zoo last week, I sat and wept
when I saw one elephant insert his trunk
into another's ass, pull out a lump,
and whip it back and forth impatiently
to free the goodies hidden in the lump.
I could have let it mean most anything,
but I was stunned again at just how little
we ask for in our lives. *Don't look! Don't look!*
Two young nuns tried to herd their giggling
schoolkids away. *Line up,* they yelled. *Let's go
and watch the monkeys in the monkey house.*

I laughed, and got a dirty look. Dear Lord,
we lurch from metaphor to metaphor,
which is—let it be so—a form of praying.

I'm usually asleep by now—the time
for supplication. Requests. As if I'd stayed
up late and called the radio and asked
they play a sentimental song. Embarrassed.
I want a lot of money and a woman.
And also, I want vanishing cream. You know—
a character like Popeye rubs it on
and disappears. Although you see right through him,
he's there. He chuckles, stumbles into things,
and smoke that's clearly visible escapes
from his invisible pipe. It makes me think,
sometimes, of you. What makes me think of me
is the poor jerk who wanders out on air
and then looks down. Below his feet, he sees
eternity, and suddenly his shoes
no longer work on nothingness, and down
he goes. As I fall past, remember me.

---

*Hudgins cites two biblical exemplars of praise in "Psalm Against
Psalms," referring to incidents in chapter 6 of the Book of Isaiah and
chapter 4 of the Book of Ezekiel. In the first, an angel touches Isaiah's
lips with a glowing ember to prepare him for his prophetic ministry. In
the second, God enjoins the prophet Ezekiel to bake his bread over hu-
man excrement as a symbol of the impure food awaiting the Jewish peo-
ple in exile.*

---

from **Psalm Against Psalms** Andrew Hudgins

Unto the pure all things are pure.

Isaiah ate the blood-red ember.
Ezekiel ate the dung. It went in fire
and came out praise. It went in shit
and came praise from his mouth. And this
is where I stick. I pray: thank, ask,
confess. But praise—dear God!—it clings
like something dirty on my tongue,
like shit. Or burns because it is a lie.
And yet I try: I pray and ask
for praise, then force the balking words
out of my mouth as if the saying them
could form the glowing coal—cool,
smooth as a ruby—on my tongue.
Or mold inside my mouth the shit
that melts like caramel—and thereby,
by magic, change my heart. Instead
I croak the harsh begrudging praise
of those who conjure grace, afraid
that it might come, afraid it won't.
But if grace tore through me and spoke,
as God in his strange redundant way
put on my tongue to praise himself,
I'd hear the words I said and learn
why I invented all the horrors of the world,
learn why I made us humans love
our hard sweet lives, then added death
to give it all intensity....

        I'm not fastidious
between extremes of fire and shit—the one
so pure it smolders on our flesh,
the other one so pure our flesh
refuses it, expels it, walks away.
That's why so few of us are prophets.

God-like, they feast on purities,
pure spirit or pure excrement.
I'm smaller, human, in between,
a leavening of dirt with fire,
and I must be, with every passing day,
more careful of what goes into my mouth,
more reckless of what issues forth.

---

*The Christian habit of praise in prayer has directed itself over time to
an array of sacred figures, all of whom for many Christians ultimately
share in holy mystery. Most familiar among these is the "dulcis Virgo"
or sweet Virgin, Mary the mother of Jesus, of Geoffrey Hill's "Hymns to
Our Lady of Chartres." But there seem to be no recorded prayers to one
of the most preeminent of sacred figures, the biblical mother of the race.
Kathleen Norris makes up the lack, and though "A Prayer to Eve" is
voiced as a petition, its unorthodox terms of address are clearly praiseful
of the first woman's attributes and example.*

---

from **Hymns to Our Lady of Chartres** Geoffrey Hill

Love is at odds. Your beauty has gone out
so many times; too vividly has flared
through the mild dreams of Herod undeterred.
Your eyes are like the eyes of the devout,

O dulcis Virgo. You are the stained world's
ransom, bear its image, live through your
perpetual exile in its courts of prayer.
"This is the carnal rose that re-enfolds

heaven into earth." They say you are disposed
to acts of grace: tumblers and holy fools.
Child-saints rejoice you, small immaculate souls,
and mundane sorrows mystically espoused.

A Prayer to Eve Kathleen Norris

Mother of fictions
and of irony,
help us to laugh.

Mother of science
and the critical method,
keep us humble.

Muse of listeners,
hope of interpreters,
inspire us to act.

Bless our metaphors,
that we might eat them.

Help us to know, Eve,
the one thing we must do.

Come with us, muse of exile,
mother of the road.

---

*In "Naming the Living God," Norris praises the cosmic origin of the cos-
mological mysteries plumbed by science. Among the ones she alludes to
is the Indeterminacy Principle, by which the position of an atomic par-
ticle changes when measuring its speed, in the same way its speed
changes when calibrating its position. The poet begins with the per-
sonal testimonies of Albert Einstein (1875–1955) and famed German
mathematician Bernhard Riemann (1826–1866).*

Naming the Living God Kathleen Norris

"The Special Theory came to me,"
Einstein said,

"as shifting forms of light."
Riemann once remarked, "I did not
invent those pairs of differential equations, I found them
in the world,
where God had hidden them."

Natural numbers stand firm,
granite laced
with ice.
Negative numbers roam, lions
about to pounce.

All things change
when you measure them. You might as well
sing, the sound of your voice
joining the others, like waters overflowing,
the name of the living God.

"Praise in Summer" by Richard Wilbur's records a poet's displeasure at his own poetic cunning. He has abused nature with metaphor, saying "this" feature of creation is like "that." "This" is "this" points to miracle enough, Wilbur insists, and is more than reason enough for praise. The strict ordering of his sonnet conveys in its own way a respect for the givenness of received forms.

Praise in Summer Richard Wilbur

Obscurely yet most surely called to praise,
As sometimes summer calls us all, I said
The hills are heavens full of branching ways
Where star-nosed moles fly overhead the dead;
I said the trees are mines in air. I said
See how the sparrow burrows in the sky!
And then I wondered why this mad *instead*
Perverts our praise to uncreation, why

Such savor's in this wrenching things awry.
Does sense so stale that it must needs derange
The world to know it? To a praiseful eye
Should it not be enough of fresh and strange
That trees grow green, and moles can course in clay,
And sparrows sweep the ceiling of our day?

A struggle to praise is compounded in Annie Dillard's long narrative poem, "Tickets For A Prayer Wheel," by a struggle merely to pray. Dillard deploys magic, aboriginal lore, meditations on nature, medieval witchcraft, surrealism, classical science and psychology, elements of pagan and Christian religion, and a touch of Gothic mystery to tell of one family's bizarre and often hilarious efforts to make contact with God. Dillard advances their story in stages roughly parallel to those of western civilization, from paganism, to rationalism and finally to revelation. In the poem's concluding section given below, the family discovers that God is present, though hidden, all along, and is ultimately known in a self-revelation so inexplicable that the poet can mark it only as a series of missing lines. The speaker's visions and ecstatic union with God, ringing with a "hundred prayers of praise," bear many of the features of Western mysticism, especially those of Teresa of Avila in her raptures of "divine espousal." Dillard's other religious imagery includes an oriflamme or glittering sacred banner, and the mandorla, a luminous oval of varying shades of blue used in religious art to signify celestial glory. In a work teeming with allusion to figures of classical and Christian history, Dillard makes a final reference to Gregory Lopez (1611–1691 A.D.), the first native Chinese Catholic bishop, whom she describes earlier in the poem as having "prayed continuously for three years, / 'Thy will be done on earth / as it is in heaven.'"

---

from **Tickets for a Prayer Wheel** Annie Dillard

You go down the hall,
and open the door,
down the hall

and open the small door,
down the dark hall
and open the smaller door,
down the hall,
small as a wire,
bare, and the final door—
flies from the wall.

*
*
*
*
*
*
*
*
*
*

God in the house
teaching us to pray:
and the family crazed
and full of breath.

We nailed a picture
by the door, on the whitewashed wall.
My father leaned close
to examine the picture,
the universe—At once
the universe rang its call
and clapped him in to itself,
to its ebon, unthinkable thrall.
God held him close
and lighted for him
the distant, dizzying stairs;
God looped him
in a sloping loop of stars.

He came back and asked
for a cup of cold water only.
He planted beans on the bookshelf;
they grew, and fed us
for a year. He said,
"I cannot bind the chains of the Pleiades,
nor loose the cords of Orion.
The one and holy God of heaven can, alone,
whose hand is his face.
We pray at his command
a prayer of praise."

The presence of God:
he picked me up
and swung me like a bell.
I saw the trees
on fire, I rang
a hundred prayers of praise.
I no longer believe
in divine playfulness.

I saw all the time of this planet
pulled like a scarf
through the sky.
Time, that lorn and furling
oriflamme . . .

Did God dilute
even his merest thought
and take a place in the scarf,
shrink and cross
to an olive continent
and eat our food at little tables for a time?
All those things
which were thought to be questions
are no longer important.
I breathe

an air like light;
I slough off questions
like a hundred suits of motley;
I wear a bright mandorla
like a gown.

We keep our paper money shut
in a box, for fear of fire.
Once, we opened the box
and Christ the lamb stepped out
and left his track of flame across the floor.

Why are we shown these things?
God teaches us to pray.

My sister
dreamed of a sculpture
showing the form of God.
He has no edges,
and the holes in him spin.
He alone is real,
and all things lie in him
as fossil shells
curl in solid shale.
My sister dreamed of God
who moves around
the spanding, spattered holes
of solar systems hollowed in his side.

I think that the dying
pray at the last
not "please"
but "thank you"
as a guest thanks his host at the door.
Falling from mountains
the people are crying
thank you,

thank you,
all down the air;
and the cold carriages
draw up for them on the rocks.

Fare away, fare away!

The Dominican
Gregorio Lopez
prayed on God's command.
A hand
raised my mother up,
and round her poured
a light like petalled water.
For thou only art holy,
thou only art the lord...
and we are drowned.

---

*The Christian ideal is to give praise in all things, and Dillard honors
this in "God" by modestly proposing a new way to count.*

God Annie Dillard

Numbers from one to ten, however, are called
"God." In other words, counting to ten you would
say, "God, God, God, God, God, God, God, God, God,
God." It is possible to distinguish among these
numbers by the tone in which each is pronounced.
"God," for example, corresponding to our "five,"
is pitched relatively high on the musical scale,
and accordingly sounds an inquisitive, even plaintive,
note. It is in sharp contrast to the number corre-
sponding to our "ten," which has a slightly accented,
basso finality, thus: "God."

The Mystical Body

S aint Paul was the first to advance the idea that the full expression of "the Christ" transcends the historical Jesus. God resurrected Jesus not just *for* his followers, Paul explains, but *in* his followers, so that all of them participate at a mystical level in the living body of the risen Christ. What this creates for believers is a community of almost infinite relatedness, for counted among its living multitude are those who have died an earthly death but are believed to continue to live in Christ. The first series of poems that follows gives a sense of how Christians experience this shared life of the living and the dead, often referred to as the communion of saints. Later poems reflect on "tradition," which is the mystical body's cumulative understanding of itself. The chapter concludes with three poems about "church," the mystical body in its local expression.

Sister Mary Appassionata Lectures
The Home Ec Class: The Feast David Citino

On time for every meal
whether I set them a place
or not, the family ghosts
assemble around the table.
My parents and theirs, dead

uncles, cousins and friends
light as steam, subtle as
anise, bay leaf or sage,
study me as I pierce and carve,
slice and chew, pause to savor.

Grease of flesh stains lips
and fingertips, coats teeth
and tongue as rust does iron
or dust the porcelain figurines
in the proper homes of

proper old ladies. Course
after course, meal after meal
and still they're unsatisfied.
Grandfather, speck of oregano
stuck between front teeth,

wipes sauce red as heart's blood
from his plate with a crust,
holds up a glass to ask for
more wine. "But you can't be
thirsty," I whisper. We're

destined to meet like this
three times each day, the family
become a rite, a thirst we'll

never slake, hunger ever
unappeased, our need, the feast.

Mostly My Nightmares Are Dull Andrew Hudgins

Mostly my nightmares are dull. On autumn nights
I rake the yard. Brown leaves fall faster, faster.
They swamp my ankles, rise up past my knees,
waist, neck, until I'm drowning in dry leaves.
A bourgeois nightmare, sure. But still
I wake up sweaty, short of breath, surprised
at just how little fear it takes to break me.
And worse, some nights I raise the dead. I say,
I didn't understand that you were dying,
but Mother simply waves my guilt away,
left-handed, as though it were tobacco smoke.
Grandmother smiles, forgives my vulgar mouth,
and Sister, dead before my birth, confides
that she too loves Ray Charles. Soon Grandma's talk
of niggers makes me snarl at her. She sulks.
Her sulking makes me yell, Mom cries, Ray sings,
and Sister lapses back into her silence.
I wake, they die again, and I walk out
into a day I'll live as carelessly
as if I'll only—fat chance—live it once.

The Wheel Wendell Berry

At the first strokes of the fiddle bow
the dancers rise from their seats.
The dance begins to shape itself
in the crowd, as couples join,
and couples join couples, their movement
together lightening their feet.
They move in the ancient circle

of the dance. The dance and the song
call each other into being. Soon
they are one—rapt in a single
rapture, so that even the night
has its clarity, and time
is the wheel that brings it round.

In this rapture the dead return.
Sorrow is gone from them.
They are light. They step
into the steps of the living
and turn with them in the dance
in the sweet enclosure
of the song, and timeless
is the wheel that brings it round.

Inheritance Kathleen Norris

Charlotte Totten 1891–1973

I

In the house are all her years:
Linen dishtowels
Ironed, starched, folded.
Fine wood:
Bird's-eye, hard rock maple
Which she oiled and rubbed.
I keep her powder jar:
I throw out her yellowed corsets
And white gloves.

I throw out the bottles of pills
For her heart, and small tins of rouge.
In the house is her King James:
Pressed leaves,
Prayers clipped from newspapers.
A photograph of a baby in a coffin.

The noon whistle blows.
I watch the minister
As he walks home to dinner.
Teach me, Lord,
To be gentle in all events, especially in disappointments;
Let me put myself aside.

II

I like the kitchen, and put my own plants
By the window.
This is where jelly bags hung in summer
With crab apple, buffalo berry:
And she set table,
Laying out a cloth,
Filling each glass with water.

Her talk was of measuring, pouring, waiting.
This is where she made divinity and caramel
At Christmas.

III

In June, 1917, men laid the sidewalk.
Children still skate on it
And learn to bicycle.

I keep her garden,
Worrying for the spent columbine and daisy
That sleep through winter
In beds of straw.

The rain barrel stands
Full of dark water, in the dark.
It opens its mouth as if to speak.

As Kathleen Norris pays homage to a single ancestor, so Maura Eichner in "Litany" honors women of courage and spiritual genius from throughout Christian history, among them the medieval poets and mystics Mechtild of Magdeburg and Hildegard of Bingen, pioneer of early religious life Mary Ward, pilgrim Marjorie Kempe, Nazi death-camp victims Edith Stein and Etty Hellesum, and mid-twentieth-century philosopher and feminist Simone Weil. The layout of Eichner's poem, recalling classic church litanies, visually replicates the idea of the communion of saints as a living census gathered to its mystical ground. The poet's final reference to "God the Mother" reflects the usage of many a late-twentieth-century Christian in designating spiritual gender: She Who Is Holy Spirit (spirit is a feminine noun, ruah, *in the Hebrew), She Who Is Wisdom (*sophía, *feminine in the Greek), She Who Is God (God's definitive self-definition in the Book of Exodus is the genderless "I Am Who Am"). Likewise, even the gender of the Jesus of history, in light of Paul's distinction made earlier, is generalized by a transfigured, cosmic Christ, an obvious premise when speaking of a christic body made up of female and male.*

Litany for the Living Maura Eichner

> Hildegard of Bingen
> Catherine of Genoa
> Catherine of Sienna
> Mechtild
> Simone Weil
> Edith Stein
> Julian of Norwich
> Teresa of Avila
> Therese of Lisieux
> Etty Hillesum
> Marjorie Kempe
> Mary Ward
> our cloud
> of witnesses

283

of flaming heart
light untouchable
dark immeasurable
mystic marriage
ground-of-being-God
the Father
God the Mother

For Christians, Wendell Berry's experience of being "rapt in a single rapture" with all human striving goes with a sense of shared historical consciousness, a "community of knowing in common," as Berry will phrase it in a poem to come. This self-awareness of the mystical body accounts for Christianity's nurture of "tradition." The Christian desire for continuity with the past, the yearning for rootedness, is not nostalgia but a conviction of the past's power, like the power imparted to living things rooted to their place in nature.

The Sycamore Wendell Berry

In the place that is my own place, whose earth
I am shaped in and must bear, there is an old tree growing,
a great sycamore that is a wondrous healer of itself.
Fences have been tied to it, nails driven into it,
hacks and whittles cut in it, the lightning has burned it.
There is no year it has flourished in
that has not harmed it. There is a hollow in it
that is its death, though its living brims whitely
at the lip of the darkness and flows outward.
Over all its scars has come the seamless white
of the bark. It bears the gnarls of its history
healed over. It has risen to a strange perfection
in the warp and bending of its long growth.
It has gathered all accidents into its purpose.
It has become the intention and radiance of its dark fate.
It is a fact, sublime, mystical and unassailable.

In all the country there is no other like it.
I recognize in it a principle, an indwelling
the same as itself, and greater, that I would be ruled by.
I see that it stands in its place, and feeds upon it,
and is fed upon, and is native, and maker.

At a Country Funeral Wendell Berry

Now the old ways that have brought us
farther than we remember sink out of sight
as under the treading of many strangers
ignorant of landmarks. Only once in a while
they are cast clear again upon the mind
as at a country funeral where, amid the soft
lights and hothouse flowers, the expensive
solemnity of experts, notes of a polite musician,
persist the usages of old neighborhood.
Friends and kinsmen come and stand and speak,
knowing the extremity they have come to,
one of their own bearing to the earth the last
of his light, his darkness and the sun's definitive mark.
They stand and think as they stood and thought
when even the gods were different.
And the organ music, though decorous
as for somebody else's grief, has its source
in the outcry of pain and hope in log churches,
and on naked hillsides by the open grave,
eastward in mountain passes, in tidelands,
and across the sea. How long a time?
Rock of Ages, cleft for me, let me hide my
self in Thee. They came, once in time,
in simple loyalty to their dead, and returned
to the world. The fields and the work
remained to be returned to. Now the entrance
of one of the old ones into the Rock
too often means a lifework perished from the land

without inheritor, and the field goes wild
and the house sits and stares. Or it passes
at cash value into the hands of strangers.
Now the old dead wait in the open coffin
for the blood kin to gather, come home
for one last time, to hear old men
whose tongues bear an essential topography
speak memories doomed to die.
But our memory of ourselves, hard earned,
is one of the land's seeds, as a seed
is the memory of the life of its kind in its place,
to pass on into life the knowledge
of what has died. What we owe the future
is not a new start, for we can only begin
with what has happened. We owe the future
the past, the long knowledge
that is the potency of time to come.
That makes of a man's grave a rich furrow.
The community of knowing in common is the seed
of our life in this place. There is not only
no better possibility, there is no
other, except for chaos and darkness,
the terrible ground of the only possible
new start. And so as the old die and the young
depart, where shall a man go who keeps
the memories of the dead, except home
again, as one would go back after a burial,
faithful to the fields, lest the dead die
a second and more final death.

---

*Berry's line from the familiar Christian hymn "Rock of Ages" alludes to
the "rock" of Christ broken on the cross, but the poem's horizon extends
to "when even the gods were different." For Berry, a farmer, his sense of
spiritual location, his place in tradition, is bound to his sense of place in
the physical world. The two are reflections and symbols of each other.
Nothing is merely local. The "usages of old neighborhood" are specific*

to locale and at the same time signatures of historic memory. *Any local breach between generations threatens the continuity of the "long knowledge / that is the potency of time to come."*

The severing of tradition, of life from root, that leads to "chaos and darkness" for Berry is the starting point of Denise Levertov's "Re-rooting." Her poem tells of an urgent struggle to restore roots to the earth that have been "rashly torn" from it. The metaphor describes Levertov's own process of turning back from the agnosticism of her early adult years to re-root the spirituality inherited from her father. Levertov has said: "My father's background of Jewish and (after his conversion) Christian scholarship and mysticism, his fervor and eloquence as a preacher, entered my imagination, even though I didn't, as a child, recognize that fact." The "revenant" or ghost in her second poem can be understood as a direct characterization of her father retrieving for the poet and her companions "brick-upon-brick / structures of early thought."

Re-rooting Denise Levertov

We were trying to put the roots back,
wild and erratic straying root-limbs,
trying to fit them into the hole that was
cleancut in clay, deep but not
wide enough; or wide but too square—trying
to get the roots back into earth
before they dried out and died.
Ineptly we pulled and pushed
striving to encompass so many rivers
of wood and fiber in one confinement without
snapping the arteries of sap, the force
of life springing in them that made them
spring away from our hands—
we knew our own life was
tied to that strength, that strength we knew would
ebb away if we could not find within us
the blessed guile to tempt

its energy back into earth,
into the quiet depths from which we had
rashly torn it, and now clumsily
struggled to thrust it back into sinuous corridors
fit for its subtleties, but obstinately
into an excavation dug by machine.
                    And I wake,
as if from dream, but discover
even this digging, better than nothing,
has not yet begun.

.

Another Revenant Denise Levertov

One long-dead
    returned for a night
        to speak to us

to me and
    a shadowy other beside me—
        we who had known him in time past—

and to a third,
    our friend, genius of listening,
        fully attentive, smiling.

While the revenant
    spoke, we looked
        back and forth to each other
            across the table,

            wicks taking flame
            one from the next, beacons
            lit on ridges of dark—

            confirming the wonder:

he was telling
    all we had not even
        thought to ask, long ago,

unsuspected luminous eloquence
    of pages long-yellowed,
        interventions

of unrecorded, brick-upon-brick
    structures of early thought
        re-collected,

rooms, towers, arches
    rising from rubble, gateways
        open, inviting entrance:

            dimensions unguessed that change
                a story the way
                    our comprehension of some unaccountable flora

            would change
                if we knew a river's course had been altered
                    before there were maps—

            altered with effort so strenuous, no-one
                long after,
                    had wanted or tried to remember it.

All we'd thought gone
    into ashes,
        clay,
            deep night—

memories to account for the
    gray unresonant
        gaps and rifts:

his memories,
>   which in his life before death had seemed
>   obliterate, buried beyond retrieval,

emerging: his gift
>   to us, and
>   yes, to himself—

visible threads
>   woven amongst us, gleaming,
>   a fabric
>   one with our listening.

Revenants of ancestral wisdom return after a period of absence for Wendell Berry as well in "Meditation in the Spring Rain." Berry remembers his grandmother remembering old Mrs. Gaines, who sang the mystical body, "One Lord, one Faith and one Cornbread." Her cornbread is a rustic variant of the matzoth, *or unleavened bread, of the Jewish Passover meal. It was this bread that Christ blessed and offered as his flesh the night before he died, calling his followers to enter into the one mystical body by eating of the loaf. His action passed into the tradition, by his authority, as the sacrament of communion, or eucharist. Its continuing enactment is a way the mystical body experiences the historical and spiritual unities of which Mrs. Gaines sings.*

Berry's poetry, like Levertov's, evolves from an earlier agnostic naturalism. "Spring Rain" records the moment of Berry's recovery of the ancestral "faith of our fathers," a phrase borrowed from the title of the old Christian hymn. Berry's memories of Mrs. Gaines combine with his experience of nature to awaken "some old exultation." The poet begins to recognize "the opening / of the flowers and the leafing-out of the trees" as but another utterance of the "great Word" of the mystical body, the Logos/Christ that was present, according to the gospel writer John, "in the beginning." Berry's conviction that the entire realm of nature seems to be witnessing the Incarnation can be observed in many of his other poems selected for this volume, and forms the centerpiece of his creation spirituality.

Meditation in the Spring Rain Wendell Berry

In the April rain I climbed up to drink
of the live water leaping off the hill,
white over the rocks. Where the mossy root
of a sycamore cups the flow, I drank
and saw the branches feathered with green.
The thickets, I said, send up their praise
at dawn. Was that what I meant—I meant
my words to have the heft and grace, the flight
and weight of the very hill, its life
rising—or was it some old exultation
that abides with me? We'll not soon escape
the faith of our fathers—no more than
crazy old Mrs. Gaines, whom my grandmother
remembers standing balanced eighty years ago
atop a fence in Port Royal, Kentucky,
singing: "One Lord, one Faith, and one
Cornbread." They had a cage built for her
in a room, "nearly as big as the room, not
cramped up," and when she grew wild
they kept her there. But mostly she went free
in the town, and they allowed the children
to go for walks with her. She strayed once
beyond where they thought she went, was lost
to them, "and they had an awful time
finding her." For her, to be free
was only to be lost. What is it about her
that draws me on, so that my mind becomes a child
to follow after her? An old woman
when my grandmother was a girl, she must have seen
the virgin forest standing here, the amplitude
of our beginning, of which no speech
remains. Out of the town's lost history,
buried in minds long buried, she has come,
brought back by a memory near death. I see her
in her dusky clothes, hair uncombed, the children

291

following. I see her wandering, muttering
to herself as her way was, among these hills
half a century before my birth, in the silence
of such speech as I know. Dawn and twilight
and dawn again trembling in the leaves
over her, she tramped the raveling verges
of her time. It was a shadowy country
that she knew, holding a darkness that was past
and a darkness to come. The fleeting lights
tattered her churchly speech to mad song.
When her poor wandering head broke the confines
of all any of them knew, they put her in a cage.
But I am glad to know it was a commodious cage,
not cramped up. And I am glad to know
that other times the town left her free
to be as she was in it, and to go her way.
May it abide a poet with as much grace!
For I too am perhaps a little mad,
standing here wet in the drizzle, listening
to the clashing syllables of the water. Surely
there is a great Word being put together here.
I begin to hear it gather in the opening
of the flowers and the leafing-out of the trees,
in the growth of bird nests in the crotches
of the branches, in the settling of the dead
leaves into the ground, in the whittling
of beetle and grub, in my thoughts
moving in the hill's flesh. Coming here,
I crossed a place where a stream flows
underground, and the sounds of the hidden water
and the water come to light braided in my ear.
I think the maker is here, creating his hill
as it will be, out of what it was.
The thickets, I say, send up their praise
at dawn! One Lord, one Faith, and one Cornbread
forever! But hush. Wait. Be as still
as the dead and the unborn in whose silence

that old one walked, muttering and singing,
followed by the children.

> For a time there
I turned away from the words I knew, and was lost.
For a time I was lost and free, speechless
in the multitudinous assembling of his Word.

"Church" is the institutional form of the mystical body. Because church happens in the neighborhood, it is also a culture and a sociology. Much of what is counted as religion among Christians has nothing much to do with religion at all but with the milieu and the lore that burgeons around it. David Citino remembers the optimism of growing up Catholic in Cleveland, steeped in a homogeneous religious culture with its high quotient of "religious imagination." Andrew Hudgins remembers a boyhood Sunday in the Baptist Church, and in a second poem, his part in a not-so-good church basement pageant, an event somewhere in the memory of almost all North American Christians.

Cleveland, Angels, Ogres, Trolls David Citino

> *Drumcliff and Rosses and choke-ful of ghosts. By bog,*
> *road, rath, hillside, sea border, they gather in all shapes:*
> *headless women, men in armor, shadow hares, fire tongued*
> *hounds, whistling seals and others. A whistling seal sank a*
> *ship the other day.*   —Yeats, The Celtic Twilight

Still today, sober and tenured as I can be,
I go back. When I close my eyes it's Cleveland,
I've fallen out of puberty, lost the beast's
rough hair and heavy hurt. Angels go with me.
To be means giving credence without question.
The mirror's a miracle even before I take off
my clothes. Aunts work wonders
with their crazy praying. Novenas shatter glasses
poised in palsied hands of drunks, the lame

293

leap and whirl like windy leaves. Kennedy
comes back, Jackie at his side unbloodied,
his skull smooth and whole as the schoolroom globe.
Old men stop to sharpen scissors or haggle
for the family's rags, their carts powered by song.
We pray for the conversion of Russia.
The whole world's Catholic, it rains new babies
every night, nothing in the world's to be
discounted and hordes of children meet each day
to learn to do and say, eyes glowing streetlamp bright
with currents of perfect fear, all joy.
Nothing tastes the same. Ogres and trolls
patrol the dark beneath each bed. Where I step
glaciers have been and may come again.
Tomorrow the sun will rise forever.

Gospel Andrew Hudgins

"Jesus will always be there. He's waiting. It's true."
He wiped his forehead, crooned, began to sway:
"Softly and tenderly Jesus is calling you.

O sinner, come home. Come start your new life anew.
I'll stand here as the organ gently plays.
Jesus will always be there. He's waiting. It's true."

I squirmed and giggled in the farthest pew,
then jabbed my best friend, smirked. He wouldn't play.
"Softly and tenderly Jesus is calling you."

Too soft for me. I picked dirt off my shoe.
I drummed my fingers and watched my best friend pray.
"Jesus will always be there. He's waiting. It's true."

Well, let him wait. I thought. He's overdue.
We get home after kickoff every Sunday.
"Softly and tenderly Jesus is calling you."

I prayed the preacher'd save a soul or two
so he'd shut up and let me go. He swayed.
Jesus is always there. He's waiting. It's true.
Softly and tenderly Jesus is calling you.

The Adoration of the Magi Andrew Hudgins

A boy—okay, it's me—wears a fringed
blue tablecloth and fidgets as Joseph
in his church Christmas play. He watches
ten-year-old magi with false beards
hold out gold, frankincense, and myrrh.
Dear God, he's desperate to pee.
Six angels with coat-hanger wings
dance by. Their tinfoil halos tilt
and slide down on their foreheads. One,
too large, has fallen past a girl's
small nose and hangs about her neck.
She pulls it up, keeps dancing. He smirks.
And each time Mary lifts her child
its doll-eyes click open and then
clack shut when she lays Jesus down.
What's wrong with me? he thinks, despairing.
Why won't my soul expand with reverence?
He hopes no one can tell by looking at him.
The pressure in his loins makes him dizzy.
He sways. The Youth Choir warbles, *Hark,
the herald angels sing.* The curtain drops,
And that grim boy bolts off, stage left,
one hand pressed hard into his crotch.

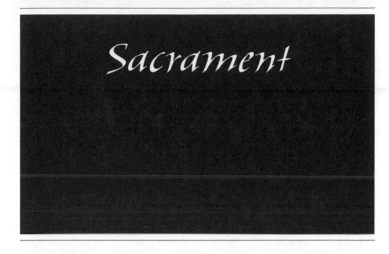

Sacrament

A number of earlier poems in this collection testify to a knowing of God that is sacramental, God experienced as a mystery of enfleshment in nature, love, in the objects and activities of sense. The meaning of the term is preserved in its more familiar churchly usage, where sacrament is a ritual having its origin in Christ that solemnizes a moment of passage. Different Christians recognize different sacraments, but where performed, a sacrament is understood as a making present of the sacred in and through the physical. For Christian poets, the sacramental elements of wine, bread, water, oil, incense, touch, gesture, music, and word are tactile openings to mystery that permeate, and are permeated by, the sacramentality of the world.

Louise Erdrich presents six of the seven traditional sacraments of the church. The first is baptism, the dying of self into the life and community of spirit, a rite of initiation Erdrich characteristically interprets in a Native American setting.

The Sacraments Louise Erdrich

Baptism, Communion, Confirmation,
Matrimony, Holy Orders, Extreme Unction

1.

As the sun dancers, in their helmets of sage,
stopped at the sun's apogee
and stood in the waterless light,
so, after loss, it came to this:
that for each year the being was destroyed,
I was to sacrifice a piece of my flesh.
The keen knife hovered
and the skin flicked in the bowl.
Then the sun, the life that consumes us,
burst into agony.

We began, the wands and the bracelets of sage,
the feathers cocked over our ears.
When the bird joined the circle and called,
we cried back, shrill breath,
through the bones in our teeth.
Her wings closed over us, her dark red
claws drew us upward by the scars,
so that we hung by the flesh,

as in the moment before birth
when the spirit is quenched
in whole pain, suspended
until there is no choice, the body

slams to earth,
the new life starts.

---

*For believers like old Mrs. Gaines in the previous chapter, the bread and
wine of communion recapitulate the bread and wine offered by Christ
as his "body" and "blood" at the last supper. (The other term for com-
munion, eucharist, means "thanksgiving" in Greek.) Eating and drink-
ing in faith joins Christians sacramentally not just to Christ but to one
another and to all who have so communed in Christ's body. The trans-
formation of natural elements implied by Christ's words when he initi-
ated the sacrament—"this is my body . . . this is my blood"—finds ex-
pression in Erdrich's poem as a metamorphosis in nature to which the
speaker is irresistibly drawn. Her bodily communion with it culminates
in an experience of wholeness and peace.*

2.

It is spring. The tiny frogs pull
their strange new bodies out
of the suckholes, the sediment of rust,
and float upward, each in a silver bubble
that breaks on the water's surface,
to one clear unceasing note of need.

Sometimes, when I hear them,
I leave our bed and stumble
among the white shafts of weeds
to the edge of the pond.
I sink to the throat,
and witness the ravenous trill
of the body transformed at last and then consumed
in a rush of music.

Sing to me, sing to me.
I have never been so cold
rising out of sleep.

3.

I was twelve, in my body
three eggs were already marked
for the future.
Two golden, one dark.
And the man,
he was selected from other men,
by a blow on the cheek
similar to mine.
That is how we knew,
from the first meeting.
There was no question.
There was the wound

4.

It was frightening, the trees in their rigid postures
using up the sun,
as the earth tilted its essential degree.
Snow covered everything. Its confusing glare
doubled the view
so that I saw you approach
my empty house
not as one man, but as a landscape
repeating along the walls of every room
papering over the cracked grief.

301

I knew as I stepped into the design,
as I joined the chain of hands,
and let the steeple of fire
be raised above our heads.
We had chosen the costliest pattern,
the strangest, the most enduring.
We were afraid as we stood between the willows,
as we shaped the standard words with our tongues.
Then it was done. The scenery multiplied
around us and we turned.
We stared calmly from the pictures.

In holy orders, the one called to ministry seeks the accomplishment of a higher will at whatever cost to self. For Erdrich's speaker, this radical encounter with mystery, "mouth painted shut," means coming to terms with an existential anxiety, like Christ's at Gethsemane.

5.

God, I was not meant to be the isolate
cry in this body.
I was meant to have your tongue in my mouth.

That is why I stand by your great plaster lips
waiting for your voice to unfold from its dark slot.

Your hand clenched in the shape of a bottle.
Your mouth painted shut on the answer.
Your eyes, two blue mirrors, in which I am perfectly denied.

I open my mouth and I speak
though it is only a thin sound, a leaf
scraping on a leaf.

6.

When the blue steam stalls over the land
and the resinous apples
turn to mash, then to a cider whose thin
twang shrivels the tongue,
the snakes hatch
twirling from the egg.

In the shattered teacup, from the silvering
boards of the barn,
in the heat of rotting mulch hay,
they soak up the particles of light

so that all winter
welded in the iron sheath
of sludge under the pond
they continue, as we do,
drawing closer to the source,
their hearts beating slower
as the days narrow
until there is this one pale aperture
and the tail sliding through

then the systole, the blackness of heaven.

The Rule Richard Wilbur

The oil for extreme unction must be blessed
On Maundy Thursday, so the rule has ruled,
And by the bishop of the diocese.
Does that revolt you? If so, you are free
To squat beneath the deadly manchineel,
That tree of caustic drops and fierce aspersion,
And fancy that you have escaped from mercy.
Things must be done in one way or another.

---

*Maundy Thursday, or Holy Thursday, falls four days before Easter
Sunday. The poisonous manchineel tree thrives in the tropics of the
Americas.*

*Missing from Louise Erdrich's sequence is the sacrament of confession,
or reconciliation as it is sometimes called today. Wishing to be recon-
ciled both with God and with those he loves, David Brendan Hopes ex-
amines his conscience before the Spirit in "A Song of Mercies." What he
seeks is not expiation of guilt but the grace of self-transformation. Like-
wise, Wendell Berry's confession of "useless words, fragments, / errors"
in "A Purification" results in more than catharsis and closure; as an au-
thenticating of self, it provides a basis for personal growth.*

---

from **A Song of Mercies** David Brendan Hopes

Mercy on me Spirit,
    for my excessiveness in all things,
    unrepentant, sorrowing that there
    was not always substance nor occasion for more.
    What I have touched I have worn out.
    Where I have gone has wished to
    see the back of me.
    What I have sought has been run to ground
    or soared off honking

where none could find it anymore.
Whom I have loved has turned from me
finally in exhaustion—
and I know that saying it this way
makes it sound, almost, a virtue,
a fire, consuming or refining, in either case white hot—
but you decide, and permit the proper mercy to descend.

Mercy on me Spirit,
  for the fierce lucidity,
  the stuff of poetry, but the man-destroyer,
  the fender-off of hearts;
  for the charity almost never withheld
  but sometimes crammed down the wrong throat,
  a feast for the merely peckish,
  the starving left with a high smile and a poem
  prostrate in the road;
  for the ingratitude that takes Arcturus and the Pleiades
  and Bach, El Greco and the red tailed hawk as merely due;
  for the pride that would unmake the world
  to make You answer me, to
  make You yield me what is mine,
  to make You love me as you must have promised
  in that swaddling hour only I remember.

Mercy on me Spirit,
  lame with anger, song by anger struck out of my mouth,
  dancer of the Kali-dance: *revenge, revenge;*
  by anger's red moon put to sleep,
  by anger's red sun wakened,
  poems wrenched into timepieces of retribution,
  nights into counting houses of Your slights and wrongs,
  reveries and friendships shattered;
  having built a house of anger to dwell within;
  having been a river of anger plowing underground;
  having been a wind of anger blackening the petals,
  freezing the boats of me in harbor;

cruel, cunning, haywire, weeping, full astray
in the Gehenna of anger, O in mercy, take it away,
having filled my mouth with dust, the Serpent
lashing its tail in the desert of its victories....

---

*Gehenna, a scriptural euphemism for "hell," is a Greek transliteration of
the Hebrew name for the Hinnom Valley southwest of Jerusalem where
the city's garbage dump smoldered and flared.*

A Purification Wendell Berry

At start of spring I open a trench
in the ground. I put into it
the winter's accumulation of paper,
pages I do not want to read
again, useless words, fragments,
errors. And I put into it
the contents of the outhouse:
light of the sun, growth of the ground,
finished with one of their journeys.
To the sky, to the wind, then,
and to the faithful trees, I confess
my sins: that I have not been happy
enough, considering my good luck;
have listened to too much noise;
have been inattentive to wonders;
have lusted after praise.
And then upon the gathered refuse
of mind and body, I close the trench,
folding shut again the dark,
the deathless earth. Beneath that seal
the old escapes into the new.

Renewal and growth are Berry's themes again in "The Mad Farmer Revolution." This time he relates them to the sacrament of communion in a mythic parable of fertility. It all begins when his protagonist gorges on communion wine in a "high lonesome," the country term for a solitary binge.

The Mad Farmer Revolution Wendell Berry

being a fragment
of the natural history of New Eden,
in homage
to Mr. Ed McClanahan, one of the locals

The mad farmer, the thirsty one,
went dry. When he had time
he threw a visionary high
lonesome on the holy communion wine.
"It is an awesome event
when an earthen man has drunk
his fill of the blood of a god,"
people said, and got out of his way.
He plowed the churchyard, the
minister's wife, three graveyards
and a golf course. In the parking lot
he planted a forest of little pines.
He sanctified the groves,
dancing at night in the oak shades
with goddesses. He led
a field of corn to creep up
and tassel like an Indian tribe
on the courthouse lawn. Pumpkins
ran out to the ends of their vines
to follow him. Ripe plums
and peaches reached into his pockets.
Flowers sprang up in his tracks
everywhere he stepped. And then

his planter's eye fell on
that parson's fair fine lady
again. "O holy plowman," cried she,
"I am all grown up in weeds.
Pray, bring me back into good tilth."
He tilled her carefully
and laid her by, and she
did bring forth others of her kind,
and others, and some more.
They sowed and reaped till all
the countryside was filled
with farmers and their brides sowing
and reaping. When they died
they became two spirits of the woods.

---

*For Denise Levertov in "This Day," communion's incarnation of body
and blood in "dry wafer" and "sour wine" triggers an awareness of
God's incarnation "in the dust," in the falterings of the created order.
She observes how the harmony of a Dutch painting integrates not just
its elements of "luxe, calme et volupté"—the "richness, quietness and
pleasure" of Charles Baudelaire's romantic utopia in his "L'Invitation
au Voyage." A "visible quietness" claims the scene's disordered elements
as well. Sacramental communion helps Levertov perceive how confu-
sion and difference are part of the "wonder" that fills her spiritual need.*

This Day Denise Levertov

i
Dry wafer,
sour wine.

This day I see

God's in the dust,
not sifted

out from confusion.

ii

Perhaps, I thought,
passing the duckpond,
perhaps—seeing the brilliantly somber water
deranged by lost feathers and bits of
drowning bread—perhaps
these imperfections (the ducklings
practised their diving,
stylized feet vigorously cycling among débris)
are part of perfection,
a pristine nuance? our eyes
our lives, too close to the canvas,
enmeshed within
the turning dance,
to see it?

iii

In so many Dutch 17th-century paintings
one perceives
a visible quietness, to which the concord
of lute and harpsichord contribute,
in which a smiling conversation
reposes;
'calme, luxe,' and—in auburn or mercurial sheen
              of vessels, autumnal wealth
              of fur-soft table-carpets,
              blue snow-gleam of Delft—
'volupte'; but also the clutter
of fruit and herbs, pots, pans, poultry,
strewn on the floor: and isn't

the quiet upon them too, in them and of them,
aren't they wholly at one with the wonder?

iv
Dry wafer,
sour wine:

this day I see

the world, a word
intricately incarnate, offers—
      ravelled, honeycombed, veined, stained—
what hunger craves,

a sorrel grass,
a crust,
water,
salt.

---

*For the speaker of David Craig's "Young Monk (Denver)," textures of
the sacred bind the communion table and everyday life as they did for
Levertov. The same again is true, in Craig's "John Says Mass," of the
communion "disc" or sacramental bread in the form of a wafer, whose
transformation Craig relates to its widest natural and historical context.
The poem is inspired by the fiftieth chapter of* The Little Flowers of Saint
Francis, *an anonymous, fourteenth-century collection of stories describ-
ing the life of Francis and his followers.*

Young Monk (Denver) David Craig

Wine, water
like the red patch, yellow body of a peach
in a bowl, sit
behind layers of fine lacquer,

two millennia of pews
in the bowels of the dark Catholic
Church.
And on the cross up front,
on the wall behind the gold,
the altar. I feel the body, the wound,
in the new water, draw;
feel the corresponding motion
without noise.

Mass and, after, outside,
capped clothespins hold the flapping
bedsheet canvas, day: yellow sun head
tucked in a coat of trailing,
above-the-trees, wrap-around blue.
Garrulous birds and the sweet
smell of pine needle.

A calling. Fine as my stride,
elevated as the caps of waves,
spray and shingle, celibate air.

This life for Life
and a walk through the trees.

John Says Mass on All Souls' Day   David Craig

John lifts the bread
The body rises
like some flaming Chariot some furnace
The disc has arms
leaping cracking like whips

Dew pops
Each leaf spreads its fingers
Ambition and dust for a moment part

311

(tales like marbles
roll along a tile floor)

Even the pig
must for a hair second step back
as a brilliant flash of light ripples across antiquity
across a sooty
opened countenance

---

*In "Death Words," Les Murray suggests the power and fecundity of
sacrament in a "bunched rite" of mourning enacted by cattle. He points
to the Catholic mass and its sacrament of communion with the phrase,
"Eat, missa est," a play on the* Ite, missa est *of the Latin rite. Translated
variously as "Go, it is the dismissal," or "Go, the mass is [ended]," the
blessing is bestowed on the assembly by the priest in the closing moments
of the ceremony. A primitive rite captures the essence of sacrament for
Andrew Hudgins too, in "The Gift." The poem's speaker takes part in an
animal sacrifice that has overtones of the sacrifice of Christ, the "lamb"
of God. In the raw physicality of the "hot, gelatinous blood," Hudgins
depicts communion not as gesture or symbol but as carnal meal, flesh of
the sanctified victim feeding the flesh of the communicant. The poem's
setting relates the christic pattern to its anthropological ground, the an-
cient rituals of sacrificial death and communal rebirth that usually co-
incided with the seasonal change from winter to spring.*

---

from **Walking to the Cattle Place: Death Words** Les Murray

Beasts, cattle, have words, neither minor nor many.
The most frightening comes with a sudden stilt jump: the blood-
    moan
straight out of earth's marrow, that *clameur,* huge-mouthed,
raised when they nose death at one of their own

and only then. The whole milking herd at that cry
will come galloping, curveting, fish-leaping in furious play-steps

312

on the thunderstruck paddock, horning one another. A hock
    dance.
A puddle of blood will trigger it, even afterbirth.

They make a shield-wall over it, the foreheads jam down
on where death has stuck, as if to horn to death Death
(dumb rising numerous straw-trace). They pour out strength
enormously on the place, heap lungs' heat on the dead one.

It is one word they enact in the horn-gate there
and the neighbor herds all running to join in it
hit the near fences, creaking. We've unpicked many million
variants from our own like wake. This is a sample.

Roughly all at once, though, from the last-comers inward
the bunched rite breaks up. They grow aimless, calm down
in straggling completion. You might say Eat, missa est.
It is uttered just once for each charnel. They will feed

a tongue's nub away from then on. Their word of power
is formal, terrible, but, for an age now, stops there.
At best, ours ramify still. Perhaps God is inevitable.
He will not necessarily come, though, again, in our species.

The Gift Andrew Hudgins

They hung the lambs and cut their white throats. Blood
flowed down their chins and into earthen bowls.
Each time one filled, another bowl was placed
beneath the stream. Inside the pit, mesquite
burned down to an orange pulse, a coat of ash.

You asked about their myths and now, at last,
they talked as they prepared the feast. They stuffed
the carcasses with masa, then packed the hole
with four lambs, three jars of blood. Green leaves

313

were tucked around the meat and everything
was buried. The dirt included excrement.

All night you hunkered on your heels, talked, smoked,
almost forgot the buried flesh because
they offered you a legend no one outside
had ever heard. The coals burned slowly. At dawn
they dug it up: the tainted meat, the jars
of hot, gelatinous blood. Already knowing
how it would double you with cramps and heaving,
you held the rough bowl in both hands, flinched once,
then drank, from courtesy, the ruinous cup,
almost eager now that you had no choice.

The Leap

C *redo quia absurdum.* "I believe," said Tertullian, "because it is absurd." The fourth-century theologian could not have phrased it more poignantly, it seems, for Christians in the postmodern twilight of the second millennium. Against an imposing secular logic stands the absurdity of the Christian hope. Beginning with Søren Kierkegaard, theologians have spoken of the "leap of faith," and though Christians believe, they do so, as Christian poets observe, with an awareness of both the fragility and the stubbornness of their belief. Verse about faith ranges from the Christian struggle with despair and doubt to faith's demands on the intellect and on the will, to the nature of human knowing, and to the roles, when making the leap, of choice and grace.

In Nathaniel Hawthorne's The Scarlet Letter, *Hester Prynne is forced to wear a scarlet "A" as a punishment for her adulterous affair with the Reverend Arthur Dimmesdale, who eventually dies in her arms. Prynne's spiritual desolation is akin to that of the contemporary speaker in Norris's "Washing Dishes Late at Night," though they find themselves there for different reasons.*

Hester Prynne Recalls a Sunday in June Kathleen Norris

Our affair had just begun,
a sweet time.
I looked forward so to seeing him.
He was preaching,
a dark figure in sunlight,
when the moment struck,
leaving me dizzy,
and I saw quite clearly
that he had it all: ritual,
law, the Word,
and I had nothing but myself.

All that
is in the past.
Now respectable women
seek my hand:
I must find each broken thread
and make it sing.

They stay and talk now
as I sew.
It's as if they expect me
to tell them something,
a secret I brought up
out of chaos.

But I've been there too long, outside
the comfort they found
in other kingdoms.
Pray for me, I tell them,
if you are my friends.

Washing Dishes Late at Night Kathleen Norris

The room tips
Where we have rearranged it,
Where lovers rode
As in a fairy tale:
Now on a dragon, now a horse.

The room cradles
Their undressings,
Their unencumbered arms and legs.
You dislodge them
With the new pictures.
I dip my hands in soapy water.

This was to be a poem about faith,
But the room tips uneasily
Around our voices,
The pale light
Where we live,
Both of us afraid.

The Theology of Doubt Scott Cairns

I have come to believe this fickleness
of belief is unavoidable. As, for these
backlot trees, the annual loss
of leaves and fruit is unavoidable.
I remember hearing that soft-soap

about faith being given
only to the faithful—mean trick,
if you believe it. This afternoon,
during my walk, which
I have come to believe is good
for me, I noticed one of those
ridiculous leaves hanging
midway up an otherwise naked oak.
The wind did what it could
to bring it down, but the slow
learner continued dancing. Then again,
once, hoping for the last
good apple, I reached among
bare branches, pulling into my hand
an apple too soft for anything
and warm to the touch, fly-blown.

---

*Doubt is different from denial. Doubt is merely a questioning of belief.
But denial, as Raimundo Luz seems to demonstrate in "My Incredulity,"
is often a fear of belief. The poem's Lazarus is drawn from the gospel
accounts, which tell of his being brought back to life by Jesus, his per-
sonal friend who wept on learning of his death. Once again, Cairns
translates from the postmodern Portuguese of his favorite, wholly imag
ined troubadour.*

The Translation of Raimundo Luz: My Incredulity Scott Cairns

Lazarus, of course,
is another story altogether.

Lazarus does not
engage my better self, nor interest me.

Drink twice from the same
wrong cup? Say the idiot boy falls down,

319

gets back up and falls
again—this is some great trick?

Our giddy crowd should swoon?
Does the first runner turn back to mock the lost?

And if he does, should we
praise him for his extravagant bad taste?

No. His sort will not
profit close attention. His story—

neither lawful nor
expedient. Tear your linens to winding cloth.

Wrap him once for all.
When you've finished with your napkin, bind his lips.

He has had his say.
Bury Lazarus as often as it takes.

Not even Christ escaped uncertainty, and in "Salvatore Mundi: Via Crucis" (Latin for "savior of the world: way of the cross"), Denise Levertov is moved with compassion for Christ's "burden of humanness" by the genius of Rembrandt's art. Two key texts from Christian scripture reveal Christ in his most vulnerable of "mortal moments." The first is his agonized prayer in the garden of Gethsemane just hours before his trial and death, in which he asks God, if God is willing, to let the cup of torment pass him by. The other is one of Christ's "seven last sayings" on the cross. In it he quotes from Psalm 22, which concludes as a paean to God but begins with the line Christ is heard to speak: "My God, my God, why have you forsaken me?"

Salvator Mundi: Via Crucis   Denise Levertov

Maybe He looked indeed
much as Rembrandt envisioned Him
in those small heads that seem in fact
portraits of more than a model.
A dark, still young, very intelligent face,
a soul-mirror gaze of deep understanding, unjudging.
That face, in extremis, would have clenched its teeth
in a grimace not shown in even the great crucifixions.
The burden of humanness (I begin to see) exacted from Him
that He taste also the humiliation of dread,
cold sweat of wanting to let the whole thing go,
like any mortal hero out of his depth,
like anyone who has taken a step too far
and wants herself back.
The painters, even the greatest, don't show how,
in the midnight Garden,
or staggering uphill under the weight of the Cross,
He went through with even the human longing
to simply cease, to not be.
Not torture of body,
not the hideous betrayals humans commit
nor the faithless weakness of friends, and surely
not the anticipation of death (not then, in agony's grip)
was Incarnation's heaviest weight,
but this sickened desire to renege,
to step back from what He, Who was God,
had promised Himself, and had entered
time and flesh to enact.
Sublime acceptance, to be absolute, had to have welled
up from those depths where purpose
drifted for mortal moments.

For Wendell Berry, the silence and intellectual darkness that in one way or another shadows the faith of Hester Prynne and Raimundo Luz and Christ can be transformed into the very conditions that nurture spiritual growth. In "Sabbaths: 1980 VI," Berry argues that the mind unaided by faith must necessarily arrive at a darkness on the ultimate questions. But held in faith as mystery, darkness can be a power that "heals," like the "living shadow" created by the poem's canopy of young trees. The trees and growing thicket reclaim an abandoned field, which like all projects of human mind and toil, "our measure," is finally to be "lost in order we are ignorant of." In urging the reader to "leave word and argument" and to "be dark and still", Berry recalls several ideas in the tradition, among them Pascal's insistence that God is known finally in the heart, not the mind, and the mystic's "dark night of the soul," where "unknowing" is the way of union with God. This is not the same as saying that faith and reason cannot co-exist. But for Berry, as for all Judeo-Christian seekers, faith cannot exist at all without the mind's willing assent to the claims of experience.

from Sabbaths: 1980 VI Wendell Berry

The intellect so ravenous to know
And in its knowing hold the very light,
Disclosing what is so and what not so,

Must finally know the dark, which is its right
And liberty; it's blind in what it sees.
Bend down, go in by this low door, despite

The thorn and briar that bar the way. The trees
Are young here in the heavy undergrowth
Upon an old field worn out by disease

Of human understanding; greed and sloth
Did bad work that this thicket now conceals,
Work lost to rain or ignorance or both.

The young trees make a darkness here that heals,
And here the forms of human thought dissolve
Into the living shadow that reveals

All orders made by mortal hand or love
Or thought come to a margin of their kind,
Are lost in order we are ignorant of

Which stirs great fear and sorrow in the mind.
The field, if it will thrive, must do so by
Exactitude of thought, by skill of hand,

And by the clouded mercy of the sky;
It is a mortal clarity between
Two darks, of Heaven and of Earth. The why

If it is *our* measure. Seen and unseen,
Its causes shape it as it is, a while.
O bent by fear and sorrow, now bend down,

Leave word and argument, be dark and still,
And come into the joy of healing shade.
Rest from your work. Be still and dark until

You grow as unopposing, unafraid
As the young trees, without thought or belief;
Until the shadow Sabbath light has made

shudders, breaks open, shines in every leaf.

Richard Wilbur also speaks of the limits of knowing in "Icarium Mare."
Three characters inhabit the poem, their stories intersecting on the Icar-
ian Sea near Greece. The first is Icarus, whose father. Daedalus, made
him the pair of wings glued together with wax that melted when Icarus
became heady with the godlike power of flight and climbed too close to
the sun. Icarus fell and drowned near Samos, which in the third cen-

tury B.C. *was the home of Aristarchus, an astronomer with the remark-
able view that the earth rotated on its axis and revolved around the sun.
Not far from Samos lies the island of Patmos, where Saint John the Di-
vine experienced his visions of the new heaven and the new earth that
fill the Book of Revelations. Wilbur contends that Aristarchus with his
instruments and John with his interior vision—his skull like a geode
whose hollow center gleams with crystal—did not attempt, as Icarus
did, to escape the gravitational pull of the earthly senses in the quest to
know, yet even then the objects of both men's "insight and calculation"
lay well beyond earth's "little shed." There is much that we can know of
the "loose change" of heaven and earth, Wilbur concludes, but of its
"bullion" there is much, as earth-bound mortals, we cannot.*

Icarium Mare Richard Wilbur

We have heard of the undimmed air
Of the True Earth above us, and how here,
   Shut in our sea-like atmosphere,
We grope like muddled fish. Perhaps from there,

   That fierce lucidity,
Came Icarus' body tumbling, flayed and trenched
   By waxen runnels, to be quenched
Near Samos riding in the actual sea,

   Where Aristarchus first
Rounded the sun in thought; near Patmos, too,
   Where John's bejeweled inward view
Descried an angel in the solar burst.

   The reckoner's instruments,
The saint's geodic skull bowed in his cave—
   Insight and calculation brave
Black distances exorbitant to sense,

Which in its little shed
Of broken light knows wonder all the same.
    Where else do lifting wings proclaim
The advent of the fire-gapped thunderhead,

    Which swells the streams to grind
What oak and olive grip their roots into,
    Shading us as we name anew
Creatures without which vision would be blind?

    This is no outer dark
But a small province haunted by the good,
    Where something may be understood
And where, within the sun's coronal arc,

    We keep our proper range,
Aspiring, with this lesser globe of sight,
    To gather tokens of the light
Not in the bullion, but in the loose change.

Wilbur's "Dubious Night" is about the poet's faith versus the faith of God. The poet intensifies the dubiousness of his night with linguistic terms denoting ambiguity, curtailment, and the oblique: diphthong (a fusing of separate vowel sounds), elision (omitting a first or last syllable when combining words), synecdoche (a part standing for the whole—"a fleet of twenty sail"). Another resonance of Wilbur's terminology is the highly dubious relation between language and a God who is ineffable, who eludes all linguistic equivalence, who can be described, and that lamely, only by trope or metaphor as being like a parent or lover or an infinite light. The "kyrie" Wilbur mentions is a mantric Christian prayer with the refrain "Lord have mercy."

A Dubious Night Richard Wilbur

A bell diphthonging in an atmosphere
Of shying night air summons some to prayer
Down in the town, two deep lone miles from here,

Yet wallows faint or sudden everywhere,
In every ear, as if the twist wind wrung
Some ten years' tangled echoes from the air.

What kyries it says are mauled among
The queer elisions of the mist and murk,
Of lights and shapes; the senses were unstrung,

Except that one star's synecdochic smirk
Burns steadily to me, that nothing's odd
And firm as ever is the masterwork.

I weary of the confidence of God.

That God's "confidence" can not only weary but intimidate believers
struggling in their faith is the subject of Louise Erdrich's "Fooling God."
The poem's speaker tries to protect herself by a strategy of manipula-
tion, presupposing a wholly anthropomorphic deity and revealing an
ambivalent faith tied to an ambivalent sense of self. Erdrich's speaker
appropriates the biblical image of the mustard grain, Christ's metaphor
for the tiny seed of faith that grows to purpose and beauty, though even
faith the size of the grain itself can "move mountains." The subject
shifts from the tortured faith of the believer to the unshakable doubt of
the skeptic in David Citino's "The Man Who Couldn't Believe."

Fooling God Louise Erdrich

I must become small and hide where he cannot reach.
I must become dull and heavy as an iron pot.

I must be tireless as rust and bold as roots
growing through the locks on doors
and crumbling the cinderblocks
of the foundations of his everlasting throne.
I must be strange as pity so he'll believe me.
I must be terrible and brush my hair
so that he finds me attractive.
Perhaps if I invoke Clare, the patron saint of television.
Perhaps if I become the images
passing through the cells of a woman's brain.

I must become very large and block his sight.
I must be sharp and impetuous as knives.
I must insert myself into the bark of his apple trees,
and cleave the bones of his cows. I must be the marrow
that he drinks into his cloud-wet body.
I must be careful and laugh when he laughs.
I must turn down the covers and guide him in.
I must fashion his children out of playdough, blue, pink, green.
I must pull them from between my legs
and set them before the television.

I must hide my memory in a mustard grain
so that he'll search for it over time until time is gone.
I must lose myself in the world's regard and disparagement.
I must remain this person and be no trouble.
None at all. So he'll forget.
I'll collect dust out of reach,
a single dish from a set, a flower made of felt,
a tablet the wrong shape to choke on.

I must become essential and file everything
under my own system,
so we can lose him and his proofs and adherents.
I must be a doubter in a city of belief
that hails his signs (the great footprints
long as limousines, the rough print on the wall).

327

On the pavement where his house begins
fainting women kneel. I'm not among them
although they polish the brass tongues of his lions
with their own tongues
and taste the everlasting life.

The Man Who Couldn't Believe David Citino

He was the sort who *entertained*
doubts. Even in early childhood
when his mother would call out
"Your daddy's home," he'd look up

from toys that were nothing more
than toys and, with a smile
both knowing and superior,
shake his head from side to side.

When Sister Mary Appassionata asked
"Why did God make you?"
he looked her straight in the eye.
"Damned if I know," he answered.

Even love was out of the question,
a series of motions out and in,
crescendo, diminuendo. "You're no worse
than the last one, and I need it,"

he'd calmly plead. "I do. I do."
It rained or shined on his parades
for meteorological reasons only.
Stars were there because they were.

Forget charmed quarks and neutrinos,
though he admitted that molecules

might exist. He could perceive
Brownian motion in the shudder

of maple leaf upon the river,
even though he suspected wind
as the rational explanation.
He found himself on earth

to consume and be consumed in turn,
to grow old and fill a hole
in some city ceremony. Afraid
of the unknown, the dark? No way.

He was all *I*. Heaven and hell
were this moment, this one, this.
He died as he lived, fearless
and alone. He didn't have a prayer.

The speaker of the sonnet from Geoffrey Hill's "Funeral Music" shares the mind and the temperament of Citino's protagonist who couldn't believe but is entirely unlike him, it seems, in that he can only *believe, in spite of himself. A skeptic at heart, he would paradoxically find more comfort in the claims of a philosopher like Averroes, Aristotle's twelfth-century Arab translator, who held that the intellect was supreme. But what of those whom Averroes could claim as his own? In "The Humanist," Hill takes an example from the Renaissance, when "man" was the measure of all things.*

---

from **Funeral Music** Geoffrey Hill

Let mind be more precious than soul; it will not
Endure. Soul grasps its price, begs its own peace,
Settles with tears and sweat, is possibly
Indestructible. That I can believe.
Though I would scorn the mere instinct of faith,

329

Expediency of assent, if I dared,
What I dare not is a waste history
Or void rule. Averroes, old heathen,
If only you had been right, if Intellect
Itself were absolute law, sufficient grace,
Our lives could be a myth of captivity
Which we might enter: an unpeopled region
Of ever new-fallen snow, a palace blazing
With perpetual silence as with torches.

The Humanist Geoffrey Hill

The *Venice* portrait: he
Broods, the achieved guest
Tired and word-perfect
At the Muses' table.

Virtue is virtù These
lips debate and praise
Some rich aphorism,
A delicate white meat.

The commonplace hands once
Thick with Plato's blood
(Tasteless! tasteless!) are laid
Dryly against the robes.

The themes of Citino and Hill are cast on a public scale by Les Murray in "Ultima Ratio." Although the poem's context in the original German is the "final solution" of the Nazis, Murray was inspired to translate Jünger's poem in 1990 after the fall of the Berlin Wall. Ratio in the Latin means plan or method, but also reason and science. For Murray and others, features of the history of both fascism and communism warn of the perils of idealizing, with Geoffrey Hill's Averroes, the Rational as Ultimate.

Ultima Ratio Les Murray

Translated from the German of
Friedrich Georg Jünger (1945)

Like vapor, the titanic scheme
is dissipated,
everything grows rusty now
that they created.

They hoped to make their craze
the lasting Plan,
now it falls apart everywhere,
sheet steel and span.

Raw chaos lies heaped up
on wide display.
Be patient. Even the fag-ends
will crumble away.

Everything they made contained
what brought their fall
and the great burden they were
crushes them all.

The demise of the rationalist premise is explored in Mindwalk, *a recent novel and film in which three vacationers in France passionately exchange ideas on the environment, the new physics and contemporary philosophy. In "After 'Mindwalk,'" Denise Levertov ponders the implications for faith in the deconstruction of the post-Enlightenment notions of coherence, matter, space-time and determinacy arising from the latest investigations of science. Blaise Pascal's "dread," roused in him three hundred years ago by the "infinite spaces" between the stars, now turns to the interior universe of our physical beings. Science defines us as "bits of the Void" still reeling from the Big Bang, Levertov's "Fiat Lux," Latin for "Let there be light." So infinitesimal and indeterminate is the stardust within us it is better comprehended as mere "flux," yet for the poet*

this makes it all the more credible, in its mystery, as a spiritual host.
Modestly, Levertov reaffirms her faith, reconciling it with the toppled
certainties of language, perception and knowledge. Deconstruction
seems as much in the poem's syntax as in its subject. Levertov arranges
words of philosophical density into a single trailing sentence torn by
qualifications and asides, a structure subverting itself, repeatedly threat-
ening collapse, until the sudden repose of the last phrase.

After "Mindwalk" Denise Levertov

Once we've laboriously
disconnected our old conjunctions—
'physical,' 'solid,' 'real,' 'material'—freed them
from antique measure to admit what,
even through eyes naked but robed
in optic devices, is not perceptible (oh,
precisely is not perceptible!): admitted
that 'large' and 'small' are bereft
of meaning, since not matter but process, process only,
gathers itself to appear
knowable: *world, universe*—

then what we feel
in moments of bleak arrest,
panic's black cloth falling
over our faces, over our breath,

is a new twist of Pascal's dread,
a shift of scrutiny,
                    its object now
inside our flesh, the *infinite spaces* discovered
within our own atoms, inside the least
particle of what we supposed
our mortal selves (and *in* and *out*side,
what are they?)—its object now

bits of the Void left over from before
the Fiat Lux, immeasurably
incorporate in our discarnate, fictive,
(yes, but sentient,) notion of substance,
inaccurate as our language,
flux which the soul alone
pervades, elusive but persistent.

Like "After 'Mindwalk'" Annie Dillard's found poem, "The Sign of Your Father," confronts the partial, fragmentary basis of knowledge, especially spiritual knowledge, and the profound mystery that is both the object and the source of faith. Dillard's sentences derive from E. Hennecke, New Testament Apocrypha, vol. 1, *edited by Wilheim Schneemeicher, English translation edited by R. McL. Wilson, 1963.*

The Sign of Your Father Annie Dillard

I

(The grain of wheat) . . .
Place shut in . . .
It was laid beneath and invisible . . .
Its wealth imponderable?

And as they were in perplexity
At his strange question, Jesus
On his way came (to the) bank
Of the (riv)er Jordan,
Stretched out (hi)s right
Hand, (fill)ed it with . . .
And sowed . . . on the . . .
And then . . . water. . . And . . .
Before (their eyes),
Brought fruit . . . much
To the jo(y?) . . .

Jesus said: "Become
Passers-by."

He said: "Lord, there are many
Around the cistern, but
Nobody in the cistern."

And we said to him, "O Lord
Are you speaking again
In parables to us?" And he said
To us, "Do not be grieved..."

II

(His) disciples ask him (and s)ay:
How should we fas(t and how
Should we pr)ay and how (...
...) and what should we observe
(Of the traditions?) Jesus says (.....
.....) do not (.....
.....) truth (.....
.....) hidden (.....

"This saying has been handed down
In a particularly sorry condition."

They all wondered and were afraid.
The Redeemer (σωτήρ) smiled
And spake to them: Of what
Are you thinking, or (ἤ) about what
Are you at a loss (απορειν), or
(ἤ) what are you seeking?

If they ask you: "What
Is the sign of your Father in you?"
You say to them: "It is a movement
And a rest (αναπαυσισ)."

Maura Eichner visualizes her faith in "Message from Inland" as an action of the will, using the "riding light" of the small seagoing vessel as her key image. But Scott Cairns's Raimundo Luz seems more to have stumbled upon faith as a gift, an empowering grace, like that of the paralytic cured by Christ who was able to pick up his mat and walk. Luz relishes the mystery of it, the "comfort" of "suspecting more than the evidence allows." In Geoffrey Hill's "Lachrimae Amantis" (Latin, "Tears of the Lover"), faith comes with wholly indiscriminate grace to its "half-faithful" speaker.

Message from Inland Maura Eichner

I am clothed
in the seamless
garment
of fog.

No gulls cry.
No nervous horn
sounds
another ship.

No fragrance
of kelp stirs,
no wind
of sea-change.

Red mud slips
like a secret
beneath
my feet.

I know
what happens

to seamless
garments.

I have lashed
a riding
light
to my heart.

The Translation of Raimundo Luz: My Good Luck Scott Cairns

Fortunately, there are mitigating circumstances.
Fortunately, Raimundo doesn't get what he deserves.
Confronted by embarrassment, I lift my bed and walk.

The comfort lies in fingering the incoherent for the true.
The comfort lies in suspecting more than evidence allows.
My only rule: if I understand something, it's no mystery.

As you might suppose, I miss my father very much;
and if I think of his dying, I can become deeply sad.
Giving yourself to appearances can do a lot of harm.

So I remember the morning my father died, and the ache
of his relief, the odd, uncanny joy which began then,
and which returns unbidden, undeserved, mercifully.

Lachrimae Amantis Geoffrey Hill

What is there in my heart that you should sue
so fiercely for its love? What kind of care
brings you as though a stranger to my door
through the long night and in the icy dew

seeking the heart that will not harbor you,
that keeps itself religiously secure?

At this dark solstice filled with frost and fire
your passion's ancient wounds must bleed anew.

So many nights the angel of my house
has fed such urgent comfort through a dream,
whispered "your lord is coming, he is close"

that I have drowsed half-faithful for a time
bathed in pure tones of promise and remorse:
"tomorrow I shall wake to welcome him."

---

*In David Brendan Hopes's "Advent Sequence," the mystery of the poet's
faith persists amid the worst extremities of sorrow and loss. Hopes ends
on a note of loving, almost ecstatic acceptance, offering to give his an-
guish "back to glory" and to forgive, against himself, the "One who is
remembrance" if ever He "reweaves... the deep ripped Way" of cross
and hope. Appearing again is the motif of hearts presented as food,
which is prominent in Hopes's later work, a re-imaging of the eucharis-
tic meal. The poem is set in winter, during the four weeks of Advent
preceding Christmas, in the Pisgah Mountain region of North Carolina
near Hopes's Asheville home.*

---

from **Advent Sequence** David Brendan Hopes

When the wolf moon howls, when the juncos,
migrants to this bitter land,
twitter their testament of somewhere worse;
when the creek is stiffened silver and
her sleepers, the frogs and chrysalides,
breathe crystal into crystal space;

when creatures caught in the open weave their last dream
with the dream of dead planets, colder, brighter,
never again to wake: Lord, I think of You.
Stars sag on Pisgah. Moon closes to the ridge,

gun-metal rolling on the mountain,
bright rim to black rim, a crushing wheel

gouged by the December of the trees.
Moon's flak bursts against the owl's wings.
Blaze and black contend.
I kneel on stone. I gather from Hominy Creek the blue
glaze shining and shifted, the finger-freezing mercury.
I gather the lights. I hoard the weapons to my hand—

pity, fury, a human face ringed with its
inevitable nimbus of tears.
After long silence I have returned—
"For You" it is best to say, but we know better.
All for an ambush, God, against Thee.
I hunch in night and make my poem.

      Go, song, I tell it.
Go to the owl cross-winged over Pisgah.
Go to the coon hound-bayed, to spider weaving
in her broil of hunger.
Go, song. Tell how heart succeeds from wound to flame.
Tell who holds his little blasphemies into the wind.

      Go tell them.
Say I lift my fist to the judging stars.
Say if they threaten I eat their hearts.
Say if they circle I meet them whirling.
Say if they condemn I vomit wind and fire.
Say whatever thing they maim, I parry healing equal.

Go song to my lovers lost by knife and plague
and sadness in the dark that called them blameless
from their birthday Edens.
Oh, unaccountably by night
I start to sing. See how the beauties float
from the ground with their dead rose laurels to listen.

338

See them lean in, shaking their gold heads,
twangling their lutes with single strings,
hearing no cry from me not cried already
by children lost in the dark woods of the world
before the worlds began.
Child, they say, *child.*

Like owls in gray roosts they natter
how all had ground to silence all the same before.
But I ask a gift of them one by one.
They listen. Sigh. They pull something
from their vault of bones. I accept.
It is their hearts. I eat.

   Go song.
Say I lift hands only to the One who is remembrance,
of turning back to glory what was burnt away.
Say if He comes walking I will greet Him running.
Say if He reweaves one ravel of the deep ripped Way,
I answer with forgiveness equal to the world.

The Holy

*H*oliness is the ultimate fulfillment of Christianity's mandate, the perfection of love to which all of its followers are called. Some answer in a way that recollects the holiness of Christ himself and these are known as saints. Their legacy is passed on largely in the form of "lives" because the narrative conveys the lesson of sainthood, the moment-to-moment practice of right action. The holy life is countercultural, often to the extent that it ends in martyrdom. But willing as they are to be tested by death, in the holism of being holy the saints participate in their humanity, and in the humanity of others, with fervor. Because of this, or because, as some put it, "saints are sinners who just keep trying," the cult of the saints manages the classic dramatic formula, to instruct and to entertain. For believers, holy ones reveal the truth of Christian living whether their stories draw on history, myth, or a little of both.

Saint Christina is the subject of one of the more colorful vignettes of Christian lore. Born to a French peasant family in 1150, at twenty-two she was pronounced dead after a seizure. David Citino describes the astonishing turn of events at her funeral mass and what happened afterward, closely following the traditional accounts. In the end, the poem's slapstick delivers the sobering witness of Christina's life, lived out eccentrically to the age of seventy, besieged by the smell of mortality everywhere.

Citino goes back a millenium before Christina for his account of the martyrdom of Saint Ignatius. Not to be confused with the sixteenth-century Jesuit founder of the same name, Ignatius was appointed bishop of Antioch by the apostle Peter and became a leading spirit for the early Christians in volatile times. He was put to death in Rome by the emperor Trajan in A.D. 107. The saint speaks not just for martyrs but for all idealists in his reflection on the legacy of his life—"Why has a man been ...?" Citino's monologue concludes with a poetic recasting of the famous "bread" speech Ignatius is said to have given as the lions came out to devour him in the arena.

Christina the Astonishing: Virgin David Citino

Death's stone rolled away from mouth and eyes,
she jerked upright in the open coffin
during Requiem, dressed in clothes
she was to wear to heaven. The place emptied
in seconds, mourners thundering down aisles
pursued by the one fate worse than death,
the priest gulping bread and wine
as he stumbled out the door. Their fear,
at once foreign and familiar, lingered,
a pall, a scream inside her head.
She was the sorriest thing on earth.
"I've been to paradise, lain with angels," she swore.
"Why've I been brought back? What time
is it? What's that awful smell?"

343

She sought apart—in belfry and burrow,
currents far enough from shore for her
to be able to dream of no one else,
mountain crags softened by wildflower, pine,
ovens warm with loaves that rose like miracles—
a parole from earth's bony penitentiary.
Naked in the baptismal font, scrubbing flesh
until it bled, she ached for a world
cleansed by forty days of rain, plagues
of locust, brimstone. It seemed
she was always downwind of somebody,
and when there was no wind the odor was there
stronger than ever, bodies living
as they died, cloying essence of the begotten,
urgent perfume of decay.

Ignatius, Bishop and Martyr David Citino

Even now at the end,
the growls of the crowd fluttering
in my gut, my only fear's that,
reading my life some day
on your knees, when it seems
the state's every fang has settled
in your flesh and the screams
of those who need are too near
for you not to hear, you'll
think me too hungry for death.

Why has a man been, if
in being no more he startles
no one, showers no timid spectator
with blood, sends no shiver
up and down the spine? I believe:
let my faith double, become
the two hard beasts

who'll grind me up until, fine
as the dust of this loud arena,
purer for a moment than any man,
I'll rise, bread of a famished Christ.

May I please you all.
May the one who sent me here
make of me one good meal.

Dietrich Bonhoeffer (1906–1945) lived and died by the measure of Ig-
natius. The German Protestant theologian and martyr preached a
costly Christian discipleship that urged dynamic participation in secu-
lar affairs. As the Nazis rose to power in the 1930s, Bonhoeffer railed
against the "cheap grace" offered by the churches that he felt was dulling
the faithful to their ethical responsibilities. The Nazis jailed Bonhoeffer
in 1943 for his part in the resistance, executing him two years later
when documents linked him to an assassination plot against Hitler.
Poet Geoffrey Hill takes Christian hope, and hopes new awareness will
arise, from Bonhoeffer's life and death.

"Christmas Trees" Geoffrey Hill

Bonhoeffer in his skylit cell
bleached by the flares' candescent fall,
pacing out his own citadel,

restores the broken themes of praise,
encourages our borrowed days,
by logic of his sacrifice.

Against wild reasons of the state
his words are quiet but not too quiet.
We hear too late or not too late.

Another twentieth-century life distinguished by its spirituality of action is that of Peter Maurin, "peasant philosopher" and "agitator." Emigrating from France in the 1920s to homestead in Canada, Maurin suffered early reversals and soon was working as an itinerant day laborer. In response to the Great Depression, Maurin developed a radical vision of empowerment for the poor and unemployed. The excerpt from David Craig's narrative poem "Peter Maurin" begins in New York City with the first meeting between Maurin and pacifist Dorothy Day (1889–1970). Realizing they shared the desire for a forum to disseminate their views, in 1933 Maurin and Day launched The Catholic Worker, *a monthly still in continuous publication. The hospitality house and farming commune they went on to establish became the basis for a movement that has spread throughout North America. Later in Craig's poem, racial activist John LaFarge seeks the philosopher-prophet in Harlem, where a biblical realm of "man lion ox eagle" exists in much-altered guise. Maurin's life provides an example of Christian holiness in its lived solidarity with the poor, and its passion for economic and social justice.*

from **Peter Maurin (1877–1949)** David Craig

> *If a thing is dull*
> *it is not Christian.*
> *—St. Philip Neri*

> *You are the salt of the earth;*
> *but if the salt has lost its taste,*
> *how shall its saltness be*
> *restored?*
> *—Jesus (Matthew 5:13)*

Peter pumped Dorothy's hand,
had a tie on.

An old coffee stain stretched,
the shirt, smoothing with working valves.
His shoulders opened like a vault.

"CLARIFICATION OF THOUGHT!" echoed
through the station like the slamming of lockers,
a dark patch where money had been,
wrinkles showing that coat's curled value.
"PERSONALIST ACTION!" thumped down stairs,
accosted strangers.

His broad head contained pines junkyards
his eyes tread silver waters carried
the weight of men
hanged black stones from the red sleeves of an oak.
Gray hair a horde of night birds
in the grating of a gathering tree.
Leather worker's skin sun-gouged,
forded rivers steel bands
around the mountains.
"VOLUNTARY POVERTY....AGRONOMIC UNIVERSITIES...
THE PROPER USE OF PROPERTY." Worn left heel,
pantleg pinned. "PACIFISM"
Shoes companion to the soil....

Jesuit John LaFarge 1937,
walking down the rat-gnawed cut
of a Harlem street toward
a storefront hospitality center
...looked up at the night sky
saw no Old Testament storm.
    Perhaps it was already here.
    Harlem sharp glint in the brown opening
    of the eye.
He saw no clouds glowing with fire coals.
No angels with four faces.
man lion ox eagle.
    The only lions the buildings
    toothless gnawing the air couched in the dark
    on stringy cords of haunch beneath
    razor white stars.

There were no cloven feet.
No eyes on the rims of great wheels.
    The only wheels here collided with potholes,
    rattled a sorry carriage a can of screws....

His heart sank.
There was no electricity no money
for candles.
But then in the streetlight
he could make out a finger voices
from inside: Peter.
The stirring of reeds
along a Babylonian canal.

"So he goes to Notre Dame, the guest of this big philosopher,
Emmanuel Chapman ya see, and the meeting, the meeting
goes fine. Smooth as a baby's butt. So anyway, later, at the bus
station Peter gets to talking and forgets which bus he's board-
ing. Instead of getting on the bus for Cincinnati he gets on the
one going to Cleveland. Talk about a death wish. Anyway,
someone points it out to him. And he says, are you ready for
this? So he says, he says, "That's alright . . . I know people in
Cleveland!"   (sound of chair falling over)....

Peter took the moment
wrapped it in a blanket:
streets garbage trucks hanging laundry,
in the form of back to back,
sleeping drunks....
He sailed mystic waters from the walls and windows,
blossoms floating on water through his
fired veins.

"Let the fire spread
hand to steel
to hand."

He agreed with a concentration camp priest who once said that
man's freedom was so precious that no one should ever exert
a personal influence to win another to an idea, that it was the
truth alone that should attract.

Eyes on you Peter said what you had to hear.
Listening was your baggage.
He gave love without sympathy because sympathy
was not love.
He learned simply
to always go to God.
He never passed a hungry man gave away coats,
socks said workers should wash the guest's feet,
the guests having already offered a freeing hand....

And the burning:
"I have written enough. It is time
for the young people to take over"
And for five years
leaves fell off the tree....

In the summer of '48 he sat quietly
beneath the pines, attended.
The previous April he had disappeared
Workers reached every corner
of the district: dives subways,
called distant friends.
He appeared four days later without words,
They put a note in his pocket,
"I am Peter Maurin,
founder of the Catholic Worker Movement."

Like Maurin, Saint Clare (1193–1253) lived in radical poverty in the
service of others. Because of her extraordinary example and gifts of
speech, Saint Francis made her the head of a new order of religious
women known as the Poor Clares. In "Saint Clare," Louise Erdrich

develops the saint's relationship with her sister Agnes, who after a time joined Clare in the convent at Basia. When their father dispatched a gang of retainers to drag Agnes home, tradition has it that the prayers of her sister foiled the men by making the slender Agnes so heavy none of them could budge her.

Saint Clare Louise Erdrich

The Call
First I heard the voice throbbing across the river.
I saw the white phosphorescence of his robe.
As he stepped from the boat, as he walked
there spread from each footfall a black ripple,
from each widening ring a wave,
from the waves a sea that covered the moon.
So I was seized in total night
and I abandoned myself in his garment
like a fish in a net. The slip knots
tightened on me and I rolled
until the sudden cry hauled me out.
Then this new element, a furnace of mirrors,
in which I watch myself burn.
The scales of my old body melt away like coins,
for I was rich, once, and my father
had already chosen my husband.

Before
I kept my silver rings in a box of porphyrite.
I ate salt on bread. I could sew.
I could mend the petals of a rose.
My nipples were pink, my sister's brown.
In the fall we filled our wide skirts with walnuts
for our mother to crack with a wooden hammer.
She put whorled meats into our mouths,
closed our lips with her finger

350

and said to Hush. So we slept
and woke to find our bodies arching into bloom.
It happened to me first,
the stain on the linen, the ceremonial
seal which was Eve's fault.
In the church at Assisi I prayed. I listened
to Brother Francis and I took his vow.
The embroidered decorations at my bodice
turned real, turned to butterflies and were dispersed.
The girdle of green silk, the gift from my father
slithered from me like a vine,
so I was something else that grew from air,
and I was light, the skeins of hair
that my mother had divided with a comb of ivory
were cut from my head and parceled to the nesting birds.

My Life As a Saint
I still have the nest, now empty,
woven of my hair, of the hollow grass,
and silken tassels at the ends of seeds.
From the window where I prayed,
I saw the house wrens gather
dark filaments from air
in the shuttles of their beaks.
The cup was made fast
to the body of the tree,
bound with the silver excrescence of the spider,
and the eggs, four in number,
ale gold and trembling,
curved in a thimble of down.

The hinged beak sprang open, tongue erect,
screaming to be fed
before the rest of the hatchling emerged.
I did not eat. I smashed my bread to crumbs upon the sill
for the parents were weary as God is weary.

351

We have the least mercy on the one
who created us,
who introduced us to this hunger.

The smallest mouth starved and the mother
swept it out like rubbish with her wing.
I found it that dawn, after lauds,
already melting into the heat of the flagstone,
a transparent teaspoon of flesh,
the tiny beak shut, the eyes still sealed
within a membrane of the clearest blue.

I buried the chick in a box of leaves.
The rest grew fat and clamorous.
I put my hand through the thorns one night and felt the bowl,
the small brown begging bowl,
waiting to be filled.

By morning, the strands of the nest disappear
into each other, shaping
an emptiness within me that I make lovely
as the immature birds make the air
by defining tunnels and the spirals
of the new sustenance. And then,
no longer hindered by the violence of their need,
they take to other trees, fling themselves
deep into the world.

Agnes
When you entered the church at Basia
holding the scepter of the almond's
white branch and when you struck
the bedrock floor, how was I to know
the prayer would be answered?
I heard the drum of hooves long in the distance,
and I held my forehead to the stone of the altar.
I asked for nothing. It is almost

impossible to ask for nothing.
I have spent my whole life trying.

I know you felt it, when his love spilled.
That ponderous light. From then on you endured
happiness, the barge you pulled
as I pull mine. This
is called density of purpose.
As you learned, you must shed everything else
in order to bear it.

That is why, toward the end of your life,
when at last there was nothing I could not relinquish,
I allowed you to spring forward without me.
Sister, I unchained myself. For I was always
the heaviest passenger,
the stone wagon of example,
the freight you dragged all the way to heaven,
and how were you to release yourself
from me, then, poor mad horse,
except by reaching the gate?

Lady Julian was a writer, visionary, and mystic, the first feminist the-
ologian to call God "Mother." She experienced fifteen visions, or "shew-
ings," on May 8, 1373, while living as a spiritual contemplative in a
small house attached to the church of Saint Julian in Norwich, England.
Denise Levertov's rendering of Julian's life centers on the most famous of
these showings, that of "a little thing, the quantity of a hazel nut," as Ju-
lian later describes in Revelations of Divine Love, *"lying in the palm of*
my hand, and to my understanding it was as round as any ball." Ju-
lian's elaboration of her showing is a mystic's vision of Oneness in
which the whole of creation subsists in each of its particulars: "I looked
thereupon and thought: 'What may this be?' And I was answered in a
general way thus: 'It is all that is made.' . . . Wouldst thou know thy
Lord's meaning in this thing? Learn it well. Love was his meaning."

---

from **The Showings: Lady Julian of Norwich, 1342–1416**
Denise Levertov

   • • •

Julian, there are vast gaps we call black holes,
unable to picture what's both dense and vacant;

and there's the dizzying multiplication of all
language can name or fail to name, unutterable
swarming of molecules. All Pascal
imagined he could not stretch his mind to imagine
is known to exceed his dread.

And there's the earth of our daily history,
its memories, its present filled with the grain
of one particular scrap of carpentered wood we happen
to be next to, its waking light on one especial leaf,
this word or that, a tune in this key not another,
beat of our hearts *now,* good or bad,
dying or being born, eroded, vanishing—

And you ask us to turn our gaze
inside out, and see
a little thing, the size of a hazelnut, and believe
it is our world? Ask us to see it lying
in God's pierced palm? That it encompasses
every awareness our minds contain? All Time?
All limitless space given form in this
medieval enigma?
                      Yes, this is indeed
what you ask, sharing
the mystery you were shown: *all that is made:*
a little thing, the size of a hazelnut, held safe
in God's pierced palm.

   • • •

What she petitioned for was never
instead of something else.
Thirty was older than it is now. She had not married
but was no starveling; if she had loved,
she had been loved. Death or some other destiny
bore him away, death or some other bride
changed him. Whatever that story,
long since she had travelled
through and beyond it. Somehow,
reading or read to, she'd spiralled
up within tall towers
of learning, steeples of discourse.
Bells in her spirit
rang new changes.

                    Swept beyond event, one longing
outstripped all others; that reality,
supreme reality,
be witnessed. To desire wounds—
three, no less, no more—
is audacity, not, five centuries early, neurosis;
it's the desire to enact metaphor, for flesh to make known
to intellect (as uttered song
      makes known to voice
      as image to eye)
make known in bone and breath
(and not die) God's agony.

. . .

"To understand her you must imagine..."
A childhood then;
the dairy's bowls of clabber, of rich cream,
ghost-white in shade, and outside
the midsummer gold, humming of dandelions.
To run back and forth, into the chill again,
the sweat of slate, a cake of butter
set on a green leaf—out once more
over slab of stone into hot light, hot

wood, the swinging gate!
A spire we think ancient split the blue
between two trees, a half-century old—
she thought it ancient.
Her father's hall, her mother's bower,
nothing was dull. The cuckoo
was changing its tune. In the church
there was glass in the windows, glass
colored like the world. You could see
Christ and his mother and his cross,
you could see his blood, the throne of God.
In the fields
calves were lowing, the shepherd was taking the sheep
to new pasture.
                    Julian perhaps
not yet her name, this child's
that vivid woman.

. . .

God's wounded hand
reached out to place in hers
the entire world, "round as a ball,
small as a hazelnut." Just so one day
of infant light remembered
her mother might have given
into her two cupped palms
a newlaid egg, warm from the hen;
just so her brother
risked to her solemn joy
his delicate treasure,
a sparrow's egg from the hedgerow,
What can this be? *the eye of her understanding* marveled.

God for a moment in our history
placed in that five-fingered
human nest
the macrocosmic egg, sublime paradox,

brown hazelnut of All that Is—
made, and belov'd, and preserved.
As still, waking each day within
our microcosm, we find it, and ourselves....

.   .   .

She lived in dark times, as we do;
war, and the black Death, hunger, strife,
torture, massacre. She knew
all of this, she felt it
sorrowfully, mournfully,
shaken as men shake
a cloth in the wind.
                  But Julian, Julian—
I turn to you:
              you clung to joy through tears and sweat
rolled down your face like the blood
you watched pour down *in beads uncountable*
as rain from the eaves:
clung like an acrobat, by your teeth, fiercely,
to a cobweb-thin high-wire, your certainty
of infinite mercy, witnessed
with your own eyes, with outward sight
in your small room, with inward sight
in your untrammeled spirit—
knowledge we long to share:
Love was his meaning.

The three "wounds" that Julian prayed for and received were a recollec-
tion of Christ's sufferings, an illness, and a "wilful longing" toward
God. Levertov interprets Julian's desire for the first two wounds, which
"healed" just before the showings, not as perversity or neurosis but as
part of an audacious craving for all dimensions of experience, "never /
instead of something else," just as she depicts Julian's childhood as an
imaginative openness to sensation and mystery.

David Brendan Hopes presents one of Julian's "shewings" as yet another wound, a dark evocation of the sufferings of her epoch and the uncertainties of human existence. The voice of Lear, king of ancient Briton—"We are not in our right minds"—is part of the poem's mix of British mythology, apocalypse, spiritual desolation, and mystical rapture.

from **Julian** David Brendan Hopes

Witch the lakemen call her, this wind
switching northwest with Pole ice
bunched at her tits, whipping the barges
   into harbor, beaching everything not anchored down.
   Only ladies are left, leave last.
The princess falls among the dragons.
The mantis snags a blown leaf with her
   saw-tooth arms, bites the pointless gold,
     swiveling her green head toward starvation.
Sisters beat southward from the Great Slave,
their gray harp wings in the moonlight.
   There is not enough to fight for.

   We are not in our right minds.
Dreams hurry day down with a prod of stars.
Heart flaps in dawn wind crying *betrayed*.
   It is not as we were promised in the sleep
     that cradled us between two worlds,
not as the bird that matined us.
Not the Garden whose plush these feet were made for.
   Madness rides the witch's broomstick.
   Madness for armor, madness for wings,
cross, crown, chrism;
madness of endurance: rock, root,
   gills waving in blackness, the sleepers under sleet,

blind fear burrowing from the cold;
madness of vengeance: ice lured into light,
traitor of algae greeing, gathering;
   seed bound in black jackets, waiting
   to spray like flak into the wind's face,
skew blast with a baffle of leaves;
madness night-locked, straightened,
   madness to hammer through:
   Lear in storm, saint kings
with snowbanks smoking in their wakes;
Christ-caught-ember
   dancing barefoot in an iron garden.

And here is a vision shown by the strangeness of God
to a devout woman, and her name is Julian,
a recluse of Norwich....

Teresa of Avila (1515–1582) is another of the great figures of Western mysticism, some might say the greatest. She was also a courageous reformer of religious life in Spain, and like Julian a brilliant writer. In "Teresa," Richard Wilbur reflect on the saint's so-called mystical espousal with Christ, which occurred during one of her raptures, leading to a "transverberation" of her heart by an angel with a flaming lance. Wilbur suggests that even Teresa, no stranger to mystical ecstasy, struggled to find a context for this experience, a physically painful, radical dying to self in amorous union with transcendence. He evaluates her cry of rapture in light of the cries of Ulysses' men when also dying to self, changed into swine on Circe's island of Aeaea. The mythic reference hints at possiblities for Teresa: the fanciful or the demonic. What validates Teresa's ecstasies for the poet is the fruit that they bore in a disciplined balance of contemplation and action. Teresa was famed for her exuberant embrace of life. When a visitor once remarked on her obvious relish in eating a pheasant, Teresa replied: "When it's time to pray, pray. When it's time to pheasant, pheasant."

Teresa Richard Wilbur

After the sun's eclipse,
The brighter angel and the spear which drew
A bridal outcry from her open lips,
    She could not prove it true,
Nor think at first of any means to test
By what she had been wedded or possessed.

    Not all cries were the same;
There was an island in mythology
Called by the very vowels of her name
    Where vagrants of the sea,
Changed by a wand, were made to squeal and cry
As heavy captives in a witch's sty.

    The proof came soon and plain:
Visions were true which quickened her to run
God's barefoot errands in the rocks of Spain
    Beneath its beating sun,
And lock the O of ecstasy within
The tempered consonants of discipline.

---

*In the lineage of Julian and Teresa as a mystic and writer, though sepa-
rated from them by hundreds of years of Christian history, is the Ameri-
can Trappist monk Thomas Merton (1915–1968). Living his adult
years in the observance of contemplative solitude at Gethsemani Abbey
outside Louisville, Kentucky, Merton turned his spiritual mastery and
literary gifts to the writing of books, essays, journals, poetry, and volu-
minous correspondence. Daniel Berrigan characteristically exploits the
occasion of a "Funeral Oration" for his friend Merton to assail the ma-
terialism of the times. By having "the compassionate Buddha" deliver
the eulogy, the poet pays homage to Merton's lifelong elucidation of both
Eastern and Western ways of spiritual enlightenment. It was while at-
tending a conference of Buddhists, Hindus, and Christians in Bangkok,
Thailand, that Merton died of electrocution at the age of fifty-three.*

---

from **The Funeral Oration as Pronounced**
by the Compassionate Buddha Daniel Berrigan

Assembled sirs. The courtesies afforded us by the Dali Lama,
the Abbot of the Trappist Fathers,
and the vergers of your cathedral, are deeply felt
and enter as a somber joy into our heart's stream.

The Christ himself (to whom all praise) were better chosen
to speak for this monk, brother and son.
Alas. The absence of your god, decreed by a thousand malevo-
    lencies
susurration, anger, skill in summoning words against him—
I hear your choice, approving; *one god at a time. Better an unknown*
    god, even
a tedious one, than that holy son, native to our flesh.
Better a subtle millennial smile, than anger and infected wounds.
Better me than he. So be it; I shall speak.

The assumption of this monk into ecstasy,
the opening of the crystal portals before that glancing spirit!
He was (I speak a high and rare praise)
not too strenuous after reward; so he attains eternal knowledge.
In his mortal journey, he refused direction from those pylons
impermeable, deadly smooth,
hard to the touch as the membrane of hell.
He detested their claim upon the soul, he exorcised their rumors....

The monk has attained god;
he had first attained man. Does the nexus trouble you, issuing as it
    does
from a mouth so neutral, so silent as mine? Be comforted.
Gioconda exists only to smile. She does so; her value mounts and
    mounts.

But the monk Merton, in his life and going forth
requires that a blow be dealt

361

your confident myths. If the gods are silent
if even to this hour, Christ and Buddha stand appalled
before your idols, if we breath the stench of your hecatombs—
still, the passage of a good man restores;
it brings the gods to earth, even to you!....

Hope?
Christ and Buddha fashion a conundrum. Hear it.
The hour of your despoiling is the hour of our return.
Until then, the world is yours, and you are Moloch's, bound hand
    and foot
upon a wheel of fire.

The monk Thomas I take up in lotus hands
to place in the eternal thought
a jewel upon my forehead.

---

*Traditions of the East might be tempted to describe Maura Eichner's
Mary the Mother of Christ as a perfection of Tao, her will not passively
yielded to fate but directed by her inner being toward a principle be-
yond appearance, where visible signs offer no compass for the journey.
David Craig relates his experience of Mary to the Tao of living the mo-
ment in spiritual poverty, the quest of the enlightened "to possess noth-
ing, / all of it."*

From a Woman's Life Maura Eichner

What Mary knew was just
enough for the usual day;
pull water, flint fire, bake
bread, smile, pray

the dark orations, sleep, wake
wait. When pain honed a nerve,

when birth or dying clotted
an hour, she leaned to the curve

of living, resilient to fear,
laughter, suffering.
Partings are a little death.
Each one's journey is a thing

wholly without precedent.
She looked at the sky
for compass. None. She, too,
created a road to travel by.

from **Marian Sector** David Craig

In the morning, when the sun
has taken its fill from tall crystal,
flowers, from gutters,
and rises, half drunk, like a cowboy
in the Hand which holds it,
and you find yourself alone, again,
at breakfast, face deep in pollen,
drowning; alive as the
white sword is drawn from its pink sheath:
your heart.

She is there, with you,
looking out past the curtains
to the stars and the roundness of the sea.

• • •

To possess nothing,
all of it.
This is your end.
To feel yourself rise in conversation,
ignore it, go on talking.

To become so small
that there is finally room
for you
on the sidewalk....

.   .   .

I saw an old woman today
downtown, and though I'm sure no one else
noticed, there was, I am positive,
a small flame which flickered
on the top of her head.

She was pushing a cart of groceries,
As I came closer to her car, bent on inspecting,
she handed me a sack of potatoes.

Before she drove away, she smiled,
and, insisted, pressing
two worn quarters
against my palm.

.   .   .

The plain wooden statue, and on the way up
to Communion, on the left cheek,
I saw a tear glistening.

She is a door
that signals procession,
the kind you feel, sometimes, mornings,
stopping your bicycle in a
graveyard, each person, one day,
rising, walking eastward
through cold grass,
dissipating mist.
You will be among them.

.   .   .

Beaded tears
on grotto floors.
We recite them, drone, as if at a funeral,
count our sins, the days we left
on the road to Sodom,
the days of wheat and barley,
of fast talking, back slapping.

They are our cry, they are
her answer.
We do not know what is to come;
we know, what is here.

---

*David Citino gives a full account of the story of Saint Agatha in classic
"Lives of the Saints" format. The cult of the implacable bride of Christ
dates back as far as the fourth century, and promulgates, for all its gore
and its horrors of male oppression, what is in many ways a Christian
archetype of integrity, courage, and spiritual commitment.*

Agatha David Citino

She was born of wealthy parents, but *her* only wealth, and
her misfortune, was the ocean sway of her hips as she walked
through the marketplace, the slow white length of ankle and
thigh, her breasts rising from a steamy bath. A loud and fat gov-
ernment man swelled for her; softly, eyes cast low onto his ani-
mal skin rugs, she said "no." So he placed her in a brothel run
by a woman named Aphrodisia—you know the type—and she
stayed long enough to know the whispered given name of every
local John. She'd sit alone each evening, legs crossed in prayer,
as content as if she were reading to herself. She was bad for
business. So, growing louder and darker, forgetting all protocol,
eyes small beneath a corrugated forehead, he ordered that she
be beaten with sticks, stretched out on the rack, kissed with the
torch. Still she remained constant, refusing to love or hate him

in the way he wished. He had her breasts cut off slowly as he watched, fists clenched. Later, while she sat alone in her cell weeping into the stained glass chapel formed by her slender hands and very little light, as she computed the value of what she'd lost and what she might gain, Peter floated in on a shaft of sunlight and returned them to her. Once again she was all woman. This pleased her. Four days later she was rolled naked over crackling coals and glowing shards of pottery. This proved too much for her.

She's a patroness of bells, bread and of course, breasts. The dates of her birth and death aren't known, nor is her place of birth—though both Catania and Palermo claim her. We can accept with certainty nothing of her story, but what will our doubt cost us?

Judging simply by a head-count of garden statuary, Francis of Assisi (1181–1226) must be just about everybody's favorite saint, second only perhaps, among some Christians, to Mary the mother of Jesus. The antic, self-styled lover of Lady Poverty was disinherited early on by his wealthy father. In a gesture of obedience, Francis took off everything he was wearing at the time and laid it at his father's feet. The bishop present at the hearing had Francis cover his nakedness with a gardener's tunic that happened to be at hand. Francis never took it off and it became the garb of his order, worn by the Franciscans today. Francis is often called the Second Christ, a title confirmed a few years before his death when he received the "stigmata" of Christ's five wounds, an event widely attested by his contemporaries. David Citino's "Francis Meets a Leper" captures the love this charismatic figure poured out on people, animals, flowers, water, stones, even fire, as Andrew Hudgins goes on to tell in "Fire and St Francis." Hudgins's poem takes the kind of comical turns marking many Saint Francis stories, and because of the episode that inspired it, Saint Francis is invoked by some Christians against fire. He is best known as patron saint of all living creatures and the ecology. His life is an upholding of Christian mystery at its most joyous.

Francis Meets a Leper David Citino

He heard the bell toll, erratic
in a palsied hand, and smelled
the goatish scent before he saw
the figure moving in mist on the road
to Assisi, a traveler gloved and shod,
as was the law, to hide the sores,
a man's inhumanity, missing fingers
and toes, and tried to unmask the face,
slack muscles showing nothing
but astonishment, lower lids keeping
eyes open always to our providential decay,
flesh soft and thick as rotten wood.
Francis saw in bleary eyes, near to him
as his mother's as she loved him,
a brother, then someone dearer, wrapped
as he'd seen others in his father's cloth
that first had profited English shepherds
and the weavers of Ghent, a skin
bleached white as bone, a flower blazing
in snow, so close to perfection it could
only decay. Francis did the only thing
he could, sun rising high enough now
to burn away the mist. He unwrapped
the face, studying lineaments fashioned
by a master's hand, image and likeness
of the death that beautifies all living.
He closed his eyes and kissed.

Fire and St. Francis Andrew Hudgins

1.

As he sat eating by the fire one night
a spark was lifted on a wisp of air
and set on the folds of cloth that wrapped his groin.

But when he felt the heat so near his flesh
he wouldn't raise his hands against the fire
or let his worried friends extinguish it.
You mustn't harm the flames or spoil their play,
he said to them. *Don't these bright creatures have
as much a right as I to be happy?*
For seconds his disciples stared as the flames
climbed up the cloth and nearer to his skin.
And he, without a qualm, turned to his bowl.
At last their knowledge of the world prevailed.
As one, they leaped on him and held him down,
smothering the fire with dirt and what was left
of the soup that had been their evening meal.
When he returned, embarrassed, to his prayers,
his genitals swung through the holes scorched in the cloth.

2.

Laid on the fire, the iron throbbed red with heat,
and then turned orange beneath the doctor's breath.
The saint's face twisted in a burst of pain,
and the doctor marked it with a dab of soot
so he would know where to apply the iron.
To calm himself, the saint spoke to the flame:
*Brother Fire, be gentle on my quenching skin
that I might have the love to suffer you.*
Composed, he signed the cross above the fire,
which bowed its many heads in seeming grace
beneath the blessing motion of his hand.

3.

He held the ember in his hand, and braced.
But soon the burning grew too great to bear,
and Francis set it gently back into the fire
and wept. His hand was oozing from the burn.
A new disciple asked him why he wept
since when you hold an ember in your hand

you know what to expect. Francis wrapped the hand
in a grimy strip of cloth torn from his robe
and said, *When I was young I had a dog*
that snapped my hand whenever I touched him,
and every time he did I held it out again.
About the hundredth time, he licked my wrist.
Perhaps he just grew tired of biting me,
or maybe with my pain I'd earned his trust.
About this fire, however, I don't know.
I dream some day the flames will flit
around my fingers like a yellow bird,
a tulip leaping on my fingertips.
But so far it won't take me for a friend.